Praise for *Is It Dyslexia?*

"*Is it Dyslexia?* is a realistic and inspiring journey that provides much needed tools ‡ a new landscape with their child's education."

—**Amy Noall,**
Psychologist, Educator, and Founder of The Scholars' Grove

"You'll find valuable information and the best practices in *Is it Dyslexia? A Comprehensive Guide to Screening, Understanding, and Supporting Children with Dyslexia*. This manual outlines a roadmap for identifying at-risk children, including early signs of dyslexia and detailed screening tools and evaluations. April McMurtrey's knowledge shines through as she guides you step by step through the screening process so that no child's struggle with dyslexia is overlooked."

—**Patrice Badami,**
MA in Childhood and Special Education, and Host of the Acorn to Tree Family Podcast

"One of the most admirable aspects of April's work lies in her dedication to empowering parents and tutors. *Is it Dyslexia?* equips them with comprehensive dyslexia questions and answers, along with step-by-step screening tasks featuring easy-to-follow instructions. These invaluable resources empower individuals to screen their loved ones or students, make well-informed decisions, and offer precise support, thereby making a profound impact on the lives of struggling readers."

—**Mary Medina,**
Owner, Breakthrough Reading Online Tutoring LLC, Certified Teacher, and Reading Specialist

"*Is it Dyslexia?* by April McMurtry is an indispensable resource for parents seeking to understand and support individuals with dyslexia. With a unique blend of personal experience and extensive research, April's book provides both comprehensive insights about dyslexia and practical screenings for personal use. Her compassionate approach empowers readers to recognize dyslexia, access crucial accommodations, debunk myths about dyslexia, and tap into the strengths often inherent in dyslexic individuals. This book's importance cannot be overstated, and it is a testament to April's expertise and dedication to making a profound difference in the lives of those affected by dyslexia."

—**Tania van Thiel Berghuys,**
Teacher, Certified Learn Reading Tutor

IS IT DYSLEXIA?

An At-Home Guide for Screening
and Supporting Children
Who Struggle to Read

APRIL McMURTREY

WILEY

Published by John Wiley & Sons, Inc., Hoboken, New Jersey.
Published simultaneously in Canada.

For general information on our other products and services or for technical support, please contact our Customer Care Department within the United States at (800) 762-2974, outside the United States at (317) 572-3993 or fax (317) 572-4002.

Wiley also publishes its books in a variety of electronic formats. Some content that appears in print may not be available in electronic formats. For more information about Wiley products, visit our web site at www.wiley.com.

Library of Congress Cataloging-in-Publication Data is Available:

ISBN 9781394194452 (Paperback)
ISBN 9781394194476 (ePDF)
ISBN 9781394194469 (ePub)

Cover Design: Wiley
Cover Image: © macondos/Adobe Stock
Author Photo: Devin Bovee

SKY10063714_010224

Contents

April McMurtrey is the developer of the Learn Reading program, a reading curriculum designed for struggling and dyslexic learners. As a professional reading and dyslexia specialist, April has helped thousands of students break through their reading barriers and unlock the world of words. Her desire is for struggling readers of all ages to have access to quality reading instruction that will change lives and strengthen generations.

Introduction

One of my very first students as a dyslexia specialist was a 75-year-old woman named Gertie. She was extremely intelligent, talented, and severely dyslexic.

Gertie had started, maintained, and managed a successful embroidery business, yet she could not write down a message quickly if someone called her on the phone or read a lengthy, written request. She could not fully participate in any family, social, religious, or community experiences that required extensive reading or writing. This left her with feelings of isolation and inferiority.

Gertie "got by" alright, but she admitted to me that there was a cost to her lack of literacy skills. That most terrible cost was directly related to her life's most treasured memory.

Out of all the experiences in her 75 years, including births, marriages, successes, family togetherness, and happy times, her favorite experience was when she found out that she was not "dumb"—she was dyslexic.

A few months later, Gertie walked excitedly into our tutoring session with a huge smile on her face. She made a grand gesture of whipping a small piece of paper out of her sweater pocket and proudly laid it on the table in front of me. She then said with a huge grin, "I have been waiting for 75 years to know how to read that word!" That word is *authentic*!

Gertie now understood the cause of her literacy struggles and how to overcome those barriers in ways she had only dreamed of before.

I was with Gertie during the last weeks of her life. Do you know what she was excited to tell me when she saw me, just before she died? She told me that she wanted to donate her brain to science, to add to the study of dyslexia, so others could benefit from her "once-thought-of-as-dumb" brain.

If you are reading this, you may be one of the millions of people who take the ability for granted, yet millions of others are desperately trying to improve their reading skills. No matter how hard they try, they can't seem to identify and break down the barriers that are preventing them from reading fluently, accurately, and confidently.

What many of these hard-working, intelligent, capable adults do not know, which would change everything if they did, is that they are very likely dyslexic.

Why would knowing you are dyslexic change everything? The answer is that there is a different way to learn to read and write if one has dyslexia. More of the same kind of instruction will not work. If it did, these intelligent, hard-working people would have caught on already. Instead, dyslexics need instruction that is highly specialized and designed the way dyslexic brains are wired. This unique type of reading instruction is very different because their brains are very different. And the outcomes are also wonderfully different!

In this book, you will learn what dyslexia is and what it is not. You will learn how to screen for it, and most importantly, what to do if it is discovered.

Hope and help have arrived.

Part I

Understanding Dyslexia

In this part of the book, you'll read a story about a family who passes down the inherited trait of dyslexia from one generation to the next. You'll follow along with the family members as they move through the struggle of not knowing why a child struggles, their questions when dyslexia is suspected, and the beautiful results when dyslexia is finally discovered.

Chapter 1

Recognizing the Signs of Dyslexia

In this chapter, you'll learn about Michael, a bright, capable boy who learns most things easily, except for reading and writing. You'll discover the signs of dyslexia so they can be easily recognized in your own child if they are present.

Michael's Story

Michael was a delightful and inquisitive toddler, born to adoring parents who read to him every night. His mother, Anna, wanted to expose her child to as many books as possible so he would get a head start in reading. Anna did not want Michael to struggle in school like she did and believed reading to him would help him to love books and eventually be good at reading. Michael's father, Jacob, also struggled in school, but he hated reading and so left storytime to his wife.

Michael hit all the development milestones in almost every way, except he was almost three and wasn't talking nearly as much as his peers, and what he did mutter was difficult to understand, especially by others. But he was bright, a joy to be around, and a cheerful, happy child.

When Michael was three, he did start talking more; however, his words were still difficult to understand most of the time. Jacob and Anna wondered if he might have a speech impediment. They decided to keep an eye on it, ask their friends who also had kids if they thought anything was wrong, and maybe ask the doctor about his speech if it didn't improve.

Anna's consistent nightly storytime did help Michael to love books! Jacob and Anna were somewhat surprised that Michael did not mind going to bed, like many of their friends' kids did. They believed it was because Anna would go to bed with him and read a story to him every night. Michael loved looking at the pictures and listening to his mom read in that special sing-song way that occurs in children's books.

Michael did not lack exposure to print. Anna not only read to Michael, but used her finger to show him that the words were read from top to bottom and from left to right. She read books about shapes and colors and letters and numbers. She read books with rhyming words and a rhythmic cadence. She read books about the alphabet and pointed out what an *A* was, and a *B*, and the sounds that those letters made.

Michael had every opportunity that a young reader could hope for to begin his literacy journey.

That's why Anna and Jacob were extremely puzzled when Michael did not thrive in preschool. They expected him to be ahead of the curve with all the print exposure he had had, both written and verbal, since the day he was born. They didn't understand what she was saying when his preschool teacher, Miss Sarah, told them that Michael had trouble with the alphabet.

"How can that be?" Anna asked. "We've taught him the alphabet over and over. He has an alphabet poster in his room. I point to letters as we read and I teach him what they are! How is it possible that he is having trouble with the alphabet?" His parents were upset and confused. They had done everything right. What happened? Was it the teacher?

Anna asked some of her friends with kids in the same preschool if they had any doubts about the teacher or how their child was progressing. Most of them had glowing reviews about Miss Sarah and said their kids were doing just fine and were ready for kindergarten. Only one friend could relate, Anna's friend, Liz. She told Anna that her daughter, Lila, was also struggling and did not know why or how to help her. Anna and Liz could think of only two possible reasons for their kids' early struggles. It was either that the teacher was not teaching them properly, or that Michael and Lila were simply late bloomers. They hoped that Kindergarten would be better. It simply had to be.

Starting Kindergarten

For kindergarten, they were thrilled when Mrs. Nelson, a seasoned teacher, seemed to do a deep dive into phonics right away. This, they felt, was exactly what Michael needed. They allowed themselves to relax a little, knowing that this experienced teacher would teach their son how to read. They kept up with all his schoolwork, practiced with him what he was learning at home, and continued to read to him every night. They were confident that Michael would learn to read this year and be well prepared for first grade. Things were looking up.

By this time, Michael had two younger siblings, Luke and Eden. His parents were continuing their pattern of nightly storytime for all the kids, and teaching the younger ones the alphabet, shapes, colors, and numbers. . . . Just like they did with Michael. Before they even entered preschool, Jacob and Anna noticed a difference in their three kids. Luke and Eden began talking much earlier and much more clearly than Michael did. They also seemed to learn the alphabet and phonics at an earlier age. Why did Michael struggle, and Luke and Eden pick things up easily? They knew it wasn't a lack of intelligence. Michael was a bright child. They also knew it wasn't their preschool teacher, or what they were doing as parents, because it was all the same. So, what was it? Why did Michael have it so hard?

As kindergarten progressed and the first progress report came home, Jacob and Anna's hearts sank. Michael was performing below the benchmarks in almost all academic areas. They comforted themselves by saying that they knew he was struggling going in and that they just needed to give Mrs. Nelson some time to work her magic.

They were hopeful when it was time for mid-year parent-teacher conferences. Michael had had half a year at school now and they were hopeful that his second report card would show improvement. At the conference, Jacob and Anna discovered that Mrs. Nelson was as pleasant and skilled as they hoped she would be. Michael's teacher told them how much she loved teaching Michael and then honestly laid out for them three concerns.

- Michael was behind in reading, and they needed to read to him every night and practice the sounds of the letters with him at home in order to bridge that gap.

- He couldn't form words that rhyme and they needed to practice that with him at home, too.

- She was referring him to speech therapy. Mrs. Nelson ended the meeting by telling them that he was a pleasant student and worked hard, but she was placing him in a special group with other kids who were behind, so he could get extra help from the aide.

They left feeling like they had both just been punched in the gut. Did Mrs. Nelson blame them for Michael's lack of reading skills? Jacob and Anna tried to tell her that they practiced the sounds of the letters regularly, but they didn't know if she believed them. Was it really their fault? Did they drop the ball with rhyming? Anna told Jacob that she read rhyming books to him all the time, and that she didn't know what more she could do. She felt terrible and was determined to somehow do better. Together, they admitted that they were surprised that she was referring him to speech therapy. Was his speech really that bad? They had become accustomed to his speech patterns and admittedly forgot to bring it up with the doctor. They decided that if the teacher recommended it, they would pursue getting Michael into speech therapy.

Jacob and Anna worked with Michael for the rest of his kindergarten year. There were letters taped up all over the house. *Fridge* starts with /f/. *Sink* starts with /s/. Michael was making progress isolating the beginning sounds of household objects, but it was hard for him to know which sound came next or to break off the ending sound of the word. To him, most of the time, one syllable was one sound. It seemed like he couldn't hear all the other sounds within the word.

They also worked with him on sight words because he wasn't learning them fast enough in class. According to his teacher, Michael should fluently read over 50 sight words by the end of his kindergarten year. He couldn't even read 10 consistently. And that was with all the extra help he was receiving.

Mrs. Nelson also said that by the end of the year, Michael should be able to recite his address and phone number, so they worked on those things for months. Jacob and Anna knew their child was smart and didn't understand why Michael had such a hard time memorizing these things when Luke, who was a year and a half younger than him, could already repeat them. Why was learning some things so hard for this intelligent boy? What was going on?

Dealing with Homework

When Michael began first grade, he was on top of the world. He loved kindergarten and knew he would love first grade too. He got his backpack ready and was excited to see his friends from last year and meet his teacher.

Miss Oaks was also a wonderful teacher and knew the importance of reading in first grade. The first thing she did was assess all her students to see where they were as readers so she could place them in appropriate reading groups. Michael was placed in the "bluebird" group, which he thought was great because his friend, Lila, was also in that group.

Michael began getting what seemed like significant amounts of homework, which was a daunting and unpleasant task for him. He didn't really like schoolwork and wasn't excited about having to do it at home, too. Jacob and Anna set time every day after school to go through his homework assignments together. As the year went on, they too began to dread homework because they found themselves getting frustrated. They felt terrible and hated that Michael often ended up in tears. Homework seemed to take much longer than it should for someone in the first grade.

There was also another surprising issue that suddenly appeared around the middle of the school year. Seemingly out of nowhere, Michael suddenly started wetting his pants in class. He had never had any sort of trouble with this in the past, but now Anna was getting called to bring Michael some dry pants almost every week! When she asked him why he was having a hard time making it to the bathroom, he just said, "I don't know." He did not need this extra pressure and embarrassment in class! Jacob and Anna were seriously beginning to worry about their oldest son. What was happening in class? What was their son going through, and how could they help him?

Anna made an appointment to see Miss Oaks. She wanted to see what insight the teacher had into what was happening in class and how, together, they could help Michael.

Miss Oaks praised Michael's behavior and mentioned that he was a joy to have in class. However, she also mentioned several things that she was concerned about now that more than half the year had gone by.

- First, she said that Michael was struggling to sound out words. He was doing better at knowing what each letter said, but when he went to try to blend those sounds together in a word, he got mixed up and couldn't do it. It was almost like he didn't know phonics at all.

- Second, Miss Oaks said Michael depends too much on guessing and sometimes doesn't even try to sound out the word when he reads. She said he could come to the word *cabin* on a page, and say, *house*, which doesn't even have ANY of the same sounds in it! He is purely and entirely guessing. This strategy is causing him to miss most of the words on a page which then completely eliminates any chance for comprehending what he reads. She told Anna that Michael does not seem to want to apply the phonics that he knows and instead seems to want to guess his way through his schoolwork. She kindly asked that Anna work with him more at home and maybe talk with him about the importance of doing his best in school.

- Third, Michael takes much longer than his peers to complete in-class assignments and so was often unable to finish. This meant he had to stay in from recess or lunch to finish his work, so he misses out on playing with his friends, having a good time, being able to relax and refresh, and enjoy being a kid. Miss Oaks told Anna that Michael struggles with his work ethic and that it seems that he doesn't care very much about school, so he slacks off during class. She asked Anna to speak with Michael about trying hard and the rewards that would bring. Miss Oaks said she would love for Michael to work hard enough to earn the reward of recess.

Anna knew Miss Oaks meant well and wanted what was best for their son, but her heart dropped and she found herself speechless. She knew Michael tried hard! She knew he wanted nothing more than to work as fast as his friends and go outside and play! Anna was so taken back by what she had just heard that she finished the meeting as soon as she could and ran out of the classroom fighting back tears.

It seems both she and Michael would do anything to get out of that classroom.

Anna then had a thought. Should I homeschool my son?

Jacob and Anna were determined to do whatever it took to help Michael succeed, even if it meant pulling him out of school and figuring out a way to homeschool him. But for now, they decided to keep him in the classroom.

They focused more and more on helping Michael become aware of his strengths and talents. He had always been good at athletics and he was brilliant at creating unique masterpieces with Legos. They decided to make sure he had plenty of time to develop the things he was good at, versus spending all of his free time trying to improve in areas where he was weak. This boy needed a good dose of positive self-esteem.

His last report card indicated that he never did master his timed math tests, or the memorization of the days of the week and months of the year in order, but his marks for behavior were excellent.

By the time Michael ended first grade, he was still below grade level in language arts and in some areas of arithmetic, but he was also the star of his soccer team and his bedroom was decorated with all of his amazing lego creations.

Though Michael spent ample time that summer doing things that he enjoyed like soccer and playing with his friends, Jacob and Anna also sent him to tutoring twice a week to try and bridge the gap between where he was performing and where he needed to be prior to entering second grade. They were always very positive with him and encouraged his efforts as much as they could.

Specific Concerns

Second grade started off great. Michael's teacher was kind and had a gentle personality. There were no reading groups, and Michael felt a little relief when school seemed a little easier than he expected. Maybe the tutoring that summer paid off!

Jacob and Anna were actually looking forward to the first parent-teacher conference. Finally, they were going to get some good news! But as they left, all three of them hung their heads in sad silence. The joy was short-lived.

After a few brief positive remarks about Michael, Mrs. Ballard then presented a list of concerns. She invited Michael to go play so she could talk to his parents alone. Jacob and Anna uncomfortably braced themselves as she began.

- Michael was unable to accurately read an analog clock, something they had been working on for over a month.
- She was concerned about some aspects of his speech. He was in second grade now and should not still be saying "frow" a ball. And no matter how hard she tried to teach him the difference between the short-*i* and the short-*e* sounds, he still could not reproduce those sounds correctly. He also consistently confused those two sounds when he tried to sound out a word.

- Michael still did not know his left from his right. He often put the wrong hand over his heart when he recited the pledge of allegiance and acted confused when she asked him which was which.

- He was still reversing several letters and numbers. He would often confuse *b* and *d* and he would also write numbers like 12 as 21, or 15 as 51 and the five would usually be reversed.

- His spelling was not only bad, but bewildering. She was concerned about his lack of ability to spell high-frequency words and the spelling he did use often had no connection to how it was actually spelled. The letters he chose to use to spell a word sometimes left her completely puzzled. It was like the letters had no meaning in the word whatsoever.

- Mrs. Ballard then threw in one more small detail that wasn't impacting his academics, but felt she should still say something. Mrs. Ballard was concerned that he still asked her or other teachers to tie his shoes. She kindly asked Jacob and Anna if they would please teach him how to tie his shoes, or else buy him some slip-ons.

When they retrieved Michael at the end of the conference, he could tell that his parents were sad and his demeanor changed instantly. He wondered what was said. And he especially wondered if that one question that was always in the back of his mind was true. . .was he really just, dumb? Did they just learn the truth?

Their trip to go get ice cream afterward didn't help lighten the mood much, but they tried to keep the conversation light and their feelings masked. They ended their outing by asking Michael if he would like to take a trip to the shoe store for a new pair of fancy slip-ons.

Anna cried that night. Ever since Michael was born, she had tried to give him a head start with reading! She exposed him to books, read to him every night, put flashcards all over the house, explained what the letter sounds were and how phonics worked. Why, then, did he still struggle? What had she not done or left out? Was this her fault? If she had done better, would he be reading at grade level? What could she have done more? Jacob tried to comfort her as she expressed her feelings and concerns, but his heart was also broken. He knew what it was like to struggle in school. He knew what it was like to panic when it was your turn to read in class. And he absolutely knew what it was like to feel like you were less smart than all the other kids in your class. He knew because he had been there and his heart ached for his little boy.

The next morning, Anna and Jacob decided to keep trying and explore additional options that they had not yet tried. They searched the internet and ordered a new phonics kit to work on with him at home. They also signed up Michael for one of those expensive tutoring clinics. If they cost that much, they must be able to truly help their students, right? They hoped that was the case anyway. They couldn't really afford it, but made sacrifices to send him there. They would do anything they could to help Michael succeed.

Michael continued using the at-home phonics lessons at home and went to the tutoring center through the end of second grade, but his grades stayed about the same. So, his parents decided to double the time at the tutoring center during the summer. Michael felt deflated. He wanted to go outside and play, not go to tutoring every day. But he also, deep down, hoped it would help.

Confidence Plummeting

When third grade came, even after all that extra help and time at the tutoring center, Michael was reading at an end-of-first grade level. He had made some progress, but not enough. He was still a full year behind.

In class, he read slower than his peers, and some kids laughed when he made mistakes like reading *dig* for *big* or *god* for *dog*. His reading was labored and inaccurate. He even misread tiny, little words that everyone was supposed to know, like *of*, *how* and *does*. Sometimes he got stuck on them, and other times he left them out altogether, without even knowing he skipped them. Then, after working extremely hard to read a page, he was in such a state of high stress that he usually had no idea what he just read.

In third grade, he was also expected to copy a lot of things from the board. He didn't understand why this took him much longer than everyone else to copy assignments. He had to look up and grab just a few letters then look down and write them down, then look back up, try to remember where he left off, grab a couple more letters, write them down, and repeat the process. He usually made mistakes when he tried to copy, so he often got assignments or dates wrong. This would make his mom mad because she didn't want him to miss assignments and get further behind.

The frustration around school came home with him and no matter what he did, he couldn't get out from under the "I'm stupid" cloud that seemed to follow him everywhere. When he was on the soccer field or when he was playing with his Legos were the only times he felt like a normal kid. All other free time was spent studying and struggling. He hated it. He hated how he felt when he couldn't do the work. And he most definitely—hated school.

By the end of third grade, Michael complained almost daily of stomachaches or headaches in the mornings, hoping his mom would not make him go to school. When he was there, he often told the teacher he was sick when it was reading time, so he could go to the nurse or go home, and not have to be humiliated in class.

Michael's self-esteem was spiraling downhill. His confidence was plummeting. He was showing signs of depression and anxiety. And his parents were at a complete loss. Was all lost for their little boy? What was going on? Was there any hope for Michael?

Getting By

During fourth and fifth grades, Jacob and Anna did everything they could to build up Michael. They encouraged him to develop his strengths. They enrolled him in anything he wanted so that he could look forward to something and at least feel good about himself in some areas. And it was working. Michael was exceptionally gifted not only athletically, but his mechanical abilities were also extraordinary. He could fix just about anything and loved taking things apart and putting them back together again. He enjoyed solving puzzles and building models. He was also a brilliant storyteller. Michael loved letting his imagination soar. He could come up with creative concepts and ideas and fold them into beautiful stories. The only problem was, he just couldn't write them down. When he tried, his writing would not even come close to reflecting the masterpiece that he could orally deliver. His writing was a smokescreen for his intelligence. It was there, you just couldn't see it.

When Michael went to junior high school, he was placed in some lower classes, which completely humiliated him. His teachers complained that he could read and spell a word just fine on one page, but not on the next and they were puzzled at his inability to decode or spell unknown words because they knew he was a bright kid. Michael's spelling was admittedly and embarrassingly atrocious. He would add or omit letters whose sounds weren't even in the word. He placed an *e* at the end of almost every unknown word because he was entirely confused about silent-*e* and so just threw it in at random, hoping some of them would end up in a correctly spelled word. He used the talk-to-text feature of his cell phone to send almost every message to his friends, hoping to disguise his spelling problem.

Though his academics hadn't improved much and he still struggled with his self-image, he had a lot of friends. Michael was extremely well liked by his peers. He was funny, empathetic, observant, and intuitive. His high social IQ and surprising maturity helped him to be, have, and keep good friends, which would be a great help to him as he entered high school the following year. He also impressed his friends, as well as his art teacher, with his ability to sketch. He didn't even know he had the skill until he took an art class and discovered he was completely drawn to art, and was better at it than most of his friends. He ended up taking a sketch book with him almost everywhere, especially English class, so he could do something that he was good at when he felt completely inept at everything academic.

Michael's people skills and his athletic ability propelled him to popularity in high school. He was the star of the track team and in his sophomore year he helped his school win the state championship. He was also mature, kind, and level-headed. These were some of the reasons he was encouraged by his friends to run for school president.

Even though Michael was good at sports and well liked by his peers, he still suffered from a low self-image, particularly around academics. He had to work twice as hard as anyone else he knew just to get acceptable grades. He struggled in almost every subject because of his reading challenges. He had to work extremely hard to figure out unknown words which was an obstacle to comprehension. He didn't understand why he still, even after all these years, had trouble decoding unfamiliar words. He made a concerted effort to listen carefully when the teacher was teaching because if he listened to the content, he could comprehend it much better than if he read it. He had to rely on what he heard because his note-taking skills were abhorrent. He often just gave up trying to write what the teacher was saying and instead focused on listening as hard as he could. Yet, even if he felt he had a pretty good grasp of the material, he still panicked on almost every test. He always felt rushed and stressed as he tried to answer the questions on exams and he absolutely dreaded questions that required an essay response.

Michael managed to just get by in most classes, but he did great in electives like art, shop, and music. Though he struggled in music to read the notes on the staff, he could play things by ear easily and discovered that he really enjoyed this new-found talent. Michael's worst classes were Spanish and English. Even though he had a private tutor for both of those subjects, he still barely made good enough grades to keep performing in sports. Maintaining his grades was a constant battle and it was absolutely not due to lack of effort. Michael tried harder than anyone he knew, and still got the poorest results on his tests and report cards.

Michael decided, with his friends' encouragement, that he would accept the opportunity to run for school president. He felt like he could do a good job because he was good at thinking outside the box and solving problems, but he was worried about the looming speech he would have to make in front of the entire school. He wasn't scared about being in front of a lot of people; he just knew that he had difficulty speaking fluently. He often had a hard time getting the words out that he wanted to say without stammering or pausing, and he sometimes confused the pronunciation of similar sounding words. He also knew that he flapped his arms and hands around wildly when he spoke, usually to help others understand what his mouth had a hard time articulating. The honest truth was he was just not a good public speaker. Or at least that's what he thought. He was afraid he would sound like an idiot in front of everyone. But, he went for it anyway! He worked hard on his speech, and presented it with just a few awkward pauses and noticeable gulps. He felt a lot more scared than he looked and ended up doing just fine. And he won.

At Michael's graduation, he didn't walk with honors, but no one clapped and cheered more loudly than Jacob and Anna. They were beyond proud of their amazing, hard-working son! He succeeded in every way he possibly could. He tried his absolute best and pushed harder than he thought he could. He had become an exceptional young man and they were beaming with love, joy, and respect for their son.

Michael was simply relieved that it was all over.

Working with His Strengths

After high school, Michael didn't attend college. Instead, because he was a natural craftsman, he started working for a cabinetmaker and became exceptionally skilled in the craft. Michael loved working with his hands and creating beautiful items from raw materials. After several years, Michael opened his own carpentry business and earned a highly respected reputation in the community. He was a successful businessman and knew that his business ran more smoothly when he delegated tasks that he was not good at (like paperwork, messaging, etc.) to others who were adept at those skills. When he concentrated on what he excelled in, creating, he and his business thrived.

Eventually, Michael got married and started a family. His first child was a son who they named John. Michael and his wife, Mary, wanted to expose John to as many books as possible from the very beginning. Michael did not want his son to go through the same academic struggles as he did. He and Mary read to John every night; they put flashcards all over the house, and they taught him his first lessons in phonics. So, they were a little surprised when his preschool teacher told them that John was behind his peers in recognizing the letters and recalling the sounds in the alphabet.

Michael's heart sank to a depth he did not know it had, but Mary recognized these early signs and knew what to do.

Signs of Dyslexia

As you can see from Michael's story, a child can go a lifetime without recognizing the signs of dyslexia. In this section of the book, you will learn exactly what dyslexia looks like so you can recognize the signs in your own family. This important knowledge will empower you to understand why your child struggles with reading and how to change the course of their academic path.

Challenges

The following are challenges for a dyslexic person.

Family History of Reading or Spelling Difficulties

Dyslexia is highly inheritable, so there will almost always be some indication of reading or spelling difficulties in a close family member. Typically, the mother or father will have some memory of struggling in school, or a recognition of their reliance on a spell check or a dislike for reading in public.

If neither parent recognizes any signs of dyslexia in themselves, then the scope can be widened to look at siblings, grandparents, aunts, uncles, and cousins.

If the family examines its members carefully, there will almost always be recognition of a family member who displays some signs of dyslexia either currently or in their early school years.

Delayed Speech Compared with Peers of the Same Age

It is not uncommon for toddlers who have dyslexia to lag behind their peers in speech development. They may be considered "late talkers."

Dyslexia is a language processing disorder. Language is processed in several ways: through speaking, reading, writing, and listening. Therefore, toddlers with dyslexia may not form three to four word sentences until well after they are three years old.

Inability to Pronounce Words Correctly after Ample Teaching/Persistent Baby Talk

A lack of strong phonemic awareness skills, a hallmark of dyslexia, is the reason why those who have the condition have extreme difficulty pronouncing certain words correctly, even after repeated correction.

In the speech of young children, this can mean so-called "baby talk" persists well past babyhood. The mispronunciation of certain words can persist through their childhood, adolescence, and even into adulthood.

When a person struggles with phonemic awareness, they struggle to discern and pronounce sounds in order. Other sounds may be inserted, omitted, or changed altogether.

A young child with dyslexia may persist in pronouncing *spaghetti* as *basketti*, *throw* as *frow*, or *packpack* for *backpack*.

Adults with dyslexia may continue to mispronounce words such as *flustrated* for *frustrated*, *supposebly* for *supposedly*, *cimannon* for *cinnamon*, or *dyklexia* for *dyslexia*.

Difficulty with the Alphabet

Students with dyslexia will likely struggle with all four requirements for learning the alphabet.

- Learning the names of the letters (including both uppercase and lowercase).
- Learning all of the sounds each of those letters makes.
- Learning the sequence of the letters.
- Learning the pencil strokes needed to create each uppercase and lowercase letter.

A preschooler may struggle to remember the order of the alphabet. They may be able to point to a particular letter when asked, but not be able to name the same letter at another time. They will likely have to sing the alphabet song aloud, to know the order, and may still yet miss several letters or become confused in the middle.

Dyslexic students may also struggle with writing the alphabet. They may form the letters from the bottom up. Or they may form a letter differently each time they write it.

A child with dyslexia may know the letter sounds, but will struggle with the difference between the name of the letter and the sound it makes when decoding a word.

Difficulty Understanding Rhyming Patterns

Phonological processing is the ability to understand and manipulate sounds to make meaningful connections in both written and spoken language. A weakness in phonological processing makes rhyming difficult, especially in young children.

Strong auditory processing skills are needed to identify, isolate, and break off chunks of sound within words or syllables and the concept of rhyming relies on this skill. To determine if two words rhyme or to produce a word that rhymes with another, one must be able to discern and identify similar ending sounds, break the sound off from the rest of the word, and replace that beginning sound with another to create a new word.

Children with dyslexia struggle with phonemic awareness, and therefore, may find these steps difficult, if not impossible. Phonemic awareness is part of phonological processing. It is an awareness of the smallest units of sound (phonemes) within a word. They may make errors such as saying *cronch* rhymes with *crunch* or that *grass* rhymes with *smash*, or that *big* rhymes with *bag*.

Trouble with Sounds

A lack of phonemic awareness (again, being aware of the smallest unit of sound within a spoken word or syllable) is the biggest reason students with dyslexia struggle with reading and spelling. They are unaware of the smallest units of sound, called phonemes, within a word or syllable. Their hearing may be perfect, but they struggle to process the sounds that they are hearing as clean, clear, separated units.

A person with dyslexia must be taught how to isolate, separate, discriminate, and manipulate all the sounds within a word before they can read and spell with confidence.

Difficulty Applying Phonics

A person with dyslexia may be just as intelligent as their peers, or more so, yet they may struggle applying the phonics that they have learned. Intelligence should not be defined by grades. Intelligence includes much more than what is reflected in a student's academic performance. It includes one's capacity for learning, reasoning skills, and problem-solving abilities, which are skills that people with dyslexia often excel in. Intelligence and dyslexia are entirely unrelated. A child with dyslexia has the same capacity to learn as a child without dyslexia; they just need the material to be explicitly taught with emphasis on phonemic awareness and phonics.

A dyslexic child may easily learn that *A* says /a/, and *B* says /b/, but when they go to apply that knowledge to read an unknown word, they are unable to do so. This is a result of their confusion regarding phonemic awareness.

A student may look at the letters in isolation and say their sounds perfectly; however, when they go to blend those sounds together, they struggle to do so. The sounds become a muddled, confusing, chaotic assortment of sounds that often doesn't even end up as a real word. This is one more reason why it is imperative that phonemic awareness is taught prior to and strengthened throughout reading instruction.

A grapheme is a letter or set of letters that makes one sound. For instance, *K* is a grapheme, as well as *CK*. They each make only one sound. Students with dyslexia must be taught that each grapheme (letter or set of letters) has a corresponding phoneme (sound). Students will then be ready to combine, or push, those sounds to read the word. This is often referred to as blending. If a student is expected to blend with precision, they must have a solid understanding that each grapheme within a word has a corresponding phoneme. They must be able to rely on the concept that every grapheme has a job, its own spot in a word, and its own mouth shape. If they do not grasp this foundational reading rule, they will never be a truly free reader.

Trouble Separating Sounds within Words

A hallmark of dyslexia is the inability to separate each sound, or phoneme, within a spoken word. If a person with dyslexia is asked to count how many sounds are in a spoken word, they will likely struggle to do so accurately.

For instance, if they try to separate and count the sounds in the word *pump*, they may only hear three: /puh/, /m/, and /p/. To them, it may be difficult to pull off the initial /p/ from the /uh/.

Or if they try to count the sounds in *chipmunk*, they may struggle to the point of giving up. To them, even repeating the sounds in the correct order when they are *looking* at the word in print may be difficult. They may look at each letter in order, but still say *chickmunk*. So when the printed letters are removed, so they are no longer able to refer to those visual clues, then they must rely solely on the sounds within the spoken word. This isolation, discrimination, and identification of spoken sounds can often seem like an impossible task to someone with dyslexia.

Difficulty with Remembering

People with dyslexia may struggle with the memorization of things that don't make sense or are arbitrary, such as a random list of names, dates, places, numbers, or in the case of the alphabet—a random list of meaningless letters.

They will have a difficult time remembering things like addresses, phone numbers, and names. They may also have trouble in school with the memorization of sight words in reading, the memorization of addition or multiplication facts, dates and places in history, or the periodic table in chemistry.

Reads below Expected Grade Level

One indication of dyslexia is reading below grade level. Students with dyslexia may struggle with all aspects of reading including phonemic awareness, applying phonics, vocabulary, and comprehension.

Some students may be able to read, but will be much slower than their peers. They prefer not to read aloud in class and may experience high anxiety when forced to do so.

There is usually a gap between their ability and their achievement with reading, and if that student is not taught in a way that is specific for a dyslexic's needs, that gap will not close and may actually continue to widen as their schooling progresses.

Assigned to Special Reading Groups or Requires Tutoring

Children with dyslexia will usually not read as fluently or accurately as their peers, and so in an effort to not embarrass them and not go too fast beyond their capabilities, these kids are often placed in a small group together so they can learn at a somewhat slower pace.

What starts off as small groups in class can eventually turn into extra tutoring with the teacher after class, being sent out for a special reading class, being recommended for special education, or the necessity of additional tutoring after school.

Dislikes and Avoids Reading

Because of their awareness of their reading challenges, and in an effort of self-preservation, people with dyslexia may go to extreme measures to avoid reading aloud and embarrassing themselves in front of others.

A child may misbehave, fake being sick, or even wet their pants in an effort to be sent out of the room before it is their turn to read aloud in class. The anxiety and fear these students feel can be overwhelming.

Weakness in Grasping Grapheme/Phoneme Correspondence

For someone with dyslexia, the letters in a word do not fully make sense. This is because they are not recognizing each and every grapheme when they hear the word spoken. Therefore, when they see the word in print, the letters do not represent what they are hearing. Thus the "meaning" of those letters is diminished or even entirely unknown. The letters simply do not correlate to what they are hearing or saying.

Guessing when Reading

If a student has dyslexia and has not been taught to read in a way that makes sense to a dyslexic, then they have no other alternative but to guess when they read.

Guessing damages a dyslexic student's ability to progress in essential reading skills such as decoding and comprehension. Guessing does not produce good readers. Guessing produces good guessers. If a student with dyslexia is not taught properly, then they will be forced to depend on guessing, which will eventually become a habit. This unfortunate spiral of guessing can produce confusion and stagnation in these reading skills.

Slow to Complete Schoolwork

Students with dyslexia often cannot complete assignments as fast as students without dyslexia, but this is not due to a lack of drive, desire, or work ethic. On the contrary, students with dyslexia typically work harder than their peers, but that extra work often goes unnoticed by their teachers.

Teachers often are unaware of the hours and hours of practice and extreme effort that go into schoolwork at home. They do not see the extra time, effort, prayers, stress, and anxiety all centered around succeeding in the classroom. They also do not see the fear, confusion, and heartbreak when they are misjudged as being lazy or slow.

Students with dyslexia are often asked to decode with accuracy and fluency when these skills have not been explicitly taught to them. Yet, the student is required to perform with precision anyway. This is why they can struggle with low self-esteem with regard to academics.

Poor Performance on Timed Math Tests

Students with dyslexia often comprehend mathematical concepts just fine; however, they underperform when that knowledge is tested with a time constraint. A student may understand how addition, subtraction, multiplication, and division work with no problem, but if they are forced to recall those facts on a timed test, they will likely struggle to do so.

Memorization of rote facts is difficult for people with dyslexia. Unless those facts have meaning and logic attached to them, they may struggle to recall them.

Struggle to Recall Sequences

People with dyslexia often struggle to recall the letters of the alphabet in order (without singing the song), the days of the week and months of the year in order, phone numbers, and other sequential lists of arbitrary numbers or facts.

Difficulty Telling Time on an Analog Clock

Due to their difficulty with direction, a person with dyslexia may struggle to tell time on a clock with hands. This requires being able to count easily by fives as well as understand that one hand indicates the hour, one the minutes, and one the seconds. Putting all of that together and wrapping it in a circle can cause a tangle of confusion for someone with dyslexia.

Difficulty Perceiving Similarities and Differences in Similar Words or Letters

A weakness in the ability to recognize the smallest units of sound within spoken words (or weak phonemic awareness skills) accounts for most of the struggles a dyslexic reader and speller will have. This includes the difficulty they may have in discerning between one sound and another.

Two common confusing sounds for people with dyslexia are the short-*i* and the short-*e* sound. A person with dyslexia will find it difficult to discern the difference when they hear those sounds, as well as when they try to pronounce them. This is why the word *pillow* may often be pronounced as *pello*w. Even though they know the correct spelling of the word, they do not comprehend that what they are seeing does not correspond with what they are saying. The subtle difference between the short-*i* sound and the short-*e* sound is often an ongoing, confusing mystery.

Other confusingly similar sounds include f/th, b/d, and m/n. This is why a student may spell the word *throw* correctly, but then say that they want to go outside and *frow* a ball. Or why an adult may have a hard time pronouncing the words *cinnamon* or *aluminum*. When they come to one of these confusing letters, they may have to stop and seriously reflect on the sound it makes before proceeding, something a person without dyslexia typically does not have to do.

Trouble Distinguishing between Left and Right

Directionality issues can make determining left from right difficult for a person with dyslexia. They will often have to use a meaningful trick to figure out which is which, such as making an *L* with their left hand or saying "I write with my right." These directionality struggles may stay with them their entire lives.

Not only can left versus right cause them to pause and think, but any implied direction can be confusing, including up/down, next/previous, and even tomorrow/yesterday.

However, left and right are only two directions out of an infinite number that can travel over an entire circle. This is why telling time on an analog clock can be a significant struggle for someone with dyslexia. This is also why it may be difficult for a child with dyslexia to learn to tie their shoes or an older child to learn the pattern to solve a math problem. Direction doesn't always flow in a line. Sometimes direction changes from left to right, then up to down, without any logic or pattern, such as in long division.

A dyslexic student may have trouble remembering that even though we read from left to right, addition, subtraction, and multiplication problems are completed from right to left; however, long division, which is literally a confusing myriad of directions, crisscrosses all over itself. This is another reason why some students with dyslexia can struggle with math as well as reading.

Letter and Number Reversals, Inversions, and Transpositions

Reversals of letters and numbers are a typical part of learning when a child is just starting to read and write. However if a student is still reversing or transposing letters and numbers past the end of first grade (provided the child has had adequate education in kindergarten and first grade), then this may be an indication that dyslexia is present.

For instance, a student may reverse the number 5 when writing, so it looks more like a 2. Or, they may write a lowercase *t* as an *f* as an example of an inversion. They may also transpose letters when spelling a word, such as writing *dose* for *does*. A student with dyslexia may still reverse *b/d* in second grade and beyond.

Poor Spelling

Poor spelling is a defining characteristic of dyslexia. Some people with dyslexia may be able to read quite well, but they may struggle with spelling their entire lives.

Poor spelling is generally a result of poor phonemic awareness skills, poor memorization skills for random facts (required to spell phonetically irregular words), and a lack of understanding of typical spelling rules.

Students with dyslexia do not learn spelling by memorizing; they learn by applying rules that make sense. If a dyslexic student is taught spelling rules in a way that creates meaningful connections, then they can usually spell words correctly using their intellect and logic. However, many dyslexics do not receive this type of specialized spelling instruction in school.

Trouble Tying Shoes

Toddlers and young children with dyslexia may struggle to learn to tie their shoes due to the requisite memorization of a sequence of steps that all include meaningless direction.

Reading Is Slow, Inaccurate, and Labor Intensive

Due to their lack of understanding of how to apply phonics, people with dyslexia will have no choice but to force their way through a passage, making errors and lacking comprehension as they go. Or, in an effort to sound as fluent as their peers, they may plunge through a passage, guessing abundantly, hoping that most of the words were correct. When they do try to apply the reading rules they've been taught, it usually still takes them much longer to read than others because they have to go through each grapheme, rule by rule, in each word. This is labor-intensive and exhausting. If dyslexic students are not being taught in the appropriate way for them, this cycle of guessing will only serve to spin their wheels and won't promote progression. More of the same strategies produces more of the same results. Unless and until these students are taught in a way that makes sense to a dyslexic brain, any gains in reading will likely be minimal.

Reading Errors Point to Directionality Challenges

Students with dyslexia will often make predictable errors involving directionality. Due to their *b/d/p/q* confusion, they may often mix up those letters, or other similar looking letters, when reading. To someone with dyslexia, the letters in a word do not easily correspond to what they hear, due to their lack of phonemic awareness skills, so the letters, then, do not make sense. This confusion, combined with their directionality issues, is why dyslexic students can sometimes seem to read words backward. They may read *saw* for *was* or *god* for *dog*. They are not seeing the word backward, but are simply confused about the sequence of the graphemes and phonemes within it.

May Have to Read a Passage Several Times to Understand It

A dyslexic person often feels they must focus on the word they are trying to read at each moment, and can sometimes, therefore, miss the big picture or comprehend what they just read. Students may have to read a passage two or three times, or more, to understand the passage. Because reading is so labor-intensive, they often miss out on the luxury of reading for meaning.

Trouble with Copying

Students with dyslexia will have trouble with both near-point and far-point copying. They may struggle just as much trying to copy something from the board onto their paper as they will in trying to copy something from the top of their paper to the bottom. They are not able to easily grasp the spelling of whole words to transfer them effortlessly. They have to look up and down constantly, trying to find where they are in the word, and then copy just a few letters at a time. This arduous cycle can cause them to make many errors when copying, like writing things twice or leaving out words or whole lines altogether.

Low Self-Esteem, Depression, and Anxiety

Depression and/or anxiety can be a natural result of the continual, unrelenting stress that reading problems can bring. People with dyslexia typically have average or above average intelligence, and so they know that they should know how to read better. These students and adults are usually aware that they are not measuring up to their potential, and don't know why they are struggling. The discrepancy between their ability and their achievement leaves them wondering if something is wrong with them, or if they perhaps aren't as intelligent as they think they are. The uncertainty that these questions bring, along with unavoidable comparisons, can lead to low self-esteem, depression, and/or anxiety.

May Read or Spell a Word Correctly and Incorrectly on the Same Page

If a person has dyslexia they are highly likely to be confused about the spelling of many words. This causes them to guess, ask others, or rely on technology for the proper spelling of words. Unless they are taught the rules of spelling to help them understand why words are spelled the way they are, then they have no choice but to use one of those alternative methods when they do not know how to spell a word. The same is true for reading, especially of words that look similar to each other, like *though*, *through*, *thought* and *thorough*. It is this lack of understanding the rules of the written language that can cause them to read or spell a word correctly on one page and incorrectly on the next. Unless a person with dyslexia is taught appropriately, they will have no other choice but to be forced to guess.

A dyslexic student's lack of phonemic awareness skills, along with a lack of receiving proper instruction of the rules of the written language, can result in the letters in a word having no meaning or logic. This is why they omit, transpose, or add letters when reading or writing; why they are confused about silent-*e*; and why they are unable to read or spell unfamiliar words correctly.

Trouble Sounding Out Unfamiliar Words

People with dyslexia will have difficulty decoding unfamiliar words due to their lack of phonemic awareness skills and the lack of understanding why the letters in the word are arranged the way they are. Unless a student with dyslexia is taught the why's of reading, they must rely solely on guessing or memorization. If they are faced with an unfamiliar word they will often try to say something that sounds like another word with a similar size and shape. This can be extremely challenging in the upper grades, when new and unfamiliar words become much more complex and commonplace.

Trouble Comprehending What They Read

A person who struggles to decode individual words may struggle with comprehension as a natural result. If reading errors are consistent throughout a passage, then it is likely that the intended meaning of the passage will be altered, misunderstood, or missed altogether. If a struggling reader guesses correctly or even reads the words correctly through laborious methods, then chances are likely that the full meaning of the passage will be missed because the reader was concentrating on each word in isolation, not on the meaning of the passage as a whole. Sometimes, however, due to their intelligence, dyslexic students are able to figure out the meaning of a passage solely on the merits of their intellect and logic.

Trouble Taking Notes in Class

Note-taking can be an extremely arduous task for people with dyslexia. This is due to their sometimes weak auditory processing skills as well as spelling difficulties. People with dyslexia can struggle to process auditory information at a fast pace. They will typically find it easier to remember what was said if it was presented slowly when it was delivered.

A dyslexic person will also have trouble with spelling in varying degrees. This uncertainty of how words are spelled causes hesitation when note-taking, and therefore, the student is less able to keep up with what was said. Later, when the student goes back to read what they wrote, they may find that their spelling and writing errors make it impossible to determine what was actually said.

Test Anxiety

Understandably it is common for students with dyslexia to become anxious about quizzes and tests. First, to prove their understanding of a topic, they must be forced to read a question about it, which involves a weakness. Then, they must write a correct answer, which involves a weakness. Or they may be asked to recall rote, random facts, which also involves a weakness. In addition, quizzes and tests are usually timed, and dyslexic students need time to process information, so this time constraint, too, involves a weakness. In short, dyslexic students are usually required to prove their knowledge

20

Is It Dyslexia?

and intelligence using only their areas of weakness. This is why their level of stress around test-taking is completely understandable. It is also, however, avoidable. Unfortunately, most methods of testing continue unchanged.

Difficulty Learning a Foreign Language

Dyslexia is characterized by difficulty processing language, so a student may naturally struggle with learning a foreign language, especially in print. A dyslexic person will have difficulty reading and spelling in their native language, which is familiar to them and which they were exposed to daily since birth. So, learning to read and write a foreign language will be even more difficult since they will be required to learn a completely new set of sounds and reading rules. They may find learning to speak a foreign language easier than learning to read and write in the new language.

Difficulty Articulating Thoughts

People with dyslexia often discover that they have a difficult time articulating what they are thinking in a fluent or eloquent way. They may find that they add filler words like *uh* and *um* as they search for an appropriate word. They also are often known to "talk with their hands," which they may feel helps to propel the meaning of their message. This extra thought-processing time, along with difficulty distinguishing between similar-sounding words when speaking, can make public speaking a daunting experience.

Family History of Dyslexia

Dyslexia is a genetic, inherited condition. One of the benefits of screening for dyslexia is an awareness of the inherited condition, which can result in a watchful eye on upcoming generations. The earlier the signs of dyslexia are spotted, the earlier appropriate instructional methods can be applied. If a child's dyslexia is caught early, they may never have to experience the negative repercussions of undiagnosed dyslexia.

Gifts

The following are areas where people with dyslexia may excel.

Great Imagination/Extremely Creative

Often people with dyslexia will be extremely creative or imaginative. They may be able to create vivid stories with incredible detail, yet not be able to write down what they said in the way that adequately represents their thoughts. A person with dyslexia will often choose to write down words that they know how to spell, rather than words that adequately express their ideas. This results in a deficient and incomplete reflection of their brilliant thoughts.

Students with dyslexia will typically perform better on oral tests than written ones. They can generally express their ideas and understanding much better verbally than in writing. Therefore, even though a student may understand the material that was taught, if they are forced to prove that knowledge on paper, they are more likely to make errors that will result in a lower grade than they would have received if allowed to prove their knowledge in other ways. Their creative writing may express wonderful ideas, yet have copious spelling errors. It is for these reasons that their intelligence, unfortunately, is not typically reflected in their writing.

Highly Observant, Intuitive, and Empathetic

People with dyslexia often know how to be a good friend, and they often keep their friends for many years. They tend to be kind because they are often gifted with a heightened sense of empathy, intuition, and are highly observant. They may also be surprisingly mature and good at seeing the big picture. All of these qualities easily enable people with dyslexia to be and have good friends.

Highly Artistic

People with dyslexia are often extremely gifted with artistic ability. Due to their exceptional skills in certain parts of the brain, students often discover that although they struggle with processing language, they excel in artistic expression. A person with dyslexia may find that they have uncommon ability in drawing, sculpture, painting, storytelling, or any other form of creative design.

Mechanical Ability

People with dyslexia are often extremely gifted with regard to mechanical ability, doing things that involve their hands, or projects requiring assembly. For this reason, they often enjoy puzzles or building models. This is also why they may be gifted in seeing the big picture of a mechanical problem and understanding how to best fix it.

Musically Gifted

Students with dyslexia may excel in certain areas involving the right hemisphere of the brain, such as musical ability and other creative expressions. A dyslexic may find it difficult to read music on a staff, yet be able to play a piece of music by ear easily and beautifully. A dyslexic may feel like the notes on a staff are an obstacle or hindrance and may find themselves drawn to the keys themselves to express themselves musically.

Gifted in Athletics

People with dyslexia can excel in several areas, such as athletics. They can be extremely gifted athletically and often outperform their peers.

Gifted in Hands-on Activities

People with dyslexia can be quite skilled with tasks involving their hands. They can be exceptional builders or crafters, and can create things with an ability that surpasses their peers. Children with dyslexia often enjoy building unique and wonderful creations out of Legos or other assembly blocks and materials. They can be exceptionally talented creators as they use their hands to build, sculpt, sew, paint, and so on.

Excellent Comprehension of Stories that Are Read or Told to Them

If a dyslexic student is permitted to listen to their lessons, rather than relying solely on reading them, then that student will be more likely to do just as well as their peers in comprehension. If students with dyslexia are allowed to listen to their texts and materials prior to presenting their knowledge of a subject, then the "playing fields" would be more evenly leveled between dyslexic students and their peers, and they could have a more equal chance of success.

Summary

Being aware of the signs of dyslexia will help you to recognize them in yourself or others. Now that you've learned the signs, if you suspect that dyslexia is present, continue with the dyslexia screening in Part 2 of this book. The results of this screening will provide you with important answers and essential next steps for you and your reader.

Chapter 2

Unraveling Misinformation about Dyslexia

Now that you know how to recognize the signs of dyslexia, you'll hear about John, Michael and Mary's son. As you read John's story, you'll learn about common myths and misconceptions surrounding dyslexia and what the truth about dyslexia really is.

John's Story

Michael and Mary loved watching their son, John, learn and grow! They loved reading to him, teaching him, and encouraging early learning while they played with their toddler. When John's kindergarten teacher told them that he was having trouble remembering the letters of the alphabet and their sounds, they were surprised because they had worked so much with him at home. Michael immediately felt his heart sink as he contemplated the agonizing academic experience that his son might have to go through if it was anything like his own experience.

Mary recognized this difficulty as being a possible early warning sign of dyslexia. Her mother and brother had dyslexia, and she was familiar with the condition and what was needed if John did have it. She took a minute to think about any other possible early warning signs. John was a late talker and did have a hard time grasping the concept of rhyming. She also thought of his difficulty remembering the names of the different shapes. All of that, coupled with the family history of reading challenges, were enough warning signs for her. She immediately talked to John about the possibility that John might have dyslexia.

Michael immediately discounted the possibility, thinking that dyslexia was a made-up, or catchall, term for kids who didn't read well. He didn't believe in dyslexia. But Mary told him about her dad and brother, how they were both screened and determined to have dyslexia, and the difference that made in their schooling.

Michael knew firsthand what a terrible schooling experience was like, so he listened, just in case there was some truth to it. He did not want John to have the same experience he had!

Together Michael and Mary looked up dyslexia on the internet and found some reputable sites. They learned that dyslexia is genetic and is neurobiological in origin. They also learned that dyslexia impacts the way a person processes language, which accounts for their struggles with reading, spelling, processing auditory input, and speaking.

Michael's heart skipped a beat. Could this be what he had? Did he have dyslexia this whole time and not know it?

Michael's thoughts began swirling. Was dyslexia real? And did he have it? He knew he could read much better now than when he was young, so was it just something you have when you're little and then grow out of it? Or do adults have dyslexia too? The first person he went to talk about this was his mother.

When Michael's mother, Anna, answered the call, Michael began by telling her the early signs of dyslexia that Mary had seen in John. He then asked her if she knew anything about dyslexia or if she ever considered that he might have had it.

At first Anna was distressed to hear that John was having some of the same struggles that Michael had at that age. But then she pondered the question he asked. Had she ever considered that Michael might have had dyslexia? She hadn't. And she told him so. "I never really heard much about dyslexia. None of your teachers mentioned it, so it never really crossed my mind," she said. "What is it exactly? Isn't that when people see things backward?" Michael answered that he didn't know a lot about it yet, but he was on a mission to learn more.

Looking for More Information in All the Wrong Places

Michael spent weeks researching and searching for more information. He began by asking friends and family if they knew anyone with dyslexia. What he discovered shocked him. Almost everyone they knew knew someone who had dyslexia! He had no idea it was so common. He thought dyslexia was a rare condition.

The more Michael dug for information, the more he became confused about what was true and what was not. He had heard from one friend that dyslexia was only found in boys, but then how could Mary's mother have it? He heard from an uncle that if you are truly dyslexic, then you can't read at all. His neighbor told him it is a vision problem and can be fixed with vision therapy. He learned from a co-worker that dyslexia is caused by a lack of phonics instruction when kids are young. Another friend told Michael not to worry, that people with dyslexia just need to try harder, that sometimes it's a result of laziness which can be "trained out of them" with a proper work ethic. That piece of information really hit hard for Michael because he knew he tried harder in school than most kids he knew. Michael was getting so much information and misinformation that his head was swimming. He had no idea what was fact and what was fiction.

Mary and her family were extremely helpful because they had been through this whole journey before. Mary's mother, Elizabeth, had struggled in school, but wasn't diagnosed with dyslexia until she was a young adult. So when Mary's brother, Luke, began showing signs of dyslexia, Elizabeth recognized the signs and knew what to do. Because of that insight, Luke did not have to endure the agony of feeling less intelligent or less capable than his peers. He was taught using instructional methods that work for dyslexic students early on and did just fine in school.

Mary and Elizabeth calmly explained to Michael what was true and what was not. Dyslexia is not exclusive to boys. Most dyslexics can read to a point. And because it is primarily a phonological processing problem, it cannot be "fixed" with vision therapy and is not caused by a lack of phonics instruction or exposure to print. They also helped Michael understand the important fact that dyslexia is not a result of laziness or a weak work ethic. In fact, most dyslexics work much harder than their peers because they have no choice if they want to succeed! They reminded Michael that dyslexic students put in hours and hours of extra time and work at home, well beyond what other kids in their class are doing, just to keep their grades above failing. They emphasized that most dyslexic students—are—*not*—lazy! Michael needed to hear all of that. It validated what he knew deep down to be true. However, he still didn't understand why all that extra effort didn't pay off for him.

Michael was beginning to hope that he did have dyslexia so there would be an answer to his lifetime of struggles, and so he could help his son to avoid them.

Michael was beginning to nurture hope, for his son, and for himself. He talked with Mary and Elizabeth about some thoughts he had kept buried in his heart his whole life. He told them, "All my life, I have always wondered why I was not as smart as everyone else around me. Why couldn't I read as well as my friends, and why I have to ask you how to spell words that others don't have any problem spelling. To me, it seemed like the only answer was that I was just not as smart as everyone else. If it turns out that I have dyslexia, does that mean I am just as smart as other people, but that it's the dyslexia that makes these things more difficult for me?" The hope in him swelled with the thought of it.

Michael excitedly wondered, *"Is it dyslexia?"*

If so, his whole world, and that of John, was about to change.

Elizabeth and Mary both gave a resounding "Yes! You are just as intelligent, or more so, than anyone else! Dyslexia just makes it difficult to learn the same way that others do. You are just as capable of reading and writing as anyone else, if you are taught in a way that makes sense to a beautifully dyslexic brain!"

Could this be? Is this possible? The ramifications of this information were overwhelming. Could it be that he was not stupid after all? He was simply dyslexic? And was there hope for his son?

Getting Answers

Mary knew exactly what to do. She arranged for both John and Michael to be screened for dyslexia. Michael was not concerned that he could have dyslexia. He was more concerned that he might not have it! He was hoping, almost more than anything, that his diagnosis would show that he did, in fact, have dyslexia. He wanted to know the reasons why he had struggled for so many years! He wanted to learn in a way that made sense! Most of all, he hoped the screening would verify the likelihood of dyslexia in John. He was just six years old, and if they could step in and teach him now, when he was young, then he would not have to struggle the way he did!

Michael thought of all those tears that John would not have to cry! He imagined all those pants he would not feel desperate enough to wet. He envisioned classrooms that he would not desperately try to be taken out of. Michael and Mary both prayed that these screening results would be a blessing to them and to future generations after them. They wanted desperately to know—is it dyslexia?

Michael and John's dyslexia screenings began with a comprehensive questionnaire. This gave the screener a good understanding of their educational, personal, and genetic history.

Each screening consisted of several tasks that measured their phonemic awareness skills, spelling knowledge, memorization skills, and of course, their reading ability. The tests for John and Michael were similar, but were adapted to their age and level of schooling.

Then, they waited for the results.

Mary felt like she already knew the answer for both Michael and John. She had seen this before and knew how to proceed once they knew for sure. Michael hoped he knew the answer. He hoped beyond hope that he and John were dyslexic.

About two weeks later, the long-awaited results came in. Both Michael and John had dyslexia. Michael could not hold back the tears. He finally had answers! He knew why he struggled for so long, and that he was not unintelligent! He now knew there was a different way to learn how to read and spell and that there was still hope for him. And most importantly, there was hope for John.

Michael and Mary did not waste any time. They immediately found a reading program that was specifically designed for students with dyslexia and they both started working on those lessons at home. When they received John's next progress report, his teacher had noted that John had already made noticeable progress and to continue doing what they were doing with him at home. It was working!

John entered first grade, second grade, third grade, and beyond never knowing what it was like to be placed in the "bluebirds" group. He never had to stay in from recess to finish his work. He never had to feel humiliated in front of his friends when he read aloud. And he never felt stupid. Instead, John thrived.

John loved school.

Years later, John's parents and grandparents went to his high school graduation with hearts soaring. As they watched John walk across the stage to receive his diploma, neither Jacob, Anna, Michael, nor Mary could hold back the tears. They knew what a walk that was, and all that it meant. As John took his diploma and shook the principal's hand, he turned around to smile and wave at his family who vigorously and tearfully waved back. Then they watched as John walked into a bright, successful, beautifully dyslexic future.

Myths about Dyslexia

There are a lot of myths about dyslexia. You may have heard misinformation from friends or the internet. In this section, you'll learn all about the myths surrounding dyslexia.

Myth: Dyslexia Is Made Up

Dyslexia is not a made-up or catchall term used to describe people who don't read well.

Dyslexia is an inherited condition that affects the processing of language. It is primarily due to phonological processing difficulties and affects a person's ability to read, spell, and speak. Dyslexia can make the processing of directionality difficult as well as the memorization and recall of rote, random facts. Dyslexia is not related to intelligence, gender, environment, or geographical location.

The scientific definition of dyslexia, which was included in the U.S. First Step Act in 2018, reads: "The term 'dyslexia' means an unexpected difficulty in reading for an individual who has the intelligence to be a much better reader, most commonly caused by a difficulty in the phonological processing (the appreciation of the individual sounds of spoken language), which affects the ability of an individual to speak, read, and spell" (Public Law 115-391) (*Overcoming Dyslexia* by Sally Shaywitz, p. 100).

The effects of dyslexia can be wide in both scope and severity. Effects can include high academic anxiety, depression, and low self-esteem. However, when dyslexia is identified as the cause of a student's academic struggles, then proper instruction can be implemented. The simple use of appropriate teaching methods can significantly, and often quite quickly, reduce the severity of those effects, and over time, may even eliminate them.

The effects of dyslexia are not all negative, however. Because of the physical differences in the brain, people with dyslexia often excel in areas such as athletics, music, interpersonal skills, and creativity. People with dyslexia also often contribute great leadership and innovation to society, and add richness and beauty to the world.

Myth: People Grow Out of Dyslexia

Since dyslexia is genetic, it remains with a person their entire life. However, the effects of dyslexia can be significantly reduced with the right teaching methods.

Some people with dyslexia have it only mildly. These are the students who may have struggled somewhat in school but grew up to be fluent readers and adequate spellers. They may go through life never knowing that they have dyslexia. If they do realize they have dyslexia, then they may have the mistaken thought that they have "grown out of it," when in reality, they learned to cope, adjust, and compensate, which is entirely possible if one's dyslexia is mild or moderate.

A dyslexic student may learn to overcome their reading challenges, but may still be confused about spelling, left versus right, long division, or telling time on an analog clock. Some of the effects of dyslexia may be reduced, but all of the effects may not entirely be eliminated.

Myth: Dyslexia Is Seeing Things Backward

A person with dyslexia may reverse *b* and *d*, or even read a word from back to front, but this is not due to an eyesight problem. It is due to their difficulty with directionality. Right versus left, up versus down, next versus previous, or any implied direction can be confusing for a dyslexic student and can therefore be misunderstood as "seeing things backward."

Myth: Dyslexia Is Rare

According to the Yale Center for Dyslexia and Creativity, "Dyslexia affects 20 percent of the population and represents 80–90 percent of all those with learning disabilities. It is the most common of all neurocognitive disorders" (see https://www.researchgate.net/publication/281351846_Achievement_Gap_in_Reading_Is_Present_as_Early_as_First_Grade_and_Persists_through_Adolescence).

According to these statistics, teachers can expect to have at least one, probably several more, dyslexic students in every class they teach.

Myth: Dyslexia Is Only Found in Boys

According to a 1990 study in the American Medical Association, by Drs. Sally and Bennett Shaywitz, it was found that "no significant differences in the prevalence of reading disability" was found in boys as compared to girls.

The study goes on to report that more boys than girls are identified by the schools. However, their data indicates that this is due to school-identified samples that are "almost unavoidably subject to referral bias."

Sally Shaywitz, in her book *Overcoming Dyslexia* (p. 33), provides one explanation for this bias. She states:

> Analysis of teacher ratings of the children's behavior revealed why girls are less readily identified than boys. There are significant differences between how teachers rate typical boys and girls. Teachers have incorporated a norm for classroom behavior that reflects the calmer behavior of normal girls. Boys who are a bit rambunctious—although still within the normal range for the behavior of boys—may be perceived as having a behavior problem and referred for further evaluation. Meanwhile, the well-mannered little Jennifers and the shy Tanishas who sit quietly in their seats but who nevertheless are failing to learn to read are often overlooked and never, or only much later, identified as dyslexic by their school systems.

Myth: People with Dyslexia Can't Read

Most people with dyslexia can read to a point. Some can read quite well. Few people with dyslexia are nonreaders.

Most dyslexics will be able to function in a world of print; however, they may feel burdened by the difficulty the written word causes them. These are the students who pass through school barely holding on to their grades and having to work twice as hard as their peers to do so. They are the students who experience high anxiety when it is time to read aloud in class and whose writing does not at all reflect their knowledge of a subject.

Even though most dyslexics can read, and some quite well, almost all dyslexics will have some trouble with spelling. Dyslexics often use spell check, speech-to-text technology, or a friend or family member to help them spell words, even when they can read those same words just fine. Spelling will almost always be more difficult for a dyslexic person than reading.

Myth: Dyslexia Can Be Fixed with Vision Therapy

Dyslexia is not a vision problem. People with dyslexia often have perfect vision. Dyslexia is also not caused by a tracking problem, and therefore, cannot be corrected solely with vision therapy.

Dyslexia is more an auditory issue than a visual one. If students with dyslexia cannot discriminate, isolate, and manipulate the individual sounds within spoken words, then trying to decipher the written word will be even more confusing.

However, people with dyslexia can have difficulty processing both visual and auditory information. They may see just fine, but they struggle to process what they are seeing, particularly if interpreting direction is required. Auditory processing is also difficult for those with dyslexia, even though their hearing may be perfect. The struggle lies in processing the information, particularly if the sights and sounds are similar.

So, even if a child wears glasses and receives vision therapy, they may still struggle to read and spell if they are not taught appropriately because of their difficulty with processing language.

Myth: Dyslexia Is Caused by a Lack of Phonics Instruction When Young

Dyslexia is an inherited condition that makes processing written and oral language difficult. A lack of phonics instruction when young does not create or cause dyslexia, nor does a lack of exposure to print as babies or toddlers.

In fact, children with dyslexia (as well as adults) often "know" phonics just fine, yet they cannot apply it due to their weak phonemic awareness skills. They will know that *A* says /a/ and *B* says /b/, but when they go to apply that knowledge to blend words, that knowledge helps them very little.

Dyslexics must strengthen phonemic awareness skills first before they can apply phonics accurately and automatically.

Myth: If People with Dyslexia Tried Harder, or Read More, They Would Succeed

Students with dyslexia do not learn to read and write the same way as their peers. They learn differently, so they need to be taught differently. If a student with dyslexia is not progressing and thriving, then the responsibility lies more with the instructor than the instructed.

Since a child is born with dyslexia, they typically miss an important pre-reading skill that is developed naturally in the non-dyslexic learner—the skill of phonemic awareness. Dyslexic students *can* learn this skill (and must!), but it must be explicitly taught to them. They do not develop the skill naturally as their peers do. If a student does not master the skill of phonemic awareness, their chances of becoming solid, automatic, and fluent readers are significantly reduced.

Teachers and parents can try to teach a dyslexic student using methods that work for nondyslexic students, but they will find that the child does not progress in the same way a nondyslexic child would. If a student is lacking phonemic awareness, they will not be able to read and spell as easily as their peers, no matter how slow the instruction or how many times it is repeated.

Myth: People with Dyslexia Are Not Smart

Dyslexia does not discriminate based on intelligence. It affects people with high as well as low IQs and all ranges in between.

Dyslexia has been traditionally defined as an unexpected difficulty with reading despite intelligence. This means that a person with dyslexia may have average or above average intelligence, yet their academic performance does not reflect that intelligence. There is an unexpected gap between their ability and their performance.

Since dyslexia is genetic, a person with a high IQ, a strong desire to learn, and ample exposure to print may still struggle with reading and writing unless and until they receive highly specialized instruction designed for the way a dyslexic brain works.

Summary

Now that you have learned the common misconceptions about dyslexia, you are in a better position to recognize what is true and what is not about the condition. You are also more equipped to teach others research-based facts and to spread the truth about dyslexia.

Chapter 3

Embracing Dyslexia

Now that you've learned how to discern myth from fact, you'll hear about Emma, John's daughter. As you read Emma's story, you'll discover that students with dyslexia can thrive and even excel in the classroom, if their dyslexia is caught and if they are taught in the way a dyslexic student needs. You'll learn exactly what works, how they learn best, and that dyslexia can be a part of a happy and successful life.

Emma's Story

After graduation, John pursued a career in agriculture management. He enjoyed his career choice and excelled in his field. He also met and married his high school sweetheart, Abigail, and together they began to raise a family.

John and Abigail had four energetic, bright, and inquisitive children. The youngest of whom was named Emma.

Emma's progress through early childhood was markedly different from that of her older siblings, and John and Abigail immediately recognized the signs of dyslexia. They were aware that dyslexia ran in John's family, so they kept a watchful eye on all of their children to identify the signs.

They noticed that Emma struggled in some academic areas, but that she excelled in many areas that were quite impressive. They had her screened as soon as possible and were not the least bit worried about a diagnosis of dyslexia. They knew that there were instructional methods that worked for students with dyslexia, and that Emma would be just fine with the proper interventions. In fact, with all of her extraordinary talents and strengths, she would be more than fine. She would be exceptional.

Emma was screened for dyslexia in kindergarten and was shown to be moderately dyslexic. This confirmed John and Abigail's suspicions, so they immediately went to work to provide her with the right interventions to help her overcome her learning challenges.

As they began to search for an appropriate reading intervention program, they discovered an extensive list of programs to choose from. They wanted a program that would not teach reading by relying on guessing. They knew that it was important that Emma be taught how to read directly and explicitly, that her learning should not be left to simply infer or naturally grasp. They also learned terms like *systematic teaching* (lessons building on each other in a logical, structured, and sequential manner), *synthetic phonics* (learning to blend, or synthesize, individual sounds together to form words), and *code-based instruction* (a focus on the letters and letter groups within words).

Choosing a Learning Path

John and Abigail discovered that many reading programs seemed to follow a systematic, explicit, and code-based approach, but they weren't sure which would be best for Emma. They wanted to know which of all these programs had everything that a dyslexic student would need. Through their research, they found that an effective reading program would include *all* of the essential components to teach a dyslexic student effectively. They knew they wanted a comprehensive reading program that included phonemic awareness, phonics, vocabulary, comprehension, and fluency development.

They did not want to have to piece together several reading programs in order to receive all of the elements of reading instruction. They were looking for a program that was not only designed for a dyslexic student, but that also incorporated all of these essential elements. The more they learned about what works for dyslexic students, the more excited they became to choose a program that had everything they needed for their daughter.

Through their research, they knew that Emma would excel with a reading program that

- Develops and strengthens phonemic awareness.
- Teaches the correct sounds of the graphemes.
- Properly teaches the role of sight words and strategies to learn them.
- Explicitly teaches how graphemes and phonemes are related to each other.
- Teaches that words are made up of individual sounds.
- Teaches how to analyze a word to determine the sound that each grapheme will make.
- Teaches how to blend, or synthesize, word parts together to form words with systematic, synthetic phonics instruction.
- Includes reading words within connected text, not solely in isolation.
- Includes explicit vocabulary instruction.
- Includes comprehension development.
- Includes instruction in expression and phrasing.
- Includes fluency exercises.

John and Abigail learned that there were some schools specifically for dyslexic students. They would have loved for Emma to experience her education in such a school, but because of the high cost and distance to the nearest school, that choice was not plausible for their family. They also interviewed several tutors who specialized in programs for dyslexic students and found several that they felt would be appropriate for Emma. However, in the end, they decided to become experts in the field of dyslexia themselves.

Self-Teaching

John and Abigail immersed themselves in learning proper teaching methods for dyslexic students. They purchased a comprehensive, dyslexia-designed reading program that met all of their needs. They applied what they were learning and taught their daughter. Emma quickly began reading accurately, fluently, and with an assured and calm confidence.

Emma excelled in school and eventually became a teacher. She devoted the rest of her life to teaching adults who struggled to read how to discover, control, embrace, and thrive with dyslexia. Emma's efforts helped illiteracy survivors all over the world overcome the same reading challenges that had brought her grandfather so much pain many years ago.

Emma was changing the world one life, and one generation, at a time.

She dedicated her efforts to her grandfather, Michael.

Systematic, Synthetic, Explicit Code-Based Instruction

A student with dyslexia does not learn how to read by guessing what a word is. Although they can easily resort to guessing, they should not be taught to read using this or any whole-language method. Children with dyslexia need to be taught how to read, not how to guess.

Whole-language instructional methods are based on the assumption that children learn to read naturally, simply by being exposed to print. This method also teaches that children should guess at what a word is based on how it looks as a whole, the context it's in, and any picture clues. It does not teach code-based phonics instruction explicitly and only lightly touches on letter-sound relationships.

Dyslexic students need systematic, explicit, code-based instruction. They need to learn not only *what* the graphemes will say, but also when and why.

Systematic, synthetic phonics instruction teaches the letter-sound relationships in a highly structured and sequential way. Students are taught how to connect the graphemes with the sounds that they will make, and when. Then, students are taught how to blend (or synthesize) those phonemes together to form words.

For instance, after a student has been taught the correct sounds for each grapheme within a given word, such as *lamp,* they will then point to and repeat each of those sounds, /l/ /a/ /m/ /p/, and next slowly push those sounds together to read the word *lamp.*

This type of phonics instruction must be taught explicitly, directly to the student. This essential code-based instruction should not be left to be inferred or learned naturally solely by exposure.

An appropriate code-based reading program for dyslexic students should include phonemic awareness exercises, explicit phonics instruction, fluency development, vocabulary lessons, and comprehension strengthening strategies.

Summary

In this chapter, you have learned that students with dyslexia can succeed academically if they are taught in the way that dyslexic learners need. You have also begun to learn what the instructional methods should look like for dyslexic students to thrive. You will learn more about these instructional methods in detail in Part 3. This critical information will help you to make informed decisions as you progress through a dyslexia screening and beyond.

Chapter 4

What to Do If You Suspect Dyslexia

Now that you've heard the stories of Michael, John, and Emma, you have seen what the life of a dyslexic student can look like with, as well as without, proper identification and instruction. Now, let's look at your own story.

Your Story

Your story might not begin the same way as Michael's or John's or Emma's, but you might have discovered some similarities in either yourself or in someone you care about.

Maybe your child, too, has difficulty reading, but their teacher told you to not worry, that they were probably just a late bloomer.

Maybe you have watched your child struggle with homework or with spelling or with memorizing math facts even though they are quite intelligent.

Maybe it is yourself that you caught a glimpse of as you read about Michael's journey through school and you remembered what it was like to dread being called on in class or to read in front of your peers.

Maybe you yearned for the hope that these good parents felt as they discovered that there is hope and help for their child!

Maybe you, too, are eager to discover whether dyslexia is the cause of your or your loved one's struggles so that you can move forward to interventions that work.

Your story might not begin the same as those you've just read about, but your story can have a similarly beautiful, hope-filled, generation-changing ending!

If you suspect dyslexia in yourself or someone you know, continue to Parts 2 and 3 of this book. You will find age-appropriate dyslexia screenings that can be administered at home. No prior training or education is required. You will receive clear, simple instructions on how to administer the screenings and how to analyze the results.

If the results of the screening show that dyslexia is likely present, you will be provided with recommendations for home and school and a step-by-step guide to moving forward successfully with dyslexia.

Summary

Now that you have learned about the signs of dyslexia, how to recognize and refute common myths, and what a dyslexic learner needs, you may be wondering if you or someone you know has dyslexia. Knowing this important information can change everything for a dyslexic learner, as you have discovered in the stories of Michael, John, and Emma. Michael went unidentified and always struggled not only academically, but emotionally as well. Emma was identified early and provided the type of instruction she needed. In Part 2 of this book, you'll find dyslexia screenings for readers of all ages. Discovering dyslexia early is, of course, ideal. However, just like Gertie in the Introduction of this book, finding out that you have dyslexia can be life changing, liberating, and a joyful discovery at any age.

Part II

Screening for Dyslexia

In this part of the book, you'll learn all about the dyslexia screening process. You'll learn how to best prepare for the screening, how to proceed through the 11 tasks, and exactly what to say throughout the process. You'll also learn about the wide range of emotions that can accompany the results of a dyslexia screening and how to best support and encourage the reader.

Chapter 5

Understanding the Dyslexia Screening Process

If someone is suspected to have dyslexia, a dyslexia screening is the first step. In this chapter, I'll introduce the screening process and then provide answers to frequently asked questions.

Introduction to the Screening Process

Screenings can be done with students as young as kindergarten age. In fact, kindergarten and first grade are ideal times to screen for dyslexia because if a child is found to fit the dyslexia profile, then specific instructional methods and academic accommodations can be made before the child struggles or fails in school.

Even though the younger the age of the student, the better, screenings can, and should, be done at any age. It is never too late to discover that dyslexia is likely the cause of a person's reading difficulties because it is never too late to begin the interventions that will help clear the chaos for a dyslexic learner.

Learning that dyslexia is present is often a relief for many dyslexic learners. It can be comforting for them to know that there are specific teaching strategies that will help them overcome the difficulties they've experienced with the printed word. When students, especially adults, find out they are dyslexic and that there is hope for their reading and spelling challenges, they often are excited about the new awareness that they are not less intelligent than their peers, like Gertie in the Introduction of the book, and that they can learn to read and spell with ease. They simply need to be taught in the way a dyslexic learner needs.

A positive result from a dyslexia screening may be difficult for some parents to face, while at the same time, be a source of joy and relief for the person being screened. It is perfectly acceptable for all emotions to be experienced, including regret for not finding out sooner.

If the results of the screening are accepted as a jumping-off point to implementing new and appropriate interventions, then usually any negative emotions become quickly overshadowed by the peace and joy that is experienced when a struggling student is finally able to "get it." It is at this new beginning that students, parents, and adults who've struggled their whole lives realize that the world of words is finally going to be theirs for the taking.

> The screenings in this book are for personal use only. Professional licenses are available for those who would like to use the screenings for professional or clinical use. To obtain a screening license, please go to https://enroll.learnreading.com/license.

Dyslexia Screening Q&A

In this section, I'll answer frequently asked questions about the screening process.

Question: How can I know if I should screen my child or student for dyslexia?

Answer: To determine whether a person should be screened for dyslexia, your first step is to complete the dyslexia screening questionnaire that corresponds to the person's grade level (not reading level). Upon completion of the questionnaire, you will be given an analysis guide to determine if you should continue with the full screening.

Question: Is my child too young to be screened?

Answer: The dyslexia screenings are appropriate for students in kindergarten through adulthood. If the student is not yet in kindergarten, dyslexia may still be present, but measuring and proving that dyslexia will be more difficult.

Question: I am an adult, and I think I have dyslexia. Can I screen myself?

Answer: Adults who would like to know if they are dyslexic should be screened by another adult. It is imperative that they not see the answers to the screening questions as it may skew their performance and results. It would also be extremely difficult to hear or notice one's own mistakes, so the results would likely be inaccurate.

Question: I don't feel qualified to administer this screening. I don't know anything about dyslexia. What if I do something wrong?

Answer: The dyslexia screening tasks are extremely user friendly for both the screener and the student. All the wording, answers, and examples are provided for you. There are also clear, explanatory videos for the screener and for the student. These short videos will teach you exactly what to do in each task. You can find those supportive videos here: https://courses.learnreading.com/courses/dyslexia-screening-videos.

Question: How long does the screening take?

Answer: The screening begins with a questionnaire, which can take anywhere from 5 to 15 minutes to complete. This is to be done prior to the screening, and the student is not needed during this portion of the screening process. The screening tasks themselves, altogether, take an average of 1 to 2 hours to complete. The screening tasks do not all have to be completed in one sitting. In fact, breaking up the tasks is recommended, so the student is given the opportunity to perform at their best. Younger or more active children may need a short break after every few tasks. These breaks can be a few minutes or even a few days. Older students or adults may want to proceed through all 11 tasks at once, and are able to easily maintain focus throughout the entire screening. The screener should gauge the reader's attention level and emotional state to determine the best pace at which the student can perform at their best.

Question: Is this screening an actual diagnosis?

Answer: No. Dyslexia is a clinical diagnosis and requires an intelligence test. This screening can be a foundational and a significant portion of a full, clinical diagnosis, but is technically incomplete without an intelligence test, which would compare the gap between a student's ability and their achievement. However, if administered correctly, the results of this screening are typically accurate.

Question: Can I use the results of this screening to demand or request formal accommodations in a public school on an IEP?

Answer: This screening is not intended for use in determining eligibility for public school intervention and is not appropriate to demand formal accommodations in the public school system. However, it is an appropriate first step in determining what informal accommodations may be requested in the classroom to support the student, should the results show that dyslexia is likely present.

Question: What if my child does have dyslexia? Then what?

Answer: If the results of this screening show that your child does fit the dyslexia profile, then you can begin immediately to pursue the recommendations in Part 3 of this book. You will receive recommendations for what to do on the very first day after the screening is completed and you have learned the results. You will also be guided through your first and next steps throughout the first week after the screening, and within the first month. Screeners will be provided with several recommendations and options that will support a dyslexic student both at home and at school.

Question: What if I'm dyslexic too? Can I still screen my child?

Answer: Yes. However, you will need to listen very carefully to the student's answers. People with dyslexia often have a difficult time hearing and discriminating between the smallest units of sound within a word, and that is exactly what many of the screening tasks are designed to measure. The correct answers, with examples, are provided for the screener; however it is very important that the screener be able to hear any mistakes that the student may make. If the screener finds that it is difficult to answer several of the screening questions correctly themselves, then they may want to hand off the administration of the dyslexia screening to someone else so as to record the most accurate results.

Question: Does this screening come with a report?

Answer: No. This at-home dyslexia screening does not include a personalized report summarizing the student's performance on each task.

Question: How will my child feel if it looks like they are dyslexic? Will it hurt their self-esteem?

Answer: Students are usually extremely relieved to know that they are, in fact, quite intelligent and that dyslexia is the cause of their reading and spelling difficulties. They are also usually excited to learn that there are ways to improve their reading and writing skills and that there is hope for a successful academic future. If the screening results indicate dyslexia is likely present, then there is a free "Congratulations!" video available for your student to watch at https://courses.learnreading.com/courses/dyslexia-screening-videos, which explains that discovering dyslexia can be wonderful, exciting, and happy news!

Summary

In this chapter, you have discovered the answers to many frequently asked questions about the dyslexia screening process. You have learned that it is an informal screening and should be used for personal use only. You have also learned about the possible emotions that can accompany the results of this screening and where to find a "Congratulations!" video to celebrate your discovery.

Chapter 6

Instructions for the Dyslexia Screening

In this chapter, we'll go through the instructions for screening for dyslexia that you can use for your child or students. All dyslexia screening videos referenced are available to view for free at https://courses.learnreading.com/courses/dyslexia-screening-videos.

Prepare for the Screening

First, make a copy of the screening packet that corresponds to the student's grade level, not reading level. If the student is dyslexic, there is a high probability that their reading level and their grade level will be different from each other. The student must be screened with the tasks corresponding to their school grade level to sufficiently measure any discrepancy between their personal versus expected achievement. If the screening is completed during the summer, administer the screening that matches the grade level the student just completed. If the person being screened is older than the seventh grade, administer the "seventh-grade and above" screening.

Next, complete the "Screening Questionnaire" later in the chapter for the person you are screening to the best of your ability. If the person to be screened is an adult, they may complete the questionnaire on their own if they are able to do so. If the screener is completing the questionnaire for a student, the student does not need to be present during this portion of the screening. If there are at least three "yes" answers on the questionnaire, the screener should proceed with the screening.

In the questionnaire, the phrase "Does (did)" is used in many questions. Please answer "yes" if the person being screened does now, or did in the past, exhibit that behavior. A person may have struggled with something in their early years, but no longer struggles with that particular task (such as learning to tie their shoes). So, even though the student no longer struggles in that area, if they did in the past, indicate "yes" on the answer sheet.

After you've answered the questionnaire and decide to proceed, you are invited to watch my free video tutorials found at https://courses.learnreading.com/courses/dyslexia-screening-videos prior to administering the screening tasks instead of, or in addition to, reviewing the written screener instructions. The video tutorials are identical to the written instructions, so watching the videos is optional in your preparation.

Also, the student is invited to watch the video tutorials prior to each task instead of, or in addition to, the verbal instructions from the screener. These videos are a supplemental option to help alleviate the pressure of both the screener and the student in determining how to properly proceed through each task. The screener will also be provided, in writing, the verbiage necessary to instruct the student prior to each task; therefore the student's viewing of these videos is optional.

It is strongly recommended that the student be presented with the information in the "Screening Explanation for the Student" sidebar (also at https://courses.learnreading.com/courses/dyslexia-screening-videos) prior to the screening. The screener will be provided this information in writing on the following pages. The screener may choose to deliver this information verbally, or have the student watch the explanatory video themselves. The "Screening Explanation for the Student" will explain to the student what the screening process will be like and how they might feel throughout the screening.

Screening Explanation for the Student

You may present this information to the student yourself or show them the "Screening Explanation for the Student" video at https://courses.learnreading.com/courses/dyslexia-screening-videos.

"I wanted to talk to you about what this screening is about today. We will be checking for something called dyslexia. If you have dyslexia that means that you learn to read and spell in a different way than some of your friends.

"If you have dyslexia, then you have more brain power in the right hemisphere! Your brain is made up of two halves, the left hemisphere and the right hemisphere. If you have dyslexia that means you are probably gifted in areas that center in the right hemisphere of your brain." (Source: https://www.sciencedirect.com/science/article/abs/pii/S0891422213000401.) Your brain is made up of two halves, the left hemisphere and the right hemisphere. If you have dyslexia that means that you have 10% more brain on the right! And that would be why you are so gifted and talented in so many things that are centered in that part of the brain.

"Maybe you are really gifted in athletics, or in art, or with music. Or maybe you're really good with people. You know how to make friends and keep them. Maybe you like being creative, or making things with your hands. Or maybe you are a Lego master! This screening will be checking to see if you have dyslexia, and if you do, then we have a plan! We can teach you how to read and spell in a way that makes sense to your brain. I'm going to be honest and tell you that this screening will be hard because it was designed to see if you process language in the way a person with dyslexia does. And if you do have dyslexia, then processing language is going to be hard.

"There might be some words that you just don't know how to read. But please try! I want you to try your best. But if you just have absolutely no idea how to answer the question, then it's okay to say, 'I don't know.' Then I will mark that down and go to the next question. That's okay! But still please try to do your very best.

"There might be some things that are a little easy for you, and other things will be hard. Go ahead and take as much time as you need to answer the questions. And also, please know that nobody is going to answer all of the questions correctly! Remember these tasks are designed to be hard, not designed for you to get them all right. So it's okay if you struggle! Everyone does! Just do your best and that will be perfect!"

It is important to present this information prior to the screening because it will help the student understand that this screening is to determine if dyslexia is the likely cause of certain academic difficulties and therefore, will probably be difficult for dyslexic learners. If the student is dyslexic, they may naturally find the questions challenging. This explainer video (or the written transcript later in the chapter) asserts that though the screening will be difficult, this does not mean the student is any less intelligent than their peers. It simply means that they may process language in a different way. It is also explained that if they are dyslexic, then there are specific instructional methods that will help them to process language in a way that makes sense to them.

Administer the Screening Tasks

It's time to administer the screening. When you're ready to administer the test, here are some tips that will give you the most accurate results:

- **Have them use a pen:** The person being screened should use a pen. This is because the screener needs to see what the student's initial attempts at answering the questions are, without the student erasing them. The screener should explain to the student that if they are unhappy with their answer, they should put a box around their answer instead of crossing it out. Then they can put the answer they wanted right next to or above their boxed error. This will help the screener to see the complete picture of any difficulty the student may have on a task.

- **Meet at a good time:** The screener should administer the screening at a time when the student is at their best in order to measure their optimal performance. The student should be allowed to take their time and not feel rushed during the screening. If the student becomes tired or upset, the screener should postpone the remaining tasks until the student is refreshed.

- **Praise and encourage:** Because this screening will be challenging for dyslexic learners, please be generous with your praise to minimize frustration, embarrassment, or demoralization. Please keep the screening as positive, upbeat, and encouraging as possible. Praise the student for sincere effort, offer breaks, and encourage them often throughout the screening process. Remember, this will be hard for them and they are trying their best.

- **Ask for lowercase:** Students with dyslexia often revert to writing a capital *B* or *D* instead of lowercase to prevent the confusion of figuring out which way the letter faces. So, in this screening, you should ask the student to use only lowercase letters. This will force the student to consider the directionality of those letters and allow you to see if that confusion exists. They may still revert to using a capital *B* or *D* even after you've asked them not to, but doing so is an indicator that they do struggle with *b/d* confusion.

- **Keep moving on:** Because the student will be working with grade-level words, not reading-level words, there is a high likelihood that they will not be able to read some of the words in the screening if they are dyslexic. If the student cannot read the words at all, ask them to simply do their best and mark the answers accordingly. If they say, "I don't know" or "I can't," or if they struggle to the point of frustration, you may mark the answer "incorrect" and move on to the next.

Make sure to offer as many breaks as is needed for the student to remain focused on the tasks.

Evaluate the Results

After all the screening tasks have been completed, I will guide you on how to analyze the results of the screening. You will be given recommendations and suggestions for your first and next steps if the student matches the dyslexia profile.

Please note that an essential part of the definition of dyslexia is that there is an unexpected underachievement in certain academic areas such as reading and spelling. People with dyslexia who have average or above average intelligence will show a surprising inability to perform certain tasks, especially those related to phonological processing.

If the person being screened does not have average to above average intelligence, then this screening will be inconclusive. It is possible that a student can have both an intellectual disability and dyslexia, but discriminating between that overlap will be extremely difficult. You may proceed with the screening, but the results may be incomplete due to the complexity of the student.

It is important to note that a student's inability to read well does not, in any way, indicate a low IQ. Intelligence and dyslexia are not related. It is important that the screener not confuse low reading ability with low intelligence.

If the results of this screening indicate that the student is found to fit the dyslexia profile, appropriate reading intervention should be provided immediately. The sooner a student receives intervention, the easier and quicker overcoming their reading challenges will be. Essential intervention and recommendations for dyslexic students are provided in Part 3 of this book.

This screening is not intended for use in determining eligibility for public school-based intervention. The results of this screening should not be used to demand or request formal accommodations in the public school system. This screening is intended for personal use only.

Summary

You'll find all the resources to complete these steps in Chapter 7. All video resources are available at https://courses.learnreading.com/courses/dyslexia-screening-videos.

The student is not needed for the following pre-screening tasks:

1. Screener copies the Grade-Level Screening Packet that includes the initial questionnaire and all of the screening tasks for that grade level.

2. Screener completes the Initial Questionnaire. If there were at least three "yes" answers, then the screener should proceed with the screening tasks.

3. Screener watches the Screener Tutorial Videos (and/or reads the instructions in the screening packet) to become familiar with how to properly administer the screening tasks.

The student begins the dyslexia screening tasks:

1. Student watches the Screening Explanation for the Student Video *or* the screener presents this information to the student verbally.

2. Student watches the Student Tutorial Video, one at a time, prior to each task, *or* the screener presents this information verbally as provided in the screening packet.

3. Screener administers the screening tasks and records the student's responses on the pages provided in the screening packet.

Chapter 7

Dyslexia Screening Packets

In this chapter, you'll find all the resources you need to conduct a screen. If you need additional help, refer to the free videos at https://courses.learnreading.com/courses/dyslexia-screening-videos.

Kindergarten Screening Packet

This packet consists of the following:

- Kindergarten Screening Questionnaire
- Kindergarten Questionnaire Answer Sheet
- Kindergarten Questionnaire Analysis

Kindergarten Screening Questionnaire

(Mark answers on the answer sheet.)

Genetics

   1. Has the student's mother had any trouble with reading or spelling?

   2. Has the student's father had any trouble with reading or spelling?

   3. Are (were) there any other immediate family members who struggle(d) with reading or spelling?

   4. Are (were) there any extended family members (parents, siblings, grandparents, cousins, aunts, uncles) who struggle(d) in school?

Articulation/Speech

   5. Did the student have a speech delay (were they a late talker)?

   6. Does the student have any articulation or speech issues?

   7. Does the student have problems forming certain words correctly?

   8. Does the student mispronounce words even after repeated correction?

   9. Does (did) the student attend speech therapy?

   10. Does the student confuse *i/e*, *m/n*, or *f/th* when they speak?

   11. Does the student have difficulty expressing themself verbally?

   12. Does the student have trouble retrieving words, use a lot of *ums* or *uhs*, or use grand gestures with their hands when speaking?

Directionality

   13. Does (did) the student have difficulty learning to tie their shoes?

Memory/Recall

   14. Does the student have trouble recalling the names of letters, numbers, shapes, or colors?

   15. Does the student have difficulty remembering their address or phone number (if taught)?

   16. Does the student have difficulty remembering sequences (such as a list of directions, days of the week, or months of the year in order)?

   17. Does the student have difficulty remembering names?

   18. Does the student have difficulty remembering the order of the alphabet?

19. Does the student have trouble recalling the names of familiar objects, instead replacing them with words like *stuff* or *things*?

20. Does the student have trouble remembering multiple-step directions?

Phonological Awareness/Auditory Processing

21. Does the student have difficulty understanding that sentences can be broken into words and words can be broken into sounds?

22. Does the student have difficulty producing a word that rhymes with another?

23. Does the student have problems repeating back three sounds accurately and in order?

24. Can the student repeat back a one-syllable nonsense word?

25. Does the student have trouble breaking off the first or last sound of a word?

26. Is the student unable to determine if two words have the same beginning or ending sound?

27. Is the student unable to count the number of sounds (phonemes) in a small word?

28. Does the student have trouble identifying and reproducing the middle sound within a word?

29. Does the student have trouble understanding the connection between letters and sounds?

Reading

30. Does the student have difficulty recalling the names of many upper- and lowercase letters?

31. Does the student have difficulty recalling the sounds of many of the upper- and lowercase letters?

32. Does the student have trouble reading sight words or high frequency words?

Spelling/Writing

33. Does the student have trouble remembering how to form many letters?

34. Does the student have trouble understanding the alphabetic principle—that the sounds in a spoken word are represented by letters in a printed word?

Additional Learning Experiences

35. Does the student need, more than others, time to process verbal information?

36. Does the student have difficulty reading printed music (if applicable)?

37. Does the student experience anxiety or high levels of stress surrounding school or academics?

Is It Dyslexia?

Strengths/Talents

38. Does the student have a high capacity for learning?

39. Is the student gifted athletically?

40. Is the student gifted musically?

41. Is the student gifted artistically?

42. Is the student extremely creative?

43. Is the student highly imaginative?

44. Does the student have surprising maturity?

45. Does the student enjoy, and are they good at, puzzles (excellent spatial reasoning)?

46. Is the student extremely curious?

47. Is the student able to easily comprehend stories that they *hear* or *listen to*?

48. Is the student able to easily remember song lyrics?

49. Is the student mechanically inclined (good with their hands, such as working with Legos)?

50. Does the student have excellent thinking and reasoning skills?

51. Does the student have the ability to produce unique, out-of-the-box ideas?

52. Is the student gifted at seeing the big picture?

53. Is the student highly empathetic?

54. Is the student highly resilient?

55. Does the student have excellent interpersonal skills (maintains friendships easily)?

Kindergarten Questionnaire Answer Sheet

Genetics

1. Yes _____   Somewhat or Unsure _____   No _____

2. Yes _____   Somewhat or Unsure _____   No _____

3. Yes _____   Somewhat or Unsure _____   No _____

4. Yes _____   Somewhat or Unsure _____   No _____

Articulation/Speech

5. Yes _____   Somewhat or Unsure _____   No _____

6. Yes _____   Somewhat or Unsure _____   No _____

7. Yes _____   Somewhat or Unsure _____   No _____

8. Yes _____   Somewhat or Unsure _____   No _____

9. Yes _____   Somewhat or Unsure _____   No _____

10. Yes _____   Somewhat or Unsure _____   No _____

11. Yes _____   Somewhat or Unsure _____   No _____

12. Yes _____   Somewhat or Unsure _____   No _____

Directionality

13. Yes _____   Somewhat or Unsure _____   No _____

Memory/Recall

14.	Yes _____	Somewhat or Unsure _____	No _____
15.	Yes _____	Somewhat or Unsure _____	No _____
16.	Yes _____	Somewhat or Unsure _____	No _____
17.	Yes _____	Somewhat or Unsure _____	No _____
18.	Yes _____	Somewhat or Unsure _____	No _____
19.	Yes _____	Somewhat or Unsure _____	No _____
20.	Yes _____	Somewhat or Unsure _____	No _____

Phonemic Awareness/Auditory Processing

21.	Yes _____	Somewhat or Unsure _____	No _____
22.	Yes _____	Somewhat or Unsure _____	No _____
23.	Yes _____	Somewhat or Unsure _____	No _____
24.	Yes _____	Somewhat or Unsure _____	No _____
25.	Yes _____	Somewhat or Unsure _____	No _____
26.	Yes _____	Somewhat or Unsure _____	No _____
27.	Yes _____	Somewhat or Unsure _____	No _____
28.	Yes _____	Somewhat or Unsure _____	No _____
29.	Yes _____	Somewhat or Unsure _____	No _____

Reading

30.	Yes _____	Somewhat or Unsure _____	No _____
31.	Yes _____	Somewhat or Unsure _____	No _____
32.	Yes _____	Somewhat or Unsure _____	No _____

Spelling/Writing

33.   Yes _____   Somewhat or Unsure _____   No _____

34.   Yes _____   Somewhat or Unsure _____   No _____

Additional Learning Experiences

35.   Yes _____   Somewhat or Unsure _____   No _____

36.   Yes _____   Somewhat or Unsure _____   No _____

37.   Yes _____   Somewhat or Unsure _____   No _____

Strengths/Talents

38.   Yes _____   Somewhat or Unsure _____   No _____

39.   Yes _____   Somewhat or Unsure _____   No _____

40.   Yes _____   Somewhat or Unsure _____   No _____

41.   Yes _____   Somewhat or Unsure _____   No _____

42.   Yes _____   Somewhat or Unsure _____   No _____

43.   Yes _____   Somewhat or Unsure _____   No _____

44.   Yes _____   Somewhat or Unsure _____   No _____

45.   Yes _____   Somewhat or Unsure _____   No _____

46.   Yes _____   Somewhat or Unsure _____   No _____

47.   Yes _____   Somewhat or Unsure _____   No _____

48.   Yes _____   Somewhat or Unsure _____   No _____

49.   Yes _____   Somewhat or Unsure _____   No _____

50.   Yes _____   Somewhat or Unsure _____   No _____

51.   Yes _____   Somewhat or Unsure _____   No _____

52.   Yes _____   Somewhat or Unsure _____   No _____

53.   Yes _____   Somewhat or Unsure _____   No _____

54.   Yes _____   Somewhat or Unsure _____   No _____

55.   Yes _____   Somewhat or Unsure _____   No _____

Kindergarten Questionnaire Analysis

All Areas except Strengths/Talents

1.	Count the number of "yes" answers in all areas **except** Strengths/Talents.	_____
2.	Count the number of "somewhat" answers in these areas and divide by 2.	_____
3.	Add lines 1 and 2 for the **TOTAL** in these areas.	_____

If the **TOTAL** in these areas is **3 or more,** then dyslexia may be present.

Strengths/Talents

4.	Count the number of "yes" answers in Strengths/Talents.	_____
5.	Count the number of "somewhat" answers and divide by 2.	_____
6.	Add lines 4 and 5 for the **TOTAL** in these areas.	_____
7.	Add lines 3 and 6 for the **GRAND TOTAL.**	_____

Any number **greater than 3** in line 7 (GRAND TOTAL) increases the likelihood that dyslexia is present.

Students with a GRAND TOTAL of **3 or greater** will benefit from immediate interventions specific for dyslexic learners. This highly specialized instruction is discussed in Part 3 of this book.

Grade 1 Screening Packet

This packet consists of the following:

- Grade 1 Screening Questionnaire
- Grade 1 Questionnaire Answer Sheet
- Grade 1 Questionnaire Analysis
- Grade 1 Student Pages (for student's written answers)
- Grade 1 Instructions and Answer Sheets (for Tasks 1–11)
- Grade 1 Results
- Grade 1 Conclusions

Grade 1 Screening Questionnaire

(Mark answers on the answer sheet.)

Genetics

1. Has the student's mother had any trouble with reading or spelling?

2. Has the student's father had any trouble with reading or spelling?

3. Are (were) there any other immediate family members who struggle(d) with reading or spelling?

4. Are (were) there any extended family members (parents, siblings, grandparents, cousins, aunts, uncles) who struggle(d) in school?

Articulation/Speech

5. Did the student have a speech delay (were they a late talker)?

6. Does (did) the student have any articulation or speech issues?

7. Does (did) the student have problems forming certain words correctly?

8. Does (did) the student mispronounce words even after repeated correction?

9. Does (did) the student attend speech therapy?

10. Does the student confuse *i/e*, *m/n*, or *f/th*, when they speak?

11. Does the student have difficulty expressing themself verbally?

12. Does the student have trouble retrieving words, use a lot of *ums* or *uhs*, or use grand gestures with their hands when speaking?

Directionality

13. Does (did) the student have difficulty learning to tie their shoes?

14. Does (did) the student have difficulty remembering the direction of mathematical operations, such as addition and subtraction moving right to left?

15. Does the student transpose number sequences, such as writing *51* for *15*?

16. Does the student reverse words when reading, such as reading *top* for *pot*?

Memory/Recall

17. Does the student have trouble recalling the names of letters, numbers, or colors?

18. Does the student have difficulty remembering an address or phone number?

19. Does the student have difficulty remembering sequences (such as a list of directions, arithmetic steps, spelling sequences, days of the week, or months of the year in order)?

20. Does the student have difficulty on timed math tests?

21. Does the student have trouble with copying (copying slowly and inaccurately)?

22. Does the student have difficulty remembering names?

23. Does the student have difficulty remembering the order of the alphabet?

24. Does the student have trouble recalling the names of familiar objects, instead replacing them with words like *stuff* or *things*?

25. Does the student have trouble remembering multiple-step directions?

26. Does the student have a hard time remembering math facts?

Phonemic Awareness/Auditory Processing

27. Does (did) the student have difficulty learning nursery rhymes or playing rhyming games?

28. Does the student have problems repeating back sounds accurately and in order?

29. Does the student have trouble breaking off the first or last sound of a word?

30. Does the student have trouble identifying the vowel sound within a word?

31. Does the student confuse the short *i* and the short *e* sound when saying or reading words?

32. Does the student have trouble understanding the connection between letters and sounds?

33. Does the student have trouble isolating and manipulating the sounds within a word?

Reading

34. Does the student read below grade level?

35. Does the student have trouble decoding unfamiliar words?

36. Is the student's reading slow and labor intensive?

37. Does the student avoid tasks that involve reading?

38. Does the student have trouble reading sight words or high frequency words?

39. Does the student forget how to read a word from one moment to the next?

40. Does the student have trouble comprehending what they read?

41. Would the student prefer *not* to be called on to read aloud in class or in public? Would they prefer to avoid reading, especially aloud?

42. Does the student guess at words based on the size, shape, context, or picture clues?

43. Does the student skip or misread small, simple words when reading?

44. Is the student easily frustrated when reading?

45. Does the student spend an unusually long time completing tasks that involve reading?

46. Does the student have trouble recognizing their mistakes when reading?

47. Does the student rarely read for pleasure?

48. Does the student omit, substitute, add, or transpose letters when reading?

Spelling/Writing

49. Does the student have trouble with spelling?

50. Does the student spend an unusually long time completing tasks that involve writing?

51. Does the student have trouble spelling sight words or high frequency words?

52. Does the student forget how to spell a word from one moment to the next?

53. Does the student have trouble remembering and applying spelling rules?

54. Does the student omit, substitute, add, or transpose letters when spelling?

Additional Learning Experiences

56. Has the student attended special academic classes, reading groups, or had outside tutoring?

57. Does the student have difficulty reading printed music?

58. Does (has) the student pretended to be sick or otherwise unable to attend school or perform academically in a classroom?

59. Does the student need, more than others, time to process verbal information?

60. Does the student have poor self-esteem resulting from poor academic performance?

61. Does the student experience anxiety or high levels of stress surrounding academics?

Strengths/Talents

62. Does the student have a high capacity for learning?

63. Is the student gifted athletically?

64. Is the student gifted musically?

65. Is the student gifted artistically?

66. Is the student extremely creative?

67. Is the student highly imaginative?

68. Does the student have surprising maturity?

69. Does the student enjoy, and are they good at, puzzles (excellent spatial reasoning)?

70. Is the student extremely curious?

71. Is the student able to easily comprehend stories that they HEAR or LISTEN TO?

72. Is the student able to easily remember song lyrics?

73. Is the student mechanically inclined (good with their hands, such as working with Legos, building models, taking things apart and putting them back together again, etc.)?

74. Does the student have excellent creative writing skills?

75. Does the student have excellent thinking and reasoning skills?

76. Does the student have the ability to produce unique, out-of-the-box ideas?

77. Is the student gifted at seeing the big picture?

78. Is the student highly empathetic?

79. Is the student highly resilient?

80. Does the student have excellent interpersonal skills (maintains friendships easily)?

Grade 1 Questionnaire Answer Sheet

Genetics

1.	Yes _____	Somewhat or Unsure _____	No _____
2.	Yes _____	Somewhat or Unsure _____	No _____
3.	Yes _____	Somewhat or Unsure _____	No _____
4.	Yes _____	Somewhat or Unsure _____	No _____

Articulation/Speech

5.	Yes _____	Somewhat or Unsure _____	No _____
6.	Yes _____	Somewhat or Unsure _____	No _____
7.	Yes _____	Somewhat or Unsure _____	No _____
8.	Yes _____	Somewhat or Unsure _____	No _____
9.	Yes _____	Somewhat or Unsure _____	No _____
10.	Yes _____	Somewhat or Unsure _____	No _____
11.	Yes _____	Somewhat or Unsure _____	No _____
12.	Yes _____	Somewhat or Unsure _____	No _____

Directionality

13.	Yes _____	Somewhat or Unsure _____	No _____
14.	Yes _____	Somewhat or Unsure _____	No _____
15.	Yes _____	Somewhat or Unsure _____	No _____
16.	Yes _____	Somewhat or Unsure _____	No _____

Memory/Recall

17.	Yes _____	Somewhat or Unsure _____	No _____
18.	Yes _____	Somewhat or Unsure _____	No _____
19.	Yes _____	Somewhat or Unsure _____	No _____
20.	Yes _____	Somewhat or Unsure _____	No _____
21.	Yes _____	Somewhat or Unsure _____	No _____
22.	Yes _____	Somewhat or Unsure _____	No _____
23.	Yes _____	Somewhat or Unsure _____	No _____
24.	Yes _____	Somewhat or Unsure _____	No _____
25.	Yes _____	Somewhat or Unsure _____	No _____
26.	Yes _____	Somewhat or Unsure _____	No _____

Phonemic Awareness/Auditory Processing

27.	Yes _____	Somewhat or Unsure _____	No _____
28.	Yes _____	Somewhat or Unsure _____	No _____
29.	Yes _____	Somewhat or Unsure _____	No _____
30.	Yes _____	Somewhat or Unsure _____	No _____
31.	Yes _____	Somewhat or Unsure _____	No _____
32.	Yes _____	Somewhat or Unsure _____	No _____
33.	Yes _____	Somewhat or Unsure _____	No _____

Reading

34.	Yes _____	Somewhat or Unsure _____	No _____
35.	Yes _____	Somewhat or Unsure _____	No _____
36.	Yes _____	Somewhat or Unsure _____	No _____
37.	Yes _____	Somewhat or Unsure _____	No _____
38.	Yes _____	Somewhat or Unsure _____	No _____
39.	Yes _____	Somewhat or Unsure _____	No _____
40.	Yes _____	Somewhat or Unsure _____	No _____
41.	Yes _____	Somewhat or Unsure _____	No _____
42.	Yes _____	Somewhat or Unsure _____	No _____
43.	Yes _____	Somewhat or Unsure _____	No _____
44.	Yes _____	Somewhat or Unsure _____	No _____
45.	Yes _____	Somewhat or Unsure _____	No _____
46.	Yes _____	Somewhat or Unsure _____	No _____
47.	Yes _____	Somewhat or Unsure _____	No _____
48.	Yes _____	Somewhat or Unsure _____	No _____

Spelling/Writing

49.	Yes _____	Somewhat or Unsure _____	No _____
50.	Yes _____	Somewhat or Unsure _____	No _____
51.	Yes _____	Somewhat or Unsure _____	No _____
52.	Yes _____	Somewhat or Unsure _____	No _____
53.	Yes _____	Somewhat or Unsure _____	No _____
54.	Yes _____	Somewhat or Unsure _____	No _____

Additional Learning Experiences

56.	Yes _____	Somewhat or Unsure _____	No _____
57.	Yes _____	Somewhat or Unsure _____	No _____
58.	Yes _____	Somewhat or Unsure _____	No _____
59.	Yes _____	Somewhat or Unsure _____	No _____
60.	Yes _____	Somewhat or Unsure _____	No _____
61.	Yes _____	Somewhat or Unsure _____	No _____

Strengths/Talents

62.	Yes _____	Somewhat or Unsure _____	No _____
63.	Yes _____	Somewhat or Unsure _____	No _____
64.	Yes _____	Somewhat or Unsure _____	No _____
65.	Yes _____	Somewhat or Unsure _____	No _____
66.	Yes _____	Somewhat or Unsure _____	No _____
67.	Yes _____	Somewhat or Unsure _____	No _____
68.	Yes _____	Somewhat or Unsure _____	No _____
69.	Yes _____	Somewhat or Unsure _____	No _____
70.	Yes _____	Somewhat or Unsure _____	No _____
71.	Yes _____	Somewhat or Unsure _____	No _____
72.	Yes _____	Somewhat or Unsure _____	No _____
73.	Yes _____	Somewhat or Unsure _____	No _____
74.	Yes _____	Somewhat or Unsure _____	No _____
75.	Yes _____	Somewhat or Unsure _____	No _____
76.	Yes _____	Somewhat or Unsure _____	No _____
77.	Yes _____	Somewhat or Unsure _____	No _____
78.	Yes _____	Somewhat or Unsure _____	No _____
79.	Yes _____	Somewhat or Unsure _____	No _____
80.	Yes _____	Somewhat or Unsure _____	No _____

Grade 1 Questionnaire Analysis

All Areas except Strengths/Talents

1.	Count the number of "yes" answers in all areas **except** Strengths/Talents.	_____
2.	Count the number of "somewhat" answers in these areas and divide by 2.	_____
3.	Add lines 1 and 2 for the **TOTAL** in these areas.	_____

If the **TOTAL** in these areas is **3 or more,** then the screener should proceed to the screening tasks.

Strengths/Talents

4.	Count the number of "yes" answers in Strengths/Talents.	_____
5.	Count the number of "somewhat" answers and divide by 2.	_____
6.	Add lines 4 and 5 for the **TOTAL** in these areas.	_____
7.	Add lines 3 and 6 for the **GRAND TOTAL.**	_____

Any number greater than 3 in line 7 (GRAND TOTAL) increases the likelihood that dyslexia is present.

Grade 1 Student Pages

(Copy these three pages for the student to write on during the screening.)

On these pages, the student will complete the work for tasks that involve writing: Tasks 1, 2, 4, 5, 6, 9, and 11. (The remaining tasks require dictation only, which the screener will record on the Screener Answer Sheet.)

Task 1: Write the Alphabet

_____

_____

_____

Task 2: Spelling Sight Words

_____

1. _____

   _____

2. _____

   _____

3. _____

   _____

4. _____

   _____

5. _____

   _____

6. _____

   _____

7. _____

   _____

8. _____

   _____

9. _____

_____

10. _____

_____

Task 4: Reading Grade-Level Words

1. *hat*

2. *wish*

3. *pen*

4. *bucks*

5. *dig*

6. *thin*

7. *brick*

8. *bulk*

9. *drop*

10. *well*

Task 5: Symbol to Sound Knowledge

1. d

2. u

3. q

4. y

5. a

6. w

7. i

8. x

9. e

10. o

Task 6: Write the Letter(s)

1. _____   6. _____
2. _____   7. _____
3. _____   8. _____
4. _____   9. _____
5. _____   10. _____

Task 9: Phonemic Awareness 2 (Isolation)

Source: https://docs.google.com/document/d/1v_W0fHCmiZ6Fm0VCZVPUsEWSAU8-YsknIDpwNJZroKY/
edit

Task 11: Reading Unfamiliar Words

1.	nam	6.	tav
2.	pob	7.	lasp
3.	brib	8.	rilth
4.	dilk	9.	wuv
5.	nilm	10.	yomp

Grade 1 Instructions and Answer Sheets

Task 1 Screener Instructions

(This information for the screener is also offered in video format at https://courses.learnreading.com/ courses/dyslexia-screening-videos.)

- Ask the student to write the alphabet in lowercase letters.

- There should be no help, no copying, no erasing, nor crossing out.

- Watch for any hints of directionality confusion when they go to write a letter. Be aware of any pauses or hesitations, especially at *b/d/p/q*.

- Watch for confusion midway through, or if they need to start again at the beginning and use the alphabet song to help them determine the next letter.

- Watch for any reversals (writing a letter backward), inversions (writing a letter upside down), or errors (omitting a letter or writing it in the wrong sequence).

- After you have carefully watched the student complete the task, record their responses by answering "true" or "no" in the spaces provided.

Task 1 Student Instructions

(You may present this information to the student yourself, or show them the "Student Instructions" video at https://courses.learnreading.com/courses/dyslexia-screening-videos.)

"In this task, you're going to write the alphabet. You're going to use a pen (or a pencil without an eraser). This is because I want to see the way your brain works, and what you write down first. So, if you don't like what you wrote and are tempted to cross it out, don't worry! Just draw a box around the answer you didn't like, so I can still see what it was, and then put the answer you do want right next to or above it. And please use only lowercase letters in this screening. Okay! Let's get started!"

Task 1 Answer Key

Directions: Ask the student to write the alphabet in lowercase letters in the space provided on the Student Pages, with no help, no copying, and no erasing.

1.	The student made it to the end without any errors.	TRUE_____ NO_____
2.	The letters all faced the correct direction. (There were no reversals or inversions.)	TRUE_____ NO_____
3.	The student wrote the alphabet easily and quickly, with no hesitations, questions, or restarts.	TRUE_____ NO_____

4.   There was no hesitation at *b/d* or *p/q*. (The student did not   TRUE_____ NO_____
      wonder which way the letter faced.)

Task 2 Screener Instructions

(This information for the screener is also offered in video format at https://courses.learnreading.com/courses/dyslexia-screening-videos.)

- You will dictate sight words for the student to spell.
- You can repeat the word and/or use it in a sentence, but no hints as to the spelling.
- Mark "correct" or "incorrect" in the spaces provided.

Task 2 Student Instructions

(You may present this information to the student yourself, or show them the "Student Instructions" video at https://courses.learnreading.com/courses/dyslexia-screening-videos.)

"You might already know that sight words are words that don't follow typical spelling rules. They can sometimes be tricky to spell. I'm going to say a few of these sight words and I'd like for you to try to spell them the best that you can."

Task 2 Answer Key

Directions: Ask the student to spell the following words in the space provided on the Student Pages, with no erasing or changing. Mark "correct" or "incorrect." (If they spelled the word incorrectly at first, then changed their mind and went to fix it, mark it "incorrect" even if their second attempt was correct.)

1.	*the*	CORRECT_____ INCORRECT_____
2.	*of*	CORRECT_____ INCORRECT_____
3.	*to* (as in "Let's go to the store.)	CORRECT_____ INCORRECT_____
4.	*you*	CORRECT_____ INCORRECT_____
5.	*was*	CORRECT_____ INCORRECT_____
6.	*are* (as in "Are you okay?")	CORRECT_____ INCORRECT_____
7.	*one* (the number)	CORRECT_____ INCORRECT_____
8.	*have*	CORRECT_____ INCORRECT_____
9.	*they*	CORRECT_____ INCORRECT_____
10.	*put* (as in "Put it over there.")	CORRECT_____ INCORRECT_____

Task 3 Screener Instructions

(This information for the screener is also offered in video format at https://courses.learnreading.com/courses/dyslexia-screening-videos.)

- You will dictate words to the student and ask them to count how many *sounds* they hear in a word (not syllables or letters).
- Mark "correct" or "incorrect" in the spaces provided. (The answer is next to the word.)

Task 3 Student Instructions

(You may present this information to the student yourself, or show them the "Student Instructions" video at https://courses.learnreading.com/courses/dyslexia-screening-videos.)

"For this task, you are simply going to be counting sounds. I am going to say a word, and you will count how many sounds you hear in that word. If you know how to spell the word, try not to think about the letters because I don't want you to count the letters, just the sounds. Sometimes there are more letters in a word than there are sounds, so just focus on the sounds, and tell me how many you hear."

Task 3 Answer Key

Directions: Ask the student how many *sounds* are in each word. (Note: they are counting individual sounds, not syllables and not letters. For instance, *chicken* has 5 sounds.)

1.	tan	(answer: 3)	CORRECT_____ INCORRECT_____
2.	blue	(answer: 3)	CORRECT_____ INCORRECT_____
3.	bench	(answer: 4)	CORRECT_____ INCORRECT_____
4.	truck	(answer: 4)	CORRECT_____ INCORRECT_____
5.	drill	(answer: 4)	CORRECT_____ INCORRECT_____
6.	straw	(answer: 4)	CORRECT_____ INCORRECT_____
7.	track	(answer: 4)	CORRECT_____ INCORRECT_____
8.	come	(answer: 3)	CORRECT_____ INCORRECT_____
9.	brick	(answer: 4)	CORRECT_____ INCORRECT_____
10.	clamp	(answer: 5)	CORRECT_____ INCORRECT_____

Task 4 Screener Instructions

(This information for the screener is also offered in video format at https://courses.learnreading.com/courses/dyslexia-screening-videos.)

- Ask the student to read the words on their Student Pages.
- Mark "correct" or "incorrect" in the spaces provided.
- If the student chose to skip a word, mark it "incorrect."

Task 4 Student Instructions

(You may present this information to the student yourself, or show them the "Student Instructions" video at https://courses.learnreading.com/courses/dyslexia-screening-videos.)

"For this task, you are going to read a list of words as best as you can. It may be a little difficult, but just do your best. If you try and still feel like you can't read the word, it's okay to say, 'Skip it,' and move on to the next word."

Task 4 Answer Key

Directions: Ask the student to READ each word as it is written for them on the Student Pages.

1.	hat	CORRECT_____	INCORRECT_____
2.	wish	CORRECT_____	INCORRECT_____
3.	pen	CORRECT_____	INCORRECT_____
4.	bucks	CORRECT_____	INCORRECT_____
5.	dig	CORRECT_____	INCORRECT_____
6.	thin	CORRECT_____	INCORRECT_____
7.	brick	CORRECT_____	INCORRECT_____
8.	bulk	CORRECT_____	INCORRECT_____
9.	drop	CORRECT_____	INCORRECT_____
10.	well	CORRECT_____	INCORRECT_____

Task 5 Screener Instructions

(This information for the screener is also offered in video format at https://courses.learnreading.com/courses/dyslexia-screening-videos.)

- Ask the student to look at each letter on their Student Page, and tell you the sound that it makes.

- When they come to the vowels, ask the student to tell you the short, or most common, sound.

- If they hesitate for longer than three seconds on any letter, mark it "incorrect."

- Mark "correct" or "incorrect" in the spaces provided. (The correct answer is provided for you.)

Task 5 Student Instructions

(You may present this information to the student yourself, or show them the "Student Instructions" video at https://courses.learnreading.com/courses/dyslexia-screening-videos.)

"For this task, I'd like you to look at a letter and then tell me the sound that it makes. When you come to a vowel, tell me the short, or most common, sound."

Task 5 Answer Key

Directions: Ask the student to look at each letter and tell you the sound each one makes. If they hesitate for longer than three seconds, mark it "incorrect." For *a, e, i, o, u,* tell them you want the short, or most common, sound. If they have any questions, tell them to just do their best.

1.	*d*	(answer: /d/ as in *dog*)	CORRECT_____	INCORRECT_____
2.	*u*	(answer: /u/ as in *under*)	CORRECT_____	INCORRECT_____
3.	*q*	(answer: /kw/ as in *queen*)	CORRECT_____	INCORRECT_____
4.	*y*	(answer: /y/ as in *yellow*)	CORRECT_____	INCORRECT_____
5.	*a*	(answer: /ă/ as in *apple*)	CORRECT_____	INCORRECT_____
6.	*w*	(answer: /w/ as in *water*)	CORRECT_____	INCORRECT_____
7.	*i*	(answer: /ĭ/ as in *index*)	CORRECT_____	INCORRECT_____
8.	*x*	(answer: /ks/ as in *fox*)	CORRECT_____	INCORRECT_____
9.	*e*	(answer: /ĕ/ as in *exit*)	CORRECT_____	INCORRECT_____
10.	*o*	(answer: /ŏ/ as in *octopus*)	CORRECT_____	INCORRECT_____

Task 6 Screener Instructions

(This information for the screener is also offered in video format at https://courses.learnreading.com/courses/dyslexia-screening-videos.)

- You will dictate a sound to the student.
- Ask the student what letter, or set of letters, makes that sound.
- The "as in" hints are for the screener only and should *not* be given to the student.
- Ask the student to write their answers in lowercase letters.
- When the student writes their answer, the letters must be facing the correct way for the answer to be marked "correct." If any letters are reversed, mark it "incorrect."

Task 6 Student Instructions

(You may present this information to the student yourself, or show them the "Student Instructions" video at https://courses.learnreading.com/courses/dyslexia-screening-videos.)

"This time I'm going to give you the sound, and you're going to write down the letter or letters that make that sound. For instance, if I said /m/ (the sound of *m*), you would write *m*. If I said /th/ (the sound of *th*), you would write *th*.

Task 6 Answer Key

Directions: For the following items, say to the student, "What letter, or letters, makes this sound?" Then pronounce the sound for them. (Do *not* say "as in..." because that is only for you to read so you are sure which sound to make. The answer is the bold letter(s) in the example word. *Q* can be written as *Q* or *QU*. Both are correct.) Have them write down their answer in lowercase letters in the space provided on the Student Pages. The letters they write down must be facing the right direction to be marked "correct."

1.	/ch/	(as in **ch**air)	CORRECT_____	INCORRECT_____
2.	/ĕ/	(as in **e**xit)	CORRECT_____	INCORRECT_____
3.	/sh/	(as in **sh**ut)	CORRECT_____	INCORRECT_____
4.	/ŏ/	(as in **o**ctopus)	CORRECT_____	INCORRECT_____
5.	/w/	(as in **w**onder)	CORRECT_____	INCORRECT_____
6.	/ĭ/	(as in **i**ndex)	CORRECT_____	INCORRECT_____
7.	/y/	(as in **y**ellow)	CORRECT_____	INCORRECT_____
8.	/ŭ/	(as in **u**nder)	CORRECT_____	INCORRECT_____
9.	/d/	(as in **d**oor)	CORRECT_____	INCORRECT_____
10.	/kw/	(as in **qu**een)	CORRECT_____	INCORRECT_____

Task 7 Screener Instructions

(This information for the screener is also offered in video format at https://courses.learnreading.com/courses/dyslexia-screening-videos.)

- Dictate three distinct sounds to the student, with clean and clear *breaks* in between each sound.
- Ask the student to repeat the sounds back to you in order.
- The "as in" hints are for the screener only and should *not* be given to the student.
- The sounds must all be repeated back with exactness to be marked "correct." If the student mispronounced or omitted any sounds, or switched the order, mark the answer "incorrect."

Task 7 Student Instructions

(You may present this information to the student yourself, or show them the "Student Instructions" video at https://courses.learnreading.com/courses/dyslexia-screening-videos.)

"For this task, I am going to say three sounds and then you just repeat them exactly as I said them and in the same order. Listen very carefully because some of the sounds may sound similar. Repeat them back to me as best you can."

Task 7 Answer Key

Directions: Ask the student to repeat the following sound sequences after you. You will pronounce all three sounds, then they should repeat the three sounds back to you. If they ask you to repeat the sequence, you may repeat it one time. If they say all three sounds back to you *exactly* right, mark it "correct." If they mispronounced (or couldn't remember) even one of the three sounds, mark it "incorrect." (Do *not* say "as in...." because that is only for you so you are sure which sound to make.)

1.	/n/ /m/ /l/ (as in: *name, milk, leg*)	CORRECT_____ INCORRECT_____
2.	/ĭ/, /ŏ/, /ĕ/ (as in: *index, octopus, exit*)	CORRECT_____ INCORRECT_____
3.	/d/ /p/ /b/ (as in: *door, pie, box*)	CORRECT_____ INCORRECT_____
4.	/sh/ /s/ /z/ (as in: *ship, sun, zebra*)	CORRECT_____ INCORRECT_____
5.	/th/ /f/ /j/ (as in: *think, fish, jam*)	CORRECT_____ INCORRECT_____
6.	/ă/ /ĕ/ /ĭ/ (as in: *apple, exit, index*)	CORRECT_____ INCORRECT_____
7.	/ŭ/ /ŏ/ /ă/ (as in: *under, octopus, apple*)	CORRECT_____ INCORRECT_____
8.	/sh/ /ch/ /th/ (as in: *ship, chop, think*)	CORRECT_____ INCORRECT_____
9.	/r/ /l/ /n/ (as in: *run, leg, net*)	CORRECT_____ INCORRECT_____
10.	/w/ /y/ /p/ (as in: *water, yellow, pot*)	CORRECT_____ INCORRECT_____

Task 8 Screener Instructions

(This information for the screener is also offered in video format at https://courses.learnreading.com/courses/dyslexia-screening-videos.)

- Important note: when you see a letter in between two slanted lines, it means the sound that that letter makes. For instance, /f/ is the *sound* of *f*, not the letter itself.
- Read the questions to the student, making sure to only say the *sound* of the letter in between the slanted lines.
- Mark "correct" or "incorrect" in the spaces provided. (The correct answer is provided for you.)

Task 8 Student Instructions

(You may present this information to the student yourself, or show them the "Student Instructions video at https://courses.learnreading.com/courses/dyslexia-screening-videos.)

"For this task, I am going to say a word. Then, I'm going to ask you to repeat the word but without one of the sounds. For example, I might say *camp*, and then ask you to say *camp* without the /m/. *Camp* without the /m/ is *Cap* (model how to do the task). So listen carefully, take your time, and try your best."

Task 8 Answer Key

Directions: Ask the student each question. When you do so, say the *sound* that they are to remove, not the letter. (FYI: a letter inside of slanted lines, like /f/, means the sound only, not the letter itself.) If they ask you to repeat the question, you may do so one time. The student should tell you the answer, not write it down.

1.	"What would *cat* say without the /k/?" (answer: *at*)	CORRECT_____ INCORRECT_____
2.	"What would *bite* say without the /t/?" (answer: *by*)	CORRECT_____ INCORRECT_____
3.	"What would *chair* say without the /ch/?" (answer: *air*)	CORRECT_____ INCORRECT_____
4.	"What would pain say without the /n/?" (answer: *pay*)	CORRECT_____ INCORRECT_____
5.	"What would *keep* say without the /p/?" (answer: *key*)	CORRECT_____ INCORRECT_____
6.	"What would *cup* say without the /k/?" (answer: *up*)	CORRECT_____ INCORRECT_____
7.	"What would *sheet* say without the /t/?" (answer: *she*)	CORRECT_____ INCORRECT_____
8.	"What would *seal* say without the /l/?" (answer: *sea*)	CORRECT_____ INCORRECT_____
9.	"What would *peach* say without the /p/?" (answer: *each*)	CORRECT_____ INCORRECT_____
10.	"What would *inch* say without the /ch/?" (answer: *in*)	CORRECT_____ INCORRECT_____

Task 9 Screener Instructions

(This information for the screener is also offered in video format at https://courses.learnreading.com/courses/dyslexia-screening-videos.)

- Ask the student to look at a picture on their Student Page; say, "What it this is a picture of?" and stretch out the sounds in that word (such as *milk* "mmmiiilllk").
- Ask the student to break apart each sound in that word and then mark the dot that represents the sound in the question that you will ask them.
- Mark "correct" or "incorrect" if they identified the correct dot that contained that sound.

Task 9 Student Instructions

(You may present this information to the student yourself, or show them the "Student Instructions" video at https://courses.learnreading.com/courses/dyslexia-screening-videos.)

"For this task, you're going to see some pictures. I want you to tell me what the picture is and then stretch out the sounds in that word. Then I want you to separate each sound in that word with nice, big breaks in between each sound. You will see dots under the picture. I'd like you to point to each dot when you say each sound in that word. Then I'm going to ask where a certain sound is, and you'll just point to, or color in, that dot."

Task 9 Answer Key

Directions: As you ask each question, ask the student to follow along with you on their Student Pages. Ask the student to look at each picture and 1) repeat what the picture is, 2) stretch out the sounds in the word, and then 3) separate the sounds within the word and mark the dot on their paper where they hear the sound in question.

1.	Where is the /oo/ in *two*?	(answer: 2nd dot)	CORRECT_____	INCORRECT_____
2.	Where is the /sh/ in *shoe*?	(answer: 1st dot)	CORRECT_____	INCORRECT_____
3.	Where is the /ee/ in *key*?	(answer: 2nd dot)	CORRECT_____	INCORRECT_____
4.	Where is the /t/ in *tie*?	(answer: 1st dot)	CORRECT_____	INCORRECT_____
5.	Where is the /ay/ in *hay*?	(answer: 2nd dot)	CORRECT_____	INCORRECT_____
6.	Where is the /ee/ in *bee*?	(answer: 2nd dot)	CORRECT_____	INCORRECT_____
7.	Where is the /t/ in *tea*?	(answer: 1st dot)	CORRECT_____	INCORRECT_____
8.	Where is the /i/ in *pie*?	(answer: 2nd dot)	CORRECT_____	INCORRECT_____

- The student had difficulty **breaking off** one sound from another in one or more of the words (if so, mark "incorrect" here). CORRECT_____ INCORRECT_____

- The student had difficulty **articulating** the correct sounds within the word (if so, mark "incorrect" here). CORRECT _____ INCORRECT _____

Task 10 Screener Instructions

(This information for the screener is also offered in video format at https://courses.learnreading.com/courses/dyslexia-screening-videos.)

- Read the word to the student. Have them repeat the word and then try to say the word backward.
- Mark "correct" or "incorrect" in the spaces provided. (The correct answer is provided for you.)

Task 10 Student Instructions

(You may present this information to the student yourself, or show them the "Student Instructions" video at https://courses.learnreading.com/courses/dyslexia-screening-videos.)

"In this task, I'm going to say a word. You will repeat the word back to me, and then try to say the word backward. For example, if I said the word *cat*. You would repeat that word *cat* and then try to say it backward. That last letter in *cat* would be the first letter if it was said backward. So *cat*, backward is *tac* (model how to do the task).

Task 10: Answer Key

Directions: 1) Read the word (or nonsense word) to the student. 2) Ask them to repeat the word back to you. Then 3) tell them to say the word backward. If they ask you to repeat the word, you may do so one time. They must say every sound in the reversed word *exactly* right to be marked "correct." (If you are unsure of the correct pronunciation of the word, a "rhymes with" word is provided for you. Do *not* share this "rhymes with" word with the student. It is only to aid the administrator.)

1.	*tea* (rhymes with *see*)	(answer: *eat*)	CORRECT_____	INCORRECT_____
2.	air (rhymes with *stare*)	(answer: *ray*)	CORRECT_____	INCORRECT_____
3.	*ile* (rhymes with *mile*)	(answer: *lie*)	CORRECT_____	INCORRECT_____
4.	*oot* (rhymes with *flute*)	(answer: *to*)	CORRECT_____	INCORRECT_____
5.	*eem* (rhymes with *team*)	(answer: *me*)	CORRECT_____	INCORRECT_____
6.	*cheap* (rhymes with *sheep*)	(answer: *peach*)	CORRECT_____	INCORRECT_____
7.	*chum* (rhymes with *plum*)	(answer: *much*)	CORRECT_____	INCORRECT_____

8.	*nape* (rhymes with *cape*)	(answer: *pain*)	CORRECT_____	INCORRECT_____
9.	*peek* (rhymes with *leak*)	(answer: *keep*)	CORRECT_____	INCORRECT_____
10.	*klim* (rhymes with *slim*)	(answer: *milk*)	CORRECT_____	INCORRECT_____

Task 11 Screener Instructions

(This information for the screener is also offered in video format at https://courses.learnreading.com/courses/dyslexia-screening-videos.)

- Ask the student to read aloud the nonsense words on their Student Pages.
- They must get each sound in the word *exactly* correct for it to be marked "correct."
- The "rhymes with" hints are for the screener only and should *not* be given to the student.

Task 11 Student Instructions

(You may present this information to the student yourself, or show them the "Student Instructions" video at https://courses.learnreading.com/courses/dyslexia-screening-videos.)

"On your Student Pages, you're going to see some nonsense words. These are crazy words that you've never seen before. To read them, just use your knowledge of what the letters say."

Task 11 Answer Key

Directions: Ask the student to read each nonsense word on their Student Pages. The student must pronounce each sound in the word *exactly* right for the word to be marked "correct." (A "rhymes with" word is provided for the screener only. Do *not* give the "rhymes with" word to the student.)

1.	*nam* (rhymes with *Sam*)	CORRECT_____	INCORRECT_____
2.	*pob* (rhymes with *cob*)	CORRECT_____	INCORRECT_____
3.	*brib* (rhymes with *crib*)	CORRECT_____	INCORRECT_____
4.	*dilk* (rhymes with *milk*)	CORRECT_____	INCORRECT_____
5.	*nilm* (rhymes with *film*)	CORRECT_____	INCORRECT_____
6.	*tav* (rhymes with *have*)	CORRECT_____	INCORRECT_____
7.	*lasp* (rhymes with *clasp*)	CORRECT_____	INCORRECT_____
8.	*rilth* (rhymes with *filth*)	CORRECT_____	INCORRECT_____
9.	*wuv* (rhymes with *love*)	CORRECT_____	INCORRECT_____
10.	*yomp* (rhymes with *chomp*)	CORRECT_____	INCORRECT_____

Grade 1 Results

Task 1: Long-Term Memory

_____

Total Incorrect (or "no" answers):   _____

_____

Task 2: Sight Words Knowledge

_____

Total Incorrect: _____

_____

Task 3: Phonemic Awareness

_____

Total Incorrect: _____

_____

Task 4: Reading Grade-Level Words

_____

Total Incorrect: _____

_____

Task 5: Symbol to Sound Knowledge

_____

Total Incorrect: _____

_____

Task 6: Sound to Symbol Knowledge

_____

Total Incorrect: _____

_____

Task 7: Auditory Discrimination/Memory

_____

Total Incorrect: _____

_____

Task 8: Phonemic Awareness

Total Incorrect: _____

Task 9: Phonemic Awareness

Total Incorrect: _____

Task 10: Phonemic Awareness

Total Incorrect: _____

Task 11: Decoding Unfamiliar Words

Total Incorrect: _____

TOTAL incorrect answers on screening tasks: _____

Results from Questionnaire, Plus Screening Tasks

1. TOTAL (line 4) on Questionnaire _____

2. TOTAL incorrect answers on Screening Tasks _____

3. **GRAND TOTAL from lines 1 and 2** _____

Grade 1 Conclusions

If the GRAND TOTAL (line 3) is **14 or greater**, then this student's performance **is** consistent with someone with dyslexia.

It can be assumed that the severity of dyslexia is in direct relation to **how much greater than 14** the GRAND TOTAL is (14 being mild and 190 being the most severe).

If the GRAND TOTAL is **less than 14**, then dyslexia is likely *not* the probable cause for the student's academic difficulties.

Grade 2 Screening Packet

This packet contains the following:

- Grade 2 Screening Questionnaire

- Grade 2 Questionnaire Answer Sheet

- Grade 2 Questionnaire Analysis

- Grade 2 Student Pages (for student's written answers)

- Grade 2 Instructions and Answer Sheets (for Tasks 1–11)

- Grade 2 Results

- Grade 2 Conclusions

Grade 2 Screening Questionnaire

(Mark answers on the answer sheet.)

Genetics

1. Does the student's mother have any trouble with reading or spelling?

2. Does the student's father have any trouble with reading or spelling?

3. Are there any other immediate family members who struggle with reading or spelling?

4. Are (or were) there any extended family members (parents, siblings, grandparents, cousins, aunts, uncles) who struggled in school?

Articulation/Speech

5. Did the student have a speech delay (were they a late talker)?

6. Does (did) the student have any articulation or speech issues?

7. Does (did) the student have problems forming certain words correctly?

8. Does (did) the student mispronounce words even after repeated correction?

9. Does (did) the student attend speech therapy?

10. Does (did) the student confuse *i/e*, *m/n*, or *f/th* when they speak?

11. Does (did) the person have difficulty saying words like *aluminum*, *cinnamon*, or *dyslexia*?

12. Does the student have difficulty expressing themself verbally?

13. Does the student have trouble retrieving words, use a lot of *ums* or *uhs*, or use grand gestures with their hands when speaking?

Directionality

14. Is (was) there any left/right confusion?

15. Are there any letter or number reversals continuing beyond the end of first grade, including *b/d* confusion?

16. Does (did) the student have difficulty learning to tie their shoes?

17. Does the student have trouble telling time on an analog clock?

18. Does (did) the student have difficulty remembering the direction of mathematical operations, such as addition and subtraction moving right to left.

19. Does the student transpose number sequences, such as writing *51* for *15*?

20. Does (did) the student reverse words when reading, such as reading *top* for *pot*?

Memory/Recall

21. Does (did) the student have trouble recalling the names of letters, numbers, or colors?

22. Does the student have difficulty remembering sequences (such as a list of directions, arithmetic steps, spelling sequences, days of the week, or months of the year in order)?

23. Does the student have difficulty on timed math tests?

24. Does the student have trouble with copying (copying slowly and inaccurately)?

25. Does the student have difficulty remembering names?

26. Does the student have difficulty remembering the order of the alphabet?

27. Does the student have trouble recalling the days of the week or months of the year in order?

28. Does the student have trouble recalling the names of familiar objects, instead replacing them with words like *stuff* or *things*?

29. Does the student have trouble remembering multiple-step directions?

30. Does the student have difficulty remembering an address or phone number?

31. Does the student have trouble with alphabetizing or with remembering the order of the alphabet?

32. Does the student have a hard time recalling math facts quickly?

Phonemic Awareness/Auditory Processing

33. Does (did) the student have difficulty learning nursery rhymes or playing rhyming games?

34. Does the student have problems repeating back sounds accurately and in order?

35. Does the student have trouble breaking off the first or last sound of a word?

36. Does the student have trouble identifying the vowel sound within a word?

37. Does the student confuse the short *i* and the short *e* sound when saying or reading words?

38. Does the student have trouble understanding the connection between letters and sounds?

39. Does the student have trouble isolating and manipulating the sounds within a word?

Reading

40. Does the student read below grade level?

41. Does the student have trouble decoding unfamiliar words?

42. Is the student's reading slow and labor intensive?

43. Does (did) the student have trouble reading sight words or high frequency words?

44. Does the student forget how to read a word from one moment to the next?

45. Does the student have trouble comprehending what they read?

46. Would the student prefer *not* to be called on to read aloud in class or in public? Would they prefer to avoid reading, especially aloud?

47. Does the student guess at words based on the size, shape, context, or picture clues?

48. Does the student skip or misread small, simple words when reading?

49. Is the student easily frustrated when reading?

50. Does the student spend an unusually long time completing tasks that involve reading?

51. Does the student omit the suffixes or endings of words?

52. Does the student have trouble recognizing their mistakes when reading?

53. Does the student rarely read for pleasure?

54. Does the student require multiple readings to comprehend the material?

55. Does the student omit, substitute, add, or transpose letters when reading?

Spelling/Writing

56. Does the student have trouble with spelling?

57. Does the student spend an unusually long time completing tasks that involve writing?

58. Does the student have trouble spelling sight words or high frequency words?

59. Does the student forget how to spell a word from one moment to the next?

60. Do others have trouble reading what the student wrote, due to spelling errors?

61. Is the student's intelligence not reflected in their writing?

62. Does the student have trouble remembering and applying spelling rules?

63. Does (did) the student use unpredictable, illogical spelling?

64. Does (did) the student omit, substitute, add, or transpose letters when spelling?

Additional Learning Experiences

65. Has the student attended special academic classes, reading groups, or had outside tutoring?

66. Does the student have difficulty reading printed music?

67. Does (has) the student pretended to be sick or otherwise unable to attend school/perform academically in a classroom?

68. Does the student need more time than others to process verbal information?

69. Does the student have poor self-esteem resulting from poor academic performance?

70. Does the student experience anxiety or high levels of stress surrounding academics?

Strengths/Talents

71. Does the student have a high capacity for learning?

72. Is the student gifted athletically?

73. Is the student gifted musically?

74. Is the student gifted artistically?

75. Is the student extremely creative?

76. Is the student highly imaginative?

77. Does the student have surprising maturity?

78. Does the student enjoy, and is good at, puzzles (excellent spatial reasoning)?

79. Is the student extremely curious?

80. Is the student able to easily comprehend stories that they *hear* or *listen to*?

81. Is the student able to easily remember song lyrics?

82. Is the student mechanically inclined (good with their hands, such as working with Legos, building models, taking things apart and putting them back together again, etc.)?

83. Does the student have excellent creative writing skills?

84. Does the student have excellent thinking and reasoning skills?

85. Does the student have the ability to produce unique, out-of-the-box ideas?

86. Is the student gifted at seeing the big picture?

87. Is the student highly empathetic?

88. Is the student highly resilient?

89. Does the student have excellent interpersonal skills (maintains friendships easily)?

Is It Dyslexia?

Grade 2 Questionnaire Answer Sheet

Genetics

1. Yes _____   Somewhat or Unsure _____   No _____
2. Yes _____   Somewhat or Unsure _____   No _____
3. Yes _____   Somewhat or Unsure _____   No _____
4. Yes _____   Somewhat or Unsure _____   No _____

Articulation/Speech

5. Yes _____   Somewhat or Unsure _____   No _____
6. Yes _____   Somewhat or Unsure _____   No _____
7. Yes _____   Somewhat or Unsure _____   No _____
8. Yes _____   Somewhat or Unsure _____   No _____
9. Yes _____   Somewhat or Unsure _____   No _____
10. Yes _____   Somewhat or Unsure _____   No _____
11. Yes _____   Somewhat or Unsure _____   No _____
12. Yes _____   Somewhat or Unsure _____   No _____
13. Yes _____   Somewhat or Unsure _____   No _____

Directionality

14. Yes _____   Somewhat or Unsure _____   No _____
15. Yes _____   Somewhat or Unsure _____   No _____
16. Yes _____   Somewhat or Unsure _____   No _____
17. Yes _____   Somewhat or Unsure _____   No _____
18. Yes _____   Somewhat or Unsure _____   No _____
19. Yes _____   Somewhat or Unsure _____   No _____
20. Yes _____   Somewhat or Unsure _____   No _____

Memory/Recall

21.	Yes _____	Somewhat or Unsure _____	No _____
22.	Yes _____	Somewhat or Unsure _____	No _____
23.	Yes _____	Somewhat or Unsure _____	No _____
24.	Yes _____	Somewhat or Unsure _____	No _____
25.	Yes _____	Somewhat or Unsure _____	No _____
26.	Yes _____	Somewhat or Unsure _____	No _____
27.	Yes _____	Somewhat or Unsure _____	No _____
28.	Yes _____	Somewhat or Unsure _____	No _____
29.	Yes _____	Somewhat or Unsure _____	No _____
30.	Yes _____	Somewhat or Unsure _____	No _____
31.	Yes _____	Somewhat or Unsure _____	No _____
32.	Yes _____	Somewhat or Unsure _____	No _____

Phonemic Awareness/Auditory Processing

33.	Yes _____	Somewhat or Unsure _____	No _____
34.	Yes _____	Somewhat or Unsure _____	No _____
35.	Yes _____	Somewhat or Unsure _____	No _____
36.	Yes _____	Somewhat or Unsure _____	No _____
37.	Yes _____	Somewhat or Unsure _____	No _____
38.	Yes _____	Somewhat or Unsure _____	No _____
39.	Yes _____	Somewhat or Unsure _____	No _____

Is It Dyslexia?

Reading

40.	Yes _____	Somewhat or Unsure _____	No _____
41.	Yes _____	Somewhat or Unsure _____	No _____
42.	Yes _____	Somewhat or Unsure _____	No _____
43.	Yes _____	Somewhat or Unsure _____	No _____
44.	Yes _____	Somewhat or Unsure _____	No _____
45.	Yes _____	Somewhat or Unsure _____	No _____
46.	Yes _____	Somewhat or Unsure _____	No _____
47.	Yes _____	Somewhat or Unsure _____	No _____
48.	Yes _____	Somewhat or Unsure _____	No _____
49.	Yes _____	Somewhat or Unsure _____	No _____
50.	Yes _____	Somewhat or Unsure _____	No _____
51.	Yes _____	Somewhat or Unsure _____	No _____
52.	Yes _____	Somewhat or Unsure _____	No _____
53.	Yes _____	Somewhat or Unsure _____	No _____
54.	Yes _____	Somewhat or Unsure _____	No _____
55.	Yes _____	Somewhat or Unsure _____	No _____

Spelling/Writing

56.	Yes _____	Somewhat or Unsure _____	No _____
57.	Yes _____	Somewhat or Unsure _____	No _____
58.	Yes _____	Somewhat or Unsure _____	No _____
59.	Yes _____	Somewhat or Unsure _____	No _____
60.	Yes _____	Somewhat or Unsure _____	No _____
61.	Yes _____	Somewhat or Unsure _____	No _____
62.	Yes _____	Somewhat or Unsure _____	No _____
63.	Yes _____	Somewhat or Unsure _____	No _____
64.	Yes _____	Somewhat or Unsure _____	No _____

Additional Learning Experiences

65.   Yes _____   Somewhat or Unsure _____   No _____

66.   Yes _____   Somewhat or Unsure _____   No _____

67.   Yes _____   Somewhat or Unsure _____   No _____

68.   Yes _____   Somewhat or Unsure _____   No _____

69.   Yes _____   Somewhat or Unsure _____   No _____

70.   Yes _____   Somewhat or Unsure _____   No _____

Strengths/Talents

71.   Yes _____   Somewhat or Unsure _____   No _____

72.   Yes _____   Somewhat or Unsure _____   No _____

73.   Yes _____   Somewhat or Unsure _____   No _____

74.   Yes _____   Somewhat or Unsure _____   No _____

75.   Yes _____   Somewhat or Unsure _____   No _____

76.   Yes _____   Somewhat or Unsure _____   No _____

77.   Yes _____   Somewhat or Unsure _____   No _____

78.   Yes _____   Somewhat or Unsure _____   No _____

79.   Yes _____   Somewhat or Unsure _____   No _____

80.   Yes _____   Somewhat or Unsure _____   No _____

81.   Yes _____   Somewhat or Unsure _____   No _____

82.   Yes _____   Somewhat or Unsure _____   No _____

83.   Yes _____   Somewhat or Unsure _____   No _____

84.   Yes _____   Somewhat or Unsure _____   No _____

85.   Yes _____   Somewhat or Unsure _____   No _____

86.   Yes _____   Somewhat or Unsure _____   No _____

87.   Yes _____   Somewhat or Unsure _____   No _____

88.   Yes _____   Somewhat or Unsure _____   No _____

89.   Yes _____   Somewhat or Unsure _____   No _____

Grade 2 Questionnaire Analysis

All Areas except Strengths/Talents

1.	Count the number of "yes" answers in all areas **except** Strengths/Talents.	_____
2.	Count the number of "somewhat" answers in these areas and divide by 2.	_____
3.	Add lines 1 and 2 for the **TOTAL** in these areas.	_____

If the **TOTAL** in these areas is **3 or more,** then the screener should proceed to the screening tasks.

Strengths/Talents

4.	Count the number of "yes" answers in Strengths/Talents.	_____
5.	Count the number of "somewhat" answers and divide by 2.	_____
6.	Add lines 4 and 5 for the **TOTAL** in these areas.	_____
7.	Add lines 3 and 6 for the **GRAND TOTAL.**	_____

Any number greater than 3 in line 7 (GRAND TOTAL) increases the likelihood that dyslexia is present.

Grade 2 Student Pages

(Copy these three pages for the student to write on during the screening.)

On these pages, the student will complete the work for tasks that involve writing: Tasks 1, 2, 4, 5, 6, 9, and 11. (The remaining tasks require dictation only, which the screener will record on the Screener Answer Sheet.)

Task 1: Write the Alphabet

_____

_____

_____

Task 2: Spelling Sight Words

_____

1. _____

   _____

2. _____

   _____

3. _____

   _____

4. _____

   _____

5. _____

   _____

6. _____

   _____

7. _____

   _____

8. _____

   _____

9. _____

_____

10. _____

_____

Task 4: Reading Grade-Level Words

1.	*clasp*	6.	*lampshade*
2.	*sped*	7.	*lantern*
3.	*slept*	8.	*velvet*
4.	*splendid*	9.	*inspect*
5.	*subtract*	10.	*distracted*

Task 5: Symbol to Sound Knowledge

1. d

2. u

3. q

4. y

5. a

6. w

7. i

8. x

9. e

10. o

Task 6: Write the Letter(s)

1.	_____	6.	_____
2.	_____	7.	_____
3.	_____	8.	_____
4.	_____	9.	_____
5.	_____	10.	_____

Task 9: Phonemic Awareness 2 (Isolation)

Source: https://docs.google.com/document/d/1v_W0fHCmiZ6Fm0VCZVPUsEWSAU8-YsknIDpwNJZroKY/edit

Task 11: Reading Unfamiliar Words

1.	*famtup*	6.	*trastly*
2.	*pob*	7.	*platcim*
3.	*drib*	8.	*crilthy*
4.	*dilk*	9.	*blondrope*
5.	*nilmtip*	10.	*spedfip*

Grade 2 Instructions and Answer Sheets

Task 1 Screener Instructions

(This information for the screener is also offered in video format at https://courses.learnreading.com/courses/dyslexia-screening-videos.)

- Ask the student to write the alphabet in lowercase letters.

- There should be no help, no copying, and no erasing or crossing out.

- Watch for any hints of directionality confusion when they go to write a letter. Be aware of any pauses or hesitations, especially at *b/d/p/q*.

- Watch for confusion midway through, or if they need to start again at the beginning and use the alphabet song to help them determine the next letter.

- Watch for any reversals (writing a letter backward), inversions (writing a letter upside down), or errors (omitting a letter or writing it in the wrong sequence).

- After you have carefully watched the student complete the task, record their responses by answering "true" or "no" in the spaces provided.

Task 1 Student Instructions

(You may present this information to the student yourself, or show them the "Student Instructions" video at https://courses.learnreading.com/courses/dyslexia-screening-videos.)

"In this task, you're going to write the alphabet. You're going to use a pen (or a pencil without an eraser). This is because I want to see the way your brain works, and what you write down first. So, if you don't like what you wrote and are tempted to cross it out, don't worry! Just draw a box around the answer you didn't like, so I can still see what it was, and then put the answer you do want right next to or above it. And please use only lowercase letters in this screening. Okay! Let's get started!"

Task 1 Answer Key

Directions: Ask the student to write the alphabet in *lowercase letters* in the space provided on the Student Pages, with no help, no copying, and no erasing.

1.	The student made it to the end without any errors.	TRUE_____	NO_____
2.	The letters all faced the correct direction. (There were no reversals or inversions.)	TRUE_____	NO_____

3.	The student wrote the alphabet easily and quickly, with no hesitations, questions, or restarts.	TRUE_____ NO_____
4.	There was no hesitation at *b/d* or *p/q*. (The student did not wonder which way the letter faced.)	TRUE_____ NO_____

Task 2 Screener Instructions

(This information for the screener is also offered in video format at https://courses.learnreading.com/courses/dyslexia-screening-videos.)

- You will dictate sight words for the student to spell.
- You can repeat the word and/or use it in a sentence, but offer no hints as to the spelling.
- Mark "correct" or "incorrect" in the spaces provided.

Task 2 Student Instructions

(You may present this information to the student yourself, or show them the "Student Instructions" video at https://courses.learnreading.com/courses/dyslexia-screening-videos.)

"You might already know that sight words are words that don't follow typical spelling rules. They can sometimes be tricky to spell. I'm going to say a few of these sight words and I'd like for you to try to spell them the best that you can."

Task 2 Answer Key

Directions: Ask the student to spell the following words in the space provided on the Student Pages, with no erasing or changing. Mark "correct" or "incorrect." (If they spelled the word incorrectly at first, then changed their mind and went to fix it, mark it "incorrect" even if their second attempt was correct.)

1.	*from*	CORRECT_____ INCORRECT_____
2.	*your* (as in "Let's go to your house.")	CORRECT_____ INCORRECT_____
3.	*word*	CORRECT_____ INCORRECT_____
4.	*said*	CORRECT_____ INCORRECT_____
5.	*there* (as in "Look over there.")	CORRECT_____ INCORRECT_____
6.	*do* (as in "Do you like that book?")	CORRECT_____ INCORRECT_____
7.	*their* (as in "We went in their car.")	CORRECT_____ INCORRECT_____
8.	*some*	CORRECT_____ INCORRECT_____

9.	would (as in "Would you go with me to the dance?")	CORRECT_____ INCORRECT_____
10.	*could*	CORRECT_____ INCORRECT_____

Grade 2: Task 3
Counting Sounds

Task 3 Screener Instructions

(This information for the screener is also offered in video format at https://courses.learnreading.com/courses/dyslexia-screening-videos).

- You will dictate words to the student and ask them to count how many SOUNDS they hear in a word (not syllables or letters).
- Mark "correct" or "incorrect" in the spaces provided. (The answer is next to the word.)

Task 3 Student Instructions

(You may present this information to the student yourself, or show them the "Student Instructions" video at https://courses.learnreading.com/courses/dyslexia-screening-videos.)

"For this task, you are simply going to be counting sounds. I am going to say a word, and you will count how many sounds you hear in that word. If you know how to spell the word, try not to think about the letters because I don't want you to count the letters, just the sounds. Sometimes there are more letters in a word than there are sounds, so just focus on the sounds, and tell me how many you hear."

Task 3 Answer Key

Directions: Ask the student how many SOUNDS are in each word. (Note: they are counting individual sounds, not syllables and not letters. For instance, *chicken* has 5 sounds.)

1.	*tan*	(answer: 3)	CORRECT_____ INCORRECT_____
2.	*blue*	(answer: 3)	CORRECT_____ INCORRECT_____
3.	*bench*	(answer: 4)	CORRECT_____ INCORRECT_____
4.	*truck*	(answer: 4)	CORRECT_____ INCORRECT_____
5.	*drill*	(answer: 4)	CORRECT_____ INCORRECT_____
6.	*straw*	(answer: 4)	CORRECT_____ INCORRECT_____
7.	*window*	(answer: 5)	CORRECT_____ INCORRECT_____

8.	*dinner*	(answer: 4)	CORRECT_____ INCORRECT_____
9.	*sticky*	(answer: 5)	CORRECT_____ INCORRECT_____
10.	*purple*	(answer: 4)	CORRECT_____ INCORRECT_____

Grade 2: Task 4
Reading Grade-Level Words

Task 4 Screener Instructions

(This information for the screener is also offered in video format at https://courses.learnreading.com/courses/dyslexia-screening-videos.)

- Ask the student to read the words on their Student Pages.
- Mark "correct" or "incorrect" in the spaces provided.

If the student chose to skip a word, mark it "incorrect."

Task 4 Student Instructions

(You may present this information to the student yourself, or show them the "Student Instructions" video at https://courses.learnreading.com/courses/dyslexia-screening-videos.)

"For this task, you are going to read a list of words as best as you can. It may be a little difficult, but just do your best. If you try and still feel like you can't read the word, it's okay to say, 'Skip it,' and move on to the next word."

Task 4 Answer Key

Directions: Ask the student to READ each word as it is written for them on the Student Pages.

1.	*clasp*	CORRECT_____ INCORRECT_____
2.	*sped*	CORRECT_____ INCORRECT_____
3.	*slept*	CORRECT_____ INCORRECT_____
4.	*splendid*	CORRECT_____ INCORRECT_____
5.	*subtract*	CORRECT_____ INCORRECT_____
6.	*lampshade*	CORRECT_____ INCORRECT_____
7.	*lantern*	CORRECT_____ INCORRECT_____
8.	*velvet*	CORRECT_____ INCORRECT_____

9.	*inspect*	CORRECT_____	INCORRECT_____
10.	*distracted*	CORRECT_____	INCORRECT_____

Grade 2: Task 5
Symbol to Sound Knowledge

Task 5 Screener Instructions

(This information for the screener is also offered in video format at https://courses.learnreading.com/courses/dyslexia-screening-videos.)

- Ask the student to look at each letter on their student page, and tell you the sound that it makes.
- When they come to the vowels, ask the student to tell you the short, or most common, sound.
- If they hesitate for longer than three seconds on any letter, mark it "incorrect."
- Mark "correct" or "incorrect" in the spaces provided. (The correct answer is provided for you.)

Task 5 Student Instructions

(You may present this information to the student yourself, or show them the "Student Instructions" video at https://courses.learnreading.com/courses/dyslexia-screening-videos.)

"For this task, I'd like you to look at a letter and then tell me the sound that it makes. When you come to a vowel, tell me the short, or most common, sound."

Task 5 Answer Key

Directions: Ask the student to look at each letter and tell you the sound each one makes. If they hesitate for longer than three seconds, mark it "incorrect." For *a, e, i, o, u*, tell them you want the short, or most common, sound. If they have any questions, tell them to just do their best.

1.	*d*	(answer: /d/ as in *dog*)	CORRECT_____	INCORRECT_____
2.	*u*	(answer: /u/ as in *under*)	CORRECT_____	INCORRECT_____
3.	*q*	(answer: /kw/ as in *queen*)	CORRECT_____	INCORRECT_____
4.	*y*	(answer: /y/ as in *yellow*)	CORRECT_____	INCORRECT_____
5.	*a*	(answer: /ă/ as in *apple*)	CORRECT_____	INCORRECT_____
6.	*w*	(answer: /w/ as in *water*)	CORRECT_____	INCORRECT_____
7.	*i*	(answer: /ĭ/ as in *index*)	CORRECT_____	INCORRECT_____
8.	*x*	(answer: /ks/ as in *fox*)	CORRECT_____	INCORRECT_____

9.	*e*	(answer: /ĕ/ as in *exit*)	CORRECT_____ INCORRECT_____
10.	*o*	(answer: /ŏ/ as in *octopus*)	CORRECT_____ INCORRECT_____

Task 6 Screener Instructions

(This information for the screener is also offered in video format at https://courses.learnreading.com/courses/dyslexia-screening-videos.)

- You will dictate a sound to the student.
- Ask the student what letter, or set of letters, makes that sound.
- The "as in" hints are for the screener only and should *not* be given to the student.
- Ask the student to write their answers in lowercase letters.
- When the student writes their answer, the letters must be facing the correct way for the answer to be marked "correct." If any letters are reversed, mark it "incorrect."

Task 6 Student Instructions

(You may present this information to the student yourself, or show them the "Student Instructions" video at https://courses.learnreading.com/courses/dyslexia-screening-videos.)

"This time I'm going to give you the sound, and you're going to write down the letter or letters that make that sound. For instance, if I said /m/ (the sound of *m*), you would write *m*. If I said /th/ (the sound of *th*), you would write *th*.

Task 6 Answer Key

Directions: For the following items, say to the student, "What letter, or letters, makes this sound?" Then pronounce the sound for them. (Do *not* say "as in..." because that is only for you to read so you are sure which sound to make. The answer is the bold letter[s] in the example word. *Q* can be written as *Q* or *QU*. Both are correct.) Have them write down their answer in lowercase letters in the space provided on the Student Pages. The letters they write down must be facing the right direction to be marked "correct."

1.	/ch/	(as in **ch**air)	CORRECT_____ INCORRECT_____
2.	/ĕ/	(as in **e**xit'	CORRECT_____ INCORRECT_____
3.	/sh/	(as in **sh**ut)	CORRECT_____ INCORRECT_____
4.	/ŏ/	(as in **o**ctopus)	CORRECT_____ INCORRECT_____

5.	/w/	(as in **wonder**)	CORRECT_____ INCORRECT_____
6.	/ĭ/	(as in **index**)	CORRECT_____ INCORRECT_____
7.	/y/	(as in **yellow**)	CORRECT_____ INCORRECT_____
8.	/ŭ/	(as in **under**)	CORRECT_____ INCORRECT_____
9.	/d/	(as in **door**)	CORRECT_____ INCORRECT_____
10.	/kw/	(as in **queen**)	CORRECT_____ INCORRECT_____

Grade 2: Task 7
Auditory Discrimination

Task 7 Screener Instructions

(This information for the screener is also offered in video format at https://courses.learnreading.com/courses/dyslexia-screening-videos.)

- Dictate three distinct sounds to the student, with clean and clear *breaks* in between each sound.
- Ask the student to repeat the sounds back to you in order.
- The "as in" hints are for the screener only and should *not* be given to the student.
- The sounds must all be repeated back with exactness to be marked "correct." If the student mispronounced or omitted any sounds, or switched the order, mark the answer "incorrect."

Task 7 Student Instructions

(You may present this information to the student yourself, or show them the "Student Instructions" video at https://courses.learnreading.com/courses/dyslexia-screening-videos.)

"For this task, I am going to say three sounds and then you just repeat them exactly as I said them and in the same order. Listen very carefully because some of the sounds may sound similar. Repeat them back to me as best you can."

Task 7 Answer Key

Directions: Ask the student to repeat the following sound sequences after you. You will pronounce all three sounds, then they should repeat the three sounds back to you. If they ask you to repeat the sequence, you may repeat it one time. If they say all three sounds back to you *exactly* right, mark it "correct." If they mispronounced (or couldn't remember) even one of the three sounds, mark it "incorrect." (Do *not* say "as in..." because that is only for you so you are sure which sound to make.)

1.	/n/ /m/ /l/ (as in: *name, milk, leg*)	CORRECT_____ INCORRECT_____
2.	/ĭ/ /ŏ/ /ĕ/ (as in: *index, octopus, exit*)	CORRECT_____ INCORRECT_____
3.	/d/ /p/ /b/ (as in: *door, pie, box*)	CORRECT_____ INCORRECT_____
4.	/sh/ /s/ /z/ (as in: *ship, sun, zebra*)	CORRECT_____ INCORRECT_____
5.	/th/ /f/ /j/ (as in: *think, fish, jam*)	CORRECT_____ INCORRECT_____
6.	/ă/ /ĕ/ /ĭ / (as in: *apple, exit, index*)	CORRECT_____ INCORRECT_____
7.	/ŭ/ /ŏ/ /ă/ (as in: *under, octopus, apple*)	CORRECT_____ INCORRECT_____
8.	/sh/ /ch/ /th/ (as in: *ship, chop, think*)	CORRECT_____ INCORRECT_____
9.	/r/ /l/ /n/ (as in: *run, leg, net*)	CORRECT_____ INCORRECT_____
10.	/w/ /y/ /p/ (as in: *water, yellow, pot*)	CORRECT_____ INCORRECT_____

Task 8 Screener Instructions

(This information for the screener is also offered in video format at https://courses.learnreading.com/courses/dyslexia-screening-videos.)

- Important note: when you see a letter in between two slanted lines, it means the sound that that letter makes. For instance, /f/ is the *sound* of *f*, not the letter itself.
- Read the questions to the student, making sure to only say the sound of the letter in between the slanted lines.
- Mark "correct" or "incorrect" in the spaces provided. (The correct answer is provided for you.)

Task 8 Student Instructions

(You may present this information to the student yourself, or show them the "Student Instructions" video at https://courses.learnreading.com/courses/dyslexia-screening-videos.)

"For this task, I am going to say a word. Then, I'm going to ask you to repeat the word but without one of the sounds. For example, I might say *camp*, and then ask you to say *camp* without the /m/. *Camp* without the /m/ is *Cap* (model how to do the task). So listen carefully, take your time, and try your best."

Task 8 Answer Key

Directions: Ask the student each question. When you do so, say the SOUND that they are to remove, not the letter. (FYI: a letter inside of slanted lines, like /f/, means the sound only, not the letter itself.) If

they ask you to repeat the question, you may do so one time. The student should tell you the answer, not write it down.

1.	"What would *cat* say without the /k/?" (answer: *at*)	CORRECT_____ INCORRECT_____
2.	"What would *bite* say without the /t/?" (answer: *by*)	CORRECT_____ INCORRECT_____
3.	"What would *flatten* say without the /l/?" (answer: *fatten*)	CORRECT_____ INCORRECT_____
4.	"What would *scram* say without the /r/?" (answer: *scam*)	CORRECT_____ INCORRECT_____
5.	"What would *feast* say without the /s/?" (answer: *feet*)	CORRECT_____ INCORRECT_____
6.	"What would *play* say without the /l/?" (answer: *pay*)	CORRECT_____ INCORRECT_____
7.	"What would *boost* say without the /s/?" (answer: *boot*)	CORRECT_____ INCORRECT_____
8.	"What would *trip* say without the /r/?" (answer: *tip*)	CORRECT_____ INCORRECT_____
9.	"What would *faxed* say without the /k/?" (answer: *fast*)	CORRECT_____ INCORRECT_____
10.	"What would *bottle* say without the /t/?" (answer: *ball*)	CORRECT_____ INCORRECT_____

Grade 2: Task 9
Phonemic Awareness/Isolation

Task 9 Screener Instructions

(This information for the screener is also offered in video format at https://courses.learnreading.com/courses/dyslexia-screening-videos.)

- Ask the student to look at a picture on their Student Page, say what it is a picture of, and stretch out the sounds in that word (such as *milk* "mmmiiiillllk").
- Ask the student to break apart each sound in that word and then mark the dot that represents the sound in the question that you will ask them.
- Mark "correct" or "incorrect" if they identified the correct dot that contained that sound.

Task 9 Student Instructions

(You may present this information to the student yourself, or show them the "Student Instructions" video at https://courses.learnreading.com/courses/dyslexia-screening-videos.)

"For this task, you're going to see some pictures. I want you to tell me what the picture is and then stretch out the sounds in that word. Then I want you to separate each sound in that word with nice, big breaks in between each sound. You will see dots under the picture. I'd like you to point to each dot when you say each sound in that word. Then I'm going to ask where a certain sound is, and you'll just point to, or color in, that dot."

Task 9 Answer Key

Directions: As you ask each question, ask the student to follow along with you on their Student Pages. Ask the student to look at each picture and 1) repeat what the picture is, 2) stretch out the sounds in the word, and then 3) separate the sounds within the word and mark the dot on their paper where they hear the sound in question.

1.	Where is the /r/ in *drill*?	(answer: 2nd dot	CORRECT_____	INCORRECT_____
2.	Where is the /l/ in *milk*?	(answer: 3rd dot)	CORRECT_____	INCORRECT_____
3.	Where is the /s/ in *toast*?	(answer: 3rd dot)	CORRECT_____	INCORRECT_____
4.	Where is the /u/ in *duck*?	(answer: 2nd dot)	CORRECT_____	INCORRECT_____
5.	Where is the /u/ in *drum*?	(answer: 3rd dot)	CORRECT_____	INCORRECT_____
6.	Where is the /l/ in *elk*?	(answer: 2nd dot)	CORRECT_____	INCORRECT_____
7.	Where is the /e/ in *shell*?	(answer: 2nd dot)	CORRECT_____	INCORRECT_____
8.	Where is the /m/ in *pump*?	(answer: 3rd dot)	CORRECT_____	INCORRECT_____

The student had difficulty **breaking off** one sound from another in one or more of the words (if so, mark "incorrect" here).   CORRECT_____ INCORRECT_____

The student had difficulty **articulating** the correct sounds within the word (if so, mark "incorrect" here).   CORRECT _____ INCORRECT _____

Task 10 Screener Instructions

(This information for the screener is also offered in video format at https://courses.learnreading.com/courses/dyslexia-screening-videos.)

- Read the word to the student. Have them repeat the word and then try to say the word backward.
- Mark "correct" or "incorrect" in the spaces provided. (The correct answer is provided for you.)

Task 10 Student Instructions

(You may present this information to the student yourself, or show them the "Student Instructions" video at https://courses.learnreading.com/courses/dyslexia-screening-videos.)

"In this task, I'm going to say a word. You will repeat the word back to me, and then try to say the word backward. For example, if I said the word cat, you would repeat that word *cat* and then try to say it backward. That last letter in cat would be the first letter if it was said backward. So *cat*, backward, is *tac* (model how to do the task).

Task 10 Answer Key

Directions: 1) Read the word (or nonsense word) to the student. 2) Ask them to repeat the word back to you. Then 3) tell them to say the word backward. If they ask you to repeat the word, you may do so one time. They must say every sound in the reversed word *exactly* right to be marked "correct." (If you are unsure of the correct pronunciation of the word, a "rhymes with" word is provided for you. Please do *not* share this "rhymes with" word with the student. It is only to aid the administrator.)

1.	*tea* (rhymes with *see*)	(answer: *eat*)	CORRECT_____	INCORRECT_____
2.	*air* (rhymes with *stare*)	(answer: *ray*)	CORRECT_____	INCORRECT_____
3.	*ile* (rhymes with *mile*)	(answer: *lie*)	CORRECT_____	INCORRECT_____
4.	*oot* (rhymes with *flute*)	(answer: *to*)	CORRECT_____	INCORRECT_____
5.	*eem* (rhymes with *team*)	(answer: *me*)	CORRECT_____	INCORRECT_____
6.	*cheap* (rhymes with *sheep*)	(answer: *peach*)	CORRECT_____	INCORRECT_____
7.	*chum* (rhymes with *plum*)	(answer: *much*)	CORRECT_____	INCORRECT_____
8.	*stop* (rhymes with *top*)	(answer: *pots*)	CORRECT_____	INCORRECT_____
9.	*gums* (rhymes with *chums*)	(answer: *smug*)	CORRECT_____	INCORRECT_____
10.	*klim* (rhymes with *slim*)	(answer: *milk*)	CORRECT_____	INCORRECT_____

Grade 2: Task 11
Decoding Unfamiliar Words

Task 11 Screener Instructions

(This information for the screener is also offered in video format at https://courses.learnreading.com/courses/dyslexia-screening-videos.)

- Ask the student to read aloud the nonsense words on their Student Pages.
- They must get each sound in the word *exactly* correct for it to be marked "correct."
- The "rhymes with" hints are for the screener only and should *not* be given to the student.

Task 11 Student Instructions

(You may present this information to the student yourself, or show them the "Student Instructions" video at https://courses.learnreading.com/courses/dyslexia-screening-videos.)

"On your Student Pages, you're going to see some nonsense words. These are crazy words that you've never seen before. To read them, just use your knowledge of what the letters say."

Task 11 Answer Key

Directions: Ask the student to READ each nonsense word on their Student Pages. The student must pronounce each sound in the word *exactly* right for the word to be marked "correct." (A "rhymes with" word is provided for the screener only. Do *not* give the "rhymes with" word to the student.)

1.	*famtup* (rhymes with *Sam cup*)	CORRECT_____ INCORRECT_____
2.	*pob* (rhymes with *cob*)	CORRECT_____ INCORRECT_____
3.	*drib* (rhymes with *crib*)	CORRECT_____ INCORRECT_____
4.	*dilk* (rhymes with *milk*)	CORRECT_____ INCORRECT_____
5.	*nilmtip* (rhymes with *film sip*)	CORRECT_____ INCORRECT_____
6.	*trastly* (rhymes with *lastly*)	CORRECT_____ INCORRECT_____
7.	*platcim* (sounds like *plat sim*)	CORRECT_____ INCORRECT_____
8.	*crilthy* (rhymes with *filthy*)	CORRECT_____ INCORRECT_____
9.	*blondrope* (sounds like *blond rope*)	CORRECT_____ INCORRECT_____
10.	*spedfip* (sounds like *sped fip*)	CORRECT_____ INCORRECT_____

Grade 2 Results

Task 1: Long-Term Memory

_____

Total Incorrect (or "no" answers):   _____
_____

Task 2: Sight Words Knowledge

_____

Total Incorrect: _____
_____

Task 3: Phonemic Awareness

_____

Total Incorrect: _____
_____

Task 4: Reading Grade-Level Words

_____

Total Incorrect: _____
_____

Task 5: Symbol to Sound Knowledge

_____

Total Incorrect: _____
_____

Task 6: Sound to Symbol Knowledge

_____

Total Incorrect: _____
_____

Task 7: Auditory Discrimination/Memory

_____

Total Incorrect: _____
_____

Task 8: Phonemic Awareness

Total Incorrect: _____

Task 9: Phonemic Awareness

Total Incorrect: _____

Task 10: Phonemic Awareness

Total Incorrect: _____

Task 11: Decoding Unfamiliar Words

Total Incorrect: _____

Results for Questionnaire Plus Screening Tasks

1.	TOTAL (line 4) on Questionnaire	_____
2.	TOTAL incorrect answers on Screening Tasks	_____
3.	**GRAND TOTAL from lines 1 and 2**	_____

Grade 2 Conclusions

If the GRAND TOTAL (line 3) **is 14 or greater**, then this student's performance is consistent with someone with dyslexia.

It can be assumed that the severity of dyslexia is in direct relation to **how much greater than 14** the GRAND TOTAL is (14 being mild and 199 being the most severe).

If the GRAND TOTAL **is less than 14**, then dyslexia is likely *not* the probable cause for the student's academic difficulties.

Grade 3 Screening Packet

This packet contains the following:

- Grade 3 Screening Questionnaire
- Grade 3 Questionnaire Answer Sheet
- Grade 3 Questionnaire Analysis
- Grade 3 Student Pages (for student's written answers)
- Grade 3 Instructions and Answer Sheets (for Tasks 1–11)
- Grade 3 Results
- Grade 3 Conclusions

Grade 3 Screening Questionnaire

(Mark answers on the answer sheet.)

Genetics

1. Does the student's mother have any trouble with reading or spelling?

2. Does the student's father have any trouble with reading or spelling?

3. Are there any other immediate family members who struggle with reading or spelling?

4. Are (or were) there any extended family members (parents, siblings, grandparents, cousins, aunts, uncles) who struggled in school?

Articulation/Speech

5. Did the student have a speech delay (were they a late talker)?

6. Does (did) the student have any articulation or speech issues?

7. Does (did) the student have problems forming certain words correctly?

8. Does (did) the student mispronounce words even after repeated correction?

9. Does (did) the student attend speech therapy?

10. Does (did) the student confuse *i/e*, *m/n*, or *f/th* when they speak?

11. Does (did) the person have difficulty saying words like *aluminum*, *cinnamon*, or *dyslexia*?

12. Does the student have difficulty expressing themself verbally?

13. Does the student have trouble retrieving words, use a lot of *ums* or *uhs*, or use grand gestures with their hands when speaking?

Directionality

14. Is (was) there any left/right confusion?

15. Are there any letter or number reversals continuing beyond the end of first grade, including *b/d* confusion?

16. Does (did) the student have difficulty learning to tie their shoes?

17. Does the student have trouble telling time on an analog clock?

18. Does (did) the student have difficulty remembering the direction of mathematical operations, such as addition and subtraction moving right to left?

19. Does the student transpose number sequences, such as writing *51* for *15*?

20. Does (did) the student reverse words when reading, such as reading *top* for *pot*?

Memory/Recall

21. Does (did) the student have trouble recalling the names of letters, numbers, or colors?

22. Does the student have difficulty remembering sequences (such as a list of directions, arithmetic steps, spelling sequences, days of the week, or months of the year in order)?

23. Does the student have difficulty on timed math tests?

24. Does the student have trouble with copying (copying slowly and inaccurately)?

25. Does the student have difficulty remembering names?

26. Does the student have difficulty remembering the order of the alphabet?

27. Does the student have trouble recalling the days of the week or months of the year in order?

28. Does the student have trouble recalling the names of familiar objects, instead replacing them with words like *stuff* or *things*?

29. Does the student have trouble remembering multiple-step directions?

30. Does the student have difficulty remembering an address or phone number?

31. Does the student have trouble with alphabetizing or with remembering the order of the alphabet?

32. Does the student have a hard time recalling math facts quickly?

Phonemic Awareness/Auditory Processing

33. Does (did) the student have difficulty learning nursery rhymes or playing rhyming games?

34. Does the student have problems repeating back sounds accurately and in order?

35. Does (did) the student have trouble breaking off the first or last sound of a word?

36. Does (did) the student have trouble identifying the vowel sound within a word?

37. Does (did) the student confuse the short *i* and the short *e* sound when saying or reading words?

38. Does (did) the student have trouble understanding the connection between letters and sounds?

39. Does (did) the student have trouble isolating and manipulating the sounds within a word?

Reading

40. Does (did) the student read below grade level?

41. Does the student have trouble decoding unfamiliar words?

42. Is the student's reading slow and labor intensive?

43. Does (did) the student have trouble reading sight words or high frequency words?

44. Does the student forget how to read a word from one moment to the next?

45. Does the student have trouble comprehending what they read?

46. Would the student prefer *not* to be called on to read aloud in class or in public? Would they prefer to avoid reading, especially aloud?

47. Does (did) the student guess at words based on the size, shape, context, or picture clues?

48. Does (did) the student skip or misread small, simple words when reading?

49. Is the student easily frustrated when reading?

50. Does the student spend an unusually long time completing tasks that involve reading?

51. Does the student omit the suffixes or endings of words?

52. Does the student have trouble recognizing their mistakes when reading?

53. Does the student rarely read for pleasure?

54. Does the student require multiple readings to comprehend the material?

55. Does the student omit, substitute, add, or transpose letters when reading?

Spelling/Writing

56. Does the student have trouble with spelling?

57. Does the student spend an unusually long time completing tasks that involve writing?

58. Does (did) the student have trouble spelling sight words or high frequency words?

59. Does (did) the student forget how to spell a word from one moment to the next?

60. Do others have trouble reading what the student wrote, due to spelling errors?

61. Is the student's intelligence not reflected in their writing?

62. When writing, will the student use words that they know how to spell, instead of those that they would prefer to use?

63. Does the student have trouble remembering and applying spelling rules?

64. Does (did) the student use unpredictable, illogical spelling?

65. Does (did) the student omit, substitute, add, or transpose letters when spelling?

66. Does the student have difficulty using spell check or a dictionary?

Additional Learning Experiences

67. Has the student attended special academic classes, reading groups, or had outside tutoring?

68. Does the student have trouble learning a foreign language in print (reading and writing in the foreign language)?

69. Does the student have difficulty reading printed music?

70. Does the student have trouble taking notes in class?

71. Does (has) the student pretended to be sick or otherwise unable to attend school/perform academically in a classroom?

72. Can the student answer questions orally, but be unable to adequately do so in print?

73. Does the student need more time than others to process verbal information?

74. Does (did) the student have poor self-esteem resulting from poor academic performance?

75. Does (did) the student experience anxiety or high levels of stress surrounding academics?

Strengths/Talents

76. Does the student have a high capacity for learning?

77. Is the student gifted athletically?

78. Is the student gifted musically?

79. Is the student gifted artistically?

80. Is the student extremely creative?

81. Is the student highly imaginative?

82. Does the student have surprising maturity?

83. Does the student enjoy, and are they good at, puzzles (excellent spatial reasoning)?

84. Is the student extremely curious?

85. Is the student able to easily comprehend stories that they *hear* or *listen to*?

86. Is the student able to easily remember song lyrics?

87. Is the student mechanically inclined (good with their hands, such as working with Legos, building models, taking things apart and putting them back together again, etc.)?

88. Does the student have excellent creative writing skills?

89. Does the student have excellent thinking and reasoning skills?

90. Does the student have the ability to produce unique, out-of-the-box ideas?

91. Is the student gifted at seeing the big picture?

92. Is the student highly empathetic?

93. Is the student highly resilient?

94. Does the student have excellent interpersonal skills (maintains friendships easily)?

Grade 3 Questionnaire Answer Sheet

Genetics

1.   Yes _____   Somewhat or Unsure _____   No _____

2.   Yes _____   Somewhat or Unsure _____   No _____

3.   Yes _____   Somewhat or Unsure _____   No _____

4.   Yes _____   Somewhat or Unsure _____   No _____

Articulation/Speech

5.   Yes _____   Somewhat or Unsure _____   No _____

6.   Yes _____   Somewhat or Unsure _____   No _____

7.   Yes _____   Somewhat or Unsure _____   No _____

8.   Yes _____   Somewhat or Unsure _____   No _____

9.   Yes _____   Somewhat or Unsure _____   No _____

10.   Yes _____   Somewhat or Unsure _____   No _____

11.   Yes _____   Somewhat or Unsure _____   No _____

12.   Yes _____   Somewhat or Unsure _____   No _____

13.   Yes _____   Somewhat or Unsure _____   No _____

Directionality

14.   Yes _____   Somewhat or Unsure _____   No _____

15.   Yes _____   Somewhat or Unsure _____   No _____

16.   Yes _____   Somewhat or Unsure _____   No _____

17.   Yes _____   Somewhat or Unsure _____   No _____

18.   Yes _____   Somewhat or Unsure _____   No _____

19.   Yes _____   Somewhat or Unsure _____   No _____

20.   Yes _____   Somewhat or Unsure _____   No _____

Is It Dyslexia?

Memory/Recall

21.	Yes _____	Somewhat or Unsure _____	No _____
22.	Yes _____	Somewhat or Unsure _____	No _____
23.	Yes _____	Somewhat or Unsure _____	No _____
24.	Yes _____	Somewhat or Unsure _____	No _____
25.	Yes _____	Somewhat or Unsure _____	No _____
26.	Yes _____	Somewhat or Unsure _____	No _____
27.	Yes _____	Somewhat or Unsure _____	No _____
28.	Yes _____	Somewhat or Unsure _____	No _____
29.	Yes _____	Somewhat or Unsure _____	No _____
30.	Yes _____	Somewhat or Unsure _____	No _____
31.	Yes _____	Somewhat or Unsure _____	No _____
32.	Yes _____	Somewhat or Unsure _____	No _____

Phonemic Awareness/Auditory Processing

33.	Yes _____	Somewhat or Unsure _____	No _____
34.	Yes _____	Somewhat or Unsure _____	No _____
35.	Yes _____	Somewhat or Unsure _____	No _____
36.	Yes _____	Somewhat or Unsure _____	No _____
37.	Yes _____	Somewhat or Unsure _____	No _____
38.	Yes _____	Somewhat or Unsure _____	No _____
39.	Yes _____	Somewhat or Unsure _____	No _____

Reading

40.	Yes _____	Somewhat or Unsure _____	No _____
41.	Yes _____	Somewhat or Unsure _____	No _____
42.	Yes _____	Somewhat or Unsure _____	No _____
43.	Yes _____	Somewhat or Unsure _____	No _____
44.	Yes _____	Somewhat or Unsure _____	No _____
45.	Yes _____	Somewhat or Unsure _____	No _____
46.	Yes _____	Somewhat or Unsure _____	No _____
47.	Yes _____	Somewhat or Unsure _____	No _____
48.	Yes _____	Somewhat or Unsure _____	No _____
49.	Yes _____	Somewhat or Unsure _____	No _____
50.	Yes _____	Somewhat or Unsure _____	No _____
51.	Yes _____	Somewhat or Unsure _____	No _____
52.	Yes _____	Somewhat or Unsure _____	No _____
53.	Yes _____	Somewhat or Unsure _____	No _____
54.	Yes _____	Somewhat or Unsure _____	No _____
55.	Yes _____	Somewhat or Unsure _____	No _____

Spelling/Writing

56.	Yes _____	Somewhat or Unsure _____	No _____
57.	Yes _____	Somewhat or Unsure _____	No _____
58.	Yes _____	Somewhat or Unsure _____	No _____
59.	Yes _____	Somewhat or Unsure _____	No _____
60.	Yes _____	Somewhat or Unsure _____	No _____
61.	Yes _____	Somewhat or Unsure _____	No _____
62.	Yes _____	Somewhat or Unsure _____	No _____
63.	Yes _____	Somewhat or Unsure _____	No _____
64.	Yes _____	Somewhat or Unsure _____	No _____

65.	Yes _____	Somewhat or Unsure _____	No _____
66.	Yes _____	Somewhat or Unsure _____	No _____

Additional Learning Experiences

67.	Yes _____	Somewhat or Unsure _____	No _____
68.	Yes _____	Somewhat or Unsure _____	No _____
69.	Yes _____	Somewhat or Unsure _____	No _____
70.	Yes _____	Somewhat or Unsure _____	No _____
71.	Yes _____	Somewhat or Unsure _____	No _____
72.	Yes _____	Somewhat or Unsure _____	No _____
73.	Yes _____	Somewhat or Unsure _____	No _____
74.	Yes _____	Somewhat or Unsure _____	No _____
75.	Yes _____	Somewhat or Unsure _____	No _____

Strengths/Talents

76.	Yes _____	Somewhat or Unsure _____	No _____
77.	Yes _____	Somewhat or Unsure _____	No _____
78.	Yes _____	Somewhat or Unsure _____	No _____
79.	Yes _____	Somewhat or Unsure _____	No _____
80.	Yes _____	Somewhat or Unsure _____	No _____
81.	Yes _____	Somewhat or Unsure _____	No _____
82.	Yes _____	Somewhat or Unsure _____	No _____
83.	Yes _____	Somewhat or Unsure _____	No _____
84.	Yes _____	Somewhat or Unsure _____	No _____
85.	Yes _____	Somewhat or Unsure _____	No _____
86.	Yes _____	Somewhat or Unsure _____	No _____
87.	Yes _____	Somewhat or Unsure _____	No _____
88.	Yes _____	Somewhat or Unsure _____	No _____

89.	Yes _____	Somewhat or Unsure _____	No _____
90.	Yes _____	Somewhat or Unsure _____	No _____
91.	Yes _____	Somewhat or Unsure _____	No _____
92.	Yes _____	Somewhat or Unsure _____	No _____
93.	Yes _____	Somewhat or Unsure _____	No _____
94.	Yes _____	Somewhat or Unsure _____	No _____

Is It Dyslexia?

Grade 3 Questionnaire Analysis

All Areas except Strengths/Talents

---

1. Count the number of "yes" answers in all areas **except** Strengths/Talents.   _____

2. Count the number of "somewhat" answers in these areas and divide by 2.   _____

3. Add lines 1 and 2 for the **TOTAL** in these areas.   _____

If the **TOTAL** in these areas is **3 or more,** then the screener should proceed to the screening tasks.

Strengths/Talents

---

4. Count the number of "yes" answers in Strengths/Talents.   _____

5. Count the number of "somewhat" answers and divide by 2.   _____

6. Add lines 4 and 5 for the **TOTAL** in these areas.   _____

7. Add lines 3 and 6 for the **GRAND TOTAL.**   _____

Any number greater than 3 in line 7 (GRAND TOTAL) increases the likelihood that dyslexia is present.

Grade 3 Student Pages

(Copy these three pages for the student to write on during the screening.)

On these pages, the student will complete the work for tasks that involve writing: Tasks: 1, 2, 4, 5, 6, 9, and 11. (The remaining tasks require dictation only, which the screener will record on the Screener Answer Sheet.)

Task 1: Write the Alphabet

_____

_____

_____

Task 2: Spelling Sight Words

_____

1. _____

_____

2. _____

_____

3. _____

_____

4. _____

_____

5. _____

_____

6. _____

_____

7. _____

_____

8. _____

_____

9. _____

_____

10. _____

_____

Task 4: Reading Grade-Level Words

1.	*sped*	6.	*momentum*
2.	*clasp*	7.	*electric*
3.	*velvet*	8.	*detest*
4.	*inspected*	9.	*multiplication*
5.	*strictly*	10.	*citrus*

Task 5: Symbol to Sound Knowledge

1. d

2. u

3. q

4. y

5. a

6. w

7. i

8. x

9. e

10. o

Task 6: Write the Letter(s)

1.	_____	6.	_____
2.	_____	7.	_____
3.	_____	8.	_____
4.	_____	9.	_____
5.	_____	10.	_____

Task 9: Phonemic Awareness 2 (Isolation)

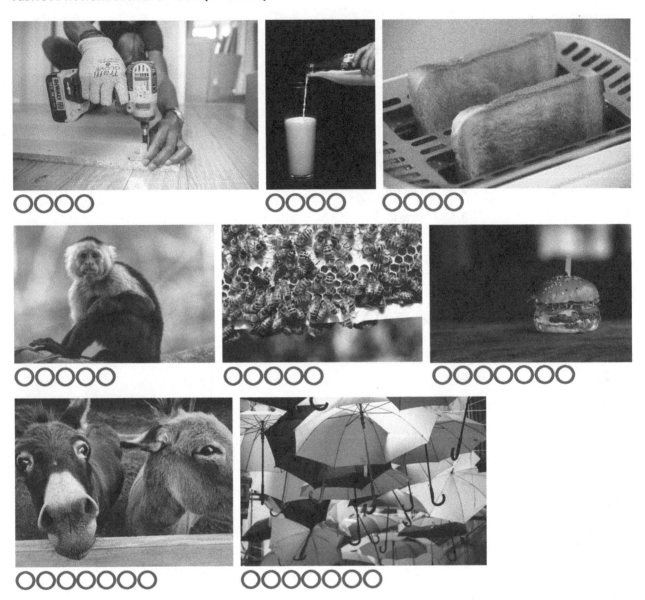

Source: https://docs.google.com/document/d/1v_W0fHCmiZ6Fm0VCZVPUsEWSAU8-YsknIDpwNJZroKY/edit

Task 11: Reading Unfamiliar Words

1.	*drib*	6.	*trats*
2.	*dilk*	7.	*flaspry*
3.	*nilmtip*	8.	*thifty*
4.	*trastly*	9.	*planstaimpy*
5.	*crilthy*	10.	*plumud*

Grade 3 Instructions and Answer Sheets

Task 1 Screener Instructions

(This information for the screener is also offered in video format at https://courses.learnreading.com/courses/dyslexia-screening-videos.)

- Ask the student to write the alphabet in lowercase letters.

- There should be no help, no copying, and no erasing or crossing out.

- Watch for any hints of directionality confusion when they go to write a letter. Be aware of any pauses or hesitations, especially at *b/d/p/q*.

- Watch for confusion midway through, or if they need to start again at the beginning and use the alphabet song to help them determine the next letter.

- Watch for any reversals (writing a letter backward), inversions (writing a letter upside down), or errors (omitting a letter or writing it in the wrong sequence).

- After you have carefully watched the student complete the task, record their responses by answering "true" or "no" in the spaces provided.

Task 1 Student Instructions

(You may present this information to the student yourself, or show them the "Student Instructions" video at https://courses.learnreading.com/courses/dyslexia-screening-videos.)

"In this task, you're going to write the alphabet. You're going to use a pen (or a pencil without an eraser). This is because I want to see the way your brain works, and what you write down first. So, if you don't like what you wrote and are tempted to cross it out, don't worry! Just draw a box around the answer you didn't like, so I can still see what it was, and then put the answer you do want right next to or above it. And please use only lowercase letters in this screening. Okay! Let's get started!"

Task 1 Answer Key

Directions: Ask the student to write the alphabet in *lowercase letters* in the space provided on the Student Pages, with no help, no copying, and no erasing.

1.	The student made it to the end without any errors.	TRUE_____	NO_____
2.	The letters all faced the correct direction. (There were no reversals or inversions.)	TRUE_____	NO_____
3.	The student wrote the alphabet easily and quickly, with no hesitations, questions, or restarts.	TRUE_____	NO_____

4.　　　There was no hesitation at *b/d* or *p/q*. (The student did not　TRUE_____ NO_____
　　　　wonder which way the letter faced.)

Task 2 Screener Instructions

(This information for the screener is also offered in video format at https://courses.learnreading.com/ courses/dyslexia-screening-videos.)

- You will dictate sight words for the student to spell.
- You can repeat the word and/or use it in a sentence, but no hints as to the spelling.
- Mark "correct" or "incorrect" in the spaces provided.

Task 2 Student Instructions

(You may present this information to the student yourself, or show them the "Student Instructions" video at https://courses.learnreading.com/courses/dyslexia-screening-videos.)

　"You might already know that sight words are words that don't follow typical spelling rules. They can sometimes be tricky to spell. I'm going to say a few of these sight words and I'd like for you to try to spell them the best that you can."

Task 2 Answer Key

Directions: Ask the student to spell the following words in the space provided on the Student Pages, with no erasing or changing. Mark "correct" or "incorrect." (If they spelled the word incorrectly at first, then changed their mind and went to fix it, mark it "incorrect" even if their second attempt was correct.)

1.	*should*	CORRECT_____ INCORRECT_____
2.	*two* (the number)	CORRECT_____ INCORRECT_____
3.	*four* (the number)	CORRECT_____ INCORRECT_____
4.	*eight* (the number)	CORRECT_____ INCORRECT_____
5.	*does*	CORRECT_____ INCORRECT_____
6.	*been* (as in "How have you been?")	CORRECT_____ INCORRECT_____
7.	*who*	CORRECT_____ INCORRECT_____
8.	*because*	CORRECT_____ INCORRECT____
9.	*come*	CORRECT_____ INCORRECT_____
10.	*love*	CORRECT_____ INCORRECT_____

　Grade 3: Task 3
　Counting Sounds

Task 3 Screener Instructions

(This information for the screener is also offered in video format at https://courses.learnreading.com/courses/dyslexia-screening-videos.)

- You will dictate words to the student and ask them to count how many sounds they hear in a word (not syllables or letters).
- Mark "correct" or "incorrect" in the spaces provided. (The answer is next to the word.)

Task 3 Student Instructions

(You may present this information to the student yourself, or show them the "Student Instructions" video at https://courses.learnreading.com/courses/dyslexia-screening-videos.)

"For this task, you are simply going to be counting sounds. I am going to say a word, and you will count how many sounds you hear in that word. If you know how to spell the word, try not to think about the letters because I don't want you to count the letters, just the sounds. Sometimes there are more letters in a word than there are sounds, so just focus on the sounds, and tell me how many you hear."

Task 3 Answer Key

Directions: Ask the student how many sounds are in each word. (Note: they are counting individual sounds, not syllables and not letters. For instance, *chicken* has 5 sounds.)

1.	*tan*	(answer: 3)	CORRECT_____ INCORRECT_____
2.	*blue*	(answer: 3)	CORRECT_____ INCORRECT_____
3.	*bench*	(answer: 4)	CORRECT_____ INCORRECT_____
4.	*truck*	(answer: 4)	CORRECT_____ INCORRECT_____
5.	*drill*	(answer: 4)	CORRECT_____ INCORRECT_____
6.	*straw*	(answer: 4)	CORRECT_____ INCORRECT_____
7.	*tractor*	(answer: 6)	CORRECT_____ INCORRECT_____
8.	*country*	(answer: 6)	CORRECT_____ INCORRECT_____
9.	*synonym*	(answer: 7)	CORRECT_____ INCORRECT_____
10.	*aluminum*	(answer: 8)	CORRECT_____ INCORRECT_____

Grade 3: Task 4
Reading Grade-Level Words

Task 4 Screener Instructions

(This information for the screener is also offered in video format at https://courses.learnreading.com/ courses/dyslexia-screening-videos.)

- Ask the student to read the words on their Student Pages.
- Mark "correct" or "incorrect" in the spaces provided.

If the student chose to skip a word, mark it "incorrect."

Task 4 Student Instructions

(You may present this information to the student yourself, or show them the "Student Instructions" video at https://courses.learnreading.com/courses/dyslexia-screening-videos.)

"For this task, you are going to read a list of words as best as you can. It may be a little difficult, but just do your best. If you try and still feel like you can't read the word, it's okay to say, 'Skip it,' and move on to the next word."

Task 4 Answer Key

Directions: Ask the student to READ each word as it is written for them on the Student Pages. If you are unsure of the pronunciation of any word, spell it into your cell phone and ask for the correct pronunciation. This is important because many words are easily missed, even by adults.

1.	sped	CORRECT_____	INCORRECT_____
2.	clasp	CORRECT_____	INCORRECT_____
3.	velvet	CORRECT_____	INCORRECT_____
4.	inspected	CORRECT_____	INCORRECT_____
5.	strictly	CORRECT_____	INCORRECT_____
6.	momentum	CORRECT_____	INCORRECT_____
7.	electric	CORRECT_____	INCORRECT_____
8.	detest	CORRECT_____	INCORRECT_____
9.	multiplication	CORRECT_____	INCORRECT_____
10.	citrus	CORRECT_____	INCORRECT_____

Grade 3: Task 5
Symbol to Sound Knowledge

Task 5 Screener Instructions

(This information for the screener is also offered in video format at https://courses.learnreading.com/courses/dyslexia-screening-videos.)

- Ask the student to look at each letter on their Student Page, and tell you the sound that it makes.
- When they come to the vowels, ask the student to tell you the short, or most common, sound.
- If they hesitate for longer than three seconds on any letter, mark it "incorrect."
- Mark "correct" or "incorrect" in the spaces provided. (The correct answer is provided for you.)

Task 5 Student Instructions

(You may present this information to the student yourself, or show them the "Student Instructions" video at https://courses.learnreading.com/courses/dyslexia-screening-videos.)

"For this task, I'd like you to look at a letter and then tell me the sound that it makes. When you come to a vowel, tell me the short, or most common, sound."

Task 5 Answer Key

Directions: Ask the student to look at each letter and tell you the sound each one makes. If they hesitate for longer than three seconds, mark it "incorrect." For *a, e, i, o, u*, tell them you want the short, or most common, sound. If they have any questions, tell them to just do their best.

1.	*d*	(answer: /d/ as in *dog*)	CORRECT_____ INCORRECT_____
2.	*u*	(answer: /u/ as in *under*)	CORRECT_____ INCORRECT_____
3.	*q*	(answer: /kw/ as in *queen*)	CORRECT_____ INCORRECT_____
4.	*y*	(answer: /y/ as in *yellow*)	CORRECT_____ INCORRECT_____
5.	*a*	(answer: /ă/ as in *apple*)	CORRECT_____ INCORRECT_____
6.	*w*	(answer: /w/ as in *water*)	CORRECT_____ INCORRECT_____
7.	*i*	(answer: /ĭ/ as in *index*)	CORRECT_____ INCORRECT_____
8.	*x*	(answer: /ks/ as in *fox*)	CORRECT_____ INCORRECT_____
9.	*e*	(answer: /ĕ/ as in *exit*)	CORRECT_____ INCORRECT_____
10.	*o*	(answer: /ŏ/ as in *octopus*)	CORRECT_____ INCORRECT_____

Grade 3: Task 6
Sound to Symbol Knowledge

Task 6 Screener Instructions

(This information for the screener is also offered in video format at https://courses.learnreading.com/courses/dyslexia-screening-videos.)

- You will dictate a sound to the student.
- Ask the student what letter, or set of letters, makes that sound.
- The "as in" hints are for the screener only and should *not* be given to the student.
- Ask the student to write their answers in lowercase letters.
- When the student writes their answer, the letters must be facing the correct way for the answer to be marked "correct." If any letters are reversed, mark it "incorrect."

Task 6 Student Instructions

(You may present this information to the student yourself, or show them the "Student Instructions" video at https://courses.learnreading.com/courses/dyslexia-screening-videos.)

"This time I'm going to give you the sound, and you're going to write down the letter or letters that make that sound. For instance, if I said /m/ (the sound of *m*), you would write *m*. If I said /th/ (the sound of *th*), you would write *th*.

Task 6 Answer Key

Directions: For the following items, say to the student, "What letter, or letters, makes this sound?" then pronounce the sound for them. (Do *not* say "as in..." because that is only for you to read so you are sure which sound to make. The answer is the bold letter(s) in the example word. *Q* can be written as *Q* or *QU*. Both are correct.) Have them write down their answer in lowercase letters in the space provided on the Student Pages. The letters they write down must be facing the right direction to be marked "correct."

1.	/ch/	(as in **ch**air)	CORRECT_____	INCORRECT_____
2.	/ĕ/	(as in **e**xit)	CORRECT_____	INCORRECT_____
3.	/sh/	(as in **sh**ut)	CORRECT_____	INCORRECT_____
4.	/ŏ/	(as in **o**ctopus)	CORRECT_____	INCORRECT_____
5.	/w/	(as in **w**onder)	CORRECT_____	INCORRECT_____
6.	/ĭ/	(as in **i**ndex)	CORRECT_____	INCORRECT_____
7.	/y/	(as in **y**ellow)	CORRECT_____	INCORRECT_____

8.	/ŭ/	(as in **under**)	CORRECT_____ INCORRECT_____
9.	/d/	(as in **d**oor)	CORRECT_____ INCORRECT_____
10.	/kw/	(as in **qu**een)	CORRECT_____ INCORRECT_____

Grade 3: Task 7
Auditory Discrimination

Task 7 Screener Instructions

(This information for the screener is also offered in video format at https://courses.learnreading.com/courses/dyslexia-screening-videos.)

- Dictate three distinct sounds to the student, with clean and clear *breaks* in between each sound.
- Ask the student to repeat the sounds back to you in order.
- The "as in" hints are for the screener only and should *not* be given to the student.
- The sounds must all be repeated back with exactness to be marked "correct." If the student mispronounced or omitted any sounds or switched the order, mark the answer "incorrect."

Task 7 Student Instructions

(You may present this information to the student yourself, or show them the "Student Instructions" video at https://courses.learnreading.com/courses/dyslexia-screening-videos.)

"For this task, I am going to say three sounds and then you just repeat them exactly as I said them and in the same order. Listen very carefully because some of the sounds may sound similar. Repeat them back to me as best you can."

Task 7 Answer Key

Directions: Ask the student to repeat the following sound sequences after you. You will pronounce ALL three sounds, then they should repeat the three sounds back to you. If they ask you to repeat the sequence, you may repeat it one time. If they say all three sounds back to you *exactly* right, mark it "correct." If they mispronounced (or couldn't remember) even one of the three sounds, mark it "incorrect." (Do *not* say "as in..." because that is only for you so you are sure which sound to make.)

1.	/n/ /m/ /l/ (as in: *name, milk, leg*)	CORRECT_____ INCORRECT_____
2.	/ĭ/ /ŏ/ /ĕ/ (as in: *index, octopus, exit*)	CORRECT_____ INCORRECT_____
3.	/d/ /p/ /b/ (as in: *door, pie, box*)	CORRECT_____ INCORRECT_____
4.	/sh/ /s/ /z/ (as in: *ship, sun, zebra*)	CORRECT_____ INCORRECT_____
5.	/th/ /f/ /j/ (as in: *think, fish, jam*)	CORRECT_____ INCORRECT_____
6.	/ă/ /ĕ/ /ĭ/ (as in: *apple, exit, index*)	CORRECT_____ INCORRECT_____
7.	/ŭ/ /ŏ/ /ă/ (as in: *under, octopus, apple*)	CORRECT_____ INCORRECT_____
8.	/sh/ /ch/ /th/ (as in: *ship, chop, think*)	CORRECT_____ INCORRECT_____
9.	/r/ /l/ /n/ (as in: *run, leg, net*)	CORRECT_____ INCORRECT_____
10.	/w/ /y/ /p/ (as in: *water, yellow, pot*)	CORRECT_____ INCORRECT_____

Grade 3: Task 8
Phonemic Awareness/Deletion

Task 8 Screener Instructions

(This information for the screener is also offered in video format at https://courses.learnreading.com/courses/dyslexia-screening-videos.)

- Important note: when you see a letter in between two slanted lines, it means the sound that that letter makes. For instance, /f/ is the *sound* of *f*, not the letter itself.
- Read the questions to the student, making sure to only say the sound of the letter in between the slanted lines.
- Mark "correct" or "incorrect" in the spaces provided. (The correct answer is provided for you.)

Task 8 Student Instructions

(You may present this information to the student yourself, or show them the "Student Instructions" video at https://courses.learnreading.com/courses/dyslexia-screening-videos.)

"For this task, I am going to say a word. Then, I'm going to ask you to repeat the word but without one of the sounds. For example, I might say *camp*, and then ask you to say *camp* without the /m/. *Camp* without the /m/ is *Cap* (model how to do the task). So listen carefully, take your time, and try your best."

Task 8 Answer Key

Directions: Ask the student each question. When you do so, say the sound that they are to remove, not the letter. (FYI: a letter inside of slanted lines, like /f/, means the sound only, not the letter itself.) If they ask you to repeat the question, you may do so one time. The student should tell you the answer, not write it down.

1.	"What would *cat* say without the /k/?" (answer: *at*)	CORRECT_____ INCORRECT_____
2.	"What would *bite* say without the /t/?" (answer: *by*)	CORRECT_____ INCORRECT_____
3.	"What would *flatten* say without the /l/?" (answer: *fatten*)	CORRECT_____ INCORRECT_____
4.	"What would *scram* say without the /r/?" (answer: *scam*)	CORRECT_____ INCORRECT_____
5.	"What would *feast* say without the /s/?" (answer: *feet*)	CORRECT_____ INCORRECT_____
6.	"What would *play* say without the /l/?" (answer: *pay*)	CORRECT_____ INCORRECT_____
7.	"What would *boost* say without the /s/?" (answer: *boot*)	CORRECT_____ INCORRECT_____
8.	"What would *trip* say without the /r/?" (answer: *tip*)	CORRECT_____ INCORRECT_____
9.	"What would *faxed* say without the /k/?" (answer: *fast*)	CORRECT_____ INCORRECT_____
10.	"What would *bottle* say without the /t/?" (answer: *ball*)	CORRECT_____ INCORRECT_____

Grade 3: Task 9
Phonemic Awareness/Isolation

Task 9 Screener Instructions

(This information for the screener is also offered in video format at https://courses.learnreading.com/courses/dyslexia-screening-videos.)

- Ask the student to look at a picture on their Student Page, say what it is a picture of, and stretch out the sounds in that word (such as *milk* "mmmiiilllk").
- Ask the student to break apart each sound in that word and then mark the dot that represents the sound in the question that you will ask them.
- Mark "correct" or "incorrect" if they identified the correct dot that contained that sound.

Task 9 Student Instructions

(You may present this information to the student yourself, or show them the "Student Instructions" video at https://courses.learnreading.com/courses/dyslexia-screening-videos.)

"For this task, you're going to see some pictures. I want you to tell me what the picture is and then stretch out the sounds in that word. Then I want you to separate each sound in that word with nice, big breaks in between each sound. You will see dots under the picture. I'd like you to point to each dot when you say each sound in that word. Then I'm going to ask where a certain sound is, and you'll just point to, or color in, that dot."

Task 9 Answer Key

Directions: As you ask each question, ask the student to follow along with you on their Student Pages. Ask the student to look at each picture and 1) repeat what the picture is, 2) stretch out the sounds in the word, and then 3) separate the sounds within the word and mark the dot on their paper where they hear the sound in question.

1.	Where is the /r/ in *drill*? (answer: 2nd dot	CORRECT_____ INCORRECT_____
2.	Where is the /l/ in *milk*? (answer: 3rd dot)	CORRECT_____ INCORRECT_____
3.	Where is the /s/ in *toast*? (answer: 3rd dot)	CORRECT_____ INCORRECT_____
4.	Where is the /k/ in *monkey*? (answer: 4th dot)	CORRECT_____ INCORRECT_____
5.	Where is the /h/ in *beehive*? (answer: 3rd dot)	CORRECT_____ INCORRECT_____
6.	Where is the /b/ in *hamburger*? (answer: 4th dot)	CORRECT_____ INCORRECT_____
7.	Where is the /ŭ/ in *animals*? (answer: 5th dot)	CORRECT_____ INCORRECT_____
8.	Where is the /r/ in *umbrella*? (answer: 4th dot)	CORRECT_____ INCORRECT_____

- The student had difficulty **breaking off** one sound from another in one or more of the words (if so, mark "incorrect" here).   CORRECT_____ INCORRECT_____

- The student had difficulty **articulating** the correct sounds within the word (if so, mark "incorrect" here).   CORRECT _____ INCORRECT _____

Task 10 Screener Instructions

(This information for the screener is also offered in video format at https://courses.learnreading.com/courses/dyslexia-screening-videos.)

- Read the word to the student. Have them repeat the word and then try to say the word backward.
- Mark "correct" or "incorrect" in the spaces provided. (The correct answer is provided for you.)

Task 10 Student Instructions

(You may present this information to the student yourself, or show them the "Student Instructions" video at https://courses.learnreading.com/courses/dyslexia-screening-videos.)

"In this task, I'm going to say a word. You will repeat the word back to me, and then try to say the word backward. For example, if I said the word *cat*. You would repeat that word *cat* and then try to say it backward. That last letter in *cat* would be the first letter if it was said backward. So *cat*, backward, is *tac* (model how to do the task).

Task 10 Answer Key

Directions: 1) Read the word (or nonsense word) to the student. 2) Ask them to repeat the word back to you. Then 3) tell them to say the word backward. If they ask you to repeat the word, you may do so one time. They must say every sound in the reversed word *exactly* right to be marked "correct." (If you are unsure of the correct pronunciation of the word, a "rhymes with" word is provided for you. Please do *not* share this "rhymes with" word with the student. It is only to aid the administrator.)

1.	*tea* (rhymes with *see*) (answer: *eat*)	CORRECT_____ INCORRECT_____
2.	*air* (rhymes with *stare*) (answer: *ray*)	CORRECT_____ INCORRECT_____
3.	*ile* (rhymes with *mile*) (answer: *lie*)	CORRECT_____ INCORRECT_____
4.	*oot* (rhymes with *flute*) (answer: *to*)	CORRECT_____ INCORRECT_____
5.	*eem* (rhymes with *team*) (answer: *me*)	CORRECT_____ INCORRECT_____
6.	*cheap* (rhymes with *sheep*) (answer: *peach*)	CORRECT_____ INCORRECT_____
7.	*chum* (rhymes with *plum*) (answer: *much*)	CORRECT_____ INCORRECT_____
8.	*stop* (rhymes with *top*) (answer: *pots*)	CORRECT_____ INCORRECT_____
9.	*gums* (rhymes with *chums*) (answer: *smug*)	CORRECT_____ INCORRECT_____
10.	*klim* (rhymes with *slim*) (answer: *milk*)	CORRECT_____ INCORRECT_____

Task 11 Screener Instructions

(This information for the screener is also offered in video format at https://courses.learnreading.com/courses/dyslexia-screening-videos.)

- Ask the student to read aloud the nonsense words on their Student Pages.
- They must get each sound in the word *exactly* correct for it to be marked "correct."
- The "rhymes with" hints are for the screener only and should *not* be given to the student.

Task 11 Student Instructions

(You may present this information to the student yourself, or show them the "Student Instructions" video at https://courses.learnreading.com/courses/dyslexia-screening-videos.)

"On your Student Pages, you're going to see some nonsense words. These are crazy words that you've never seen before. To read them, just use your knowledge of what the letters say."

Task 11 Answer Key

Directions: Ask the student to READ each nonsense word on their Student Pages. The student must pronounce each sound in the word *exactly* right for the word to be marked "correct." (A "rhymes with" word is provided for the screener only. Do *not* give the "rhymes with" word to the student.)

1.	*drib* (rhymes with *crib*)	CORRECT_____ INCORRECT_____
2.	*dilk* (rhymes with *milk*)	CORRECT_____ INCORRECT_____
3.	*nilmtip* (rhymes with *film sip*)	CORRECT_____ INCORRECT_____
4.	*trastly* (rhymes with *lastly*)	CORRECT_____ INCORRECT_____
5.	*crilthy* (rhymes with *filthy*)	CORRECT_____ INCORRECT_____
6.	*trats* (rhymes with *rats*)	CORRECT_____ INCORRECT_____
7.	*flaspry* (rhymes with *clasp ree*)	CORRECT_____ INCORRECT_____
8.	*thifty* (rhymes with *fifty*)	CORRECT_____ INCORRECT_____
9.	*planstaimpy* (sounds like *plăns tame pee*)	CORRECT_____ INCORRECT_____
10.	*plumud* (sounds like *plew mud*)	CORRECT_____ INCORRECT_____

Grade 3 Results

Task 1: Long-Term Memory

_____

Total Incorrect (or "no" answers):   _____

Task 2: Sight Words Knowledge

_____

Total Incorrect: _____

Task 3: Phonemic Awareness

_____

Total Incorrect: _____

Task 4: Reading Grade-Level Words

_____

Total Incorrect: _____

Task 5: Symbol to Sound Knowledge

_____

Total Incorrect: _____

Task 6: Sound to Symbol Knowledge

_____

Total Incorrect: _____

Task 7: Auditory Discrimination/Memory

_____

Total Incorrect: _____

Task 8: Phonemic Awareness

Total Incorrect: _____

Task 9: Phonemic Awareness

Total Incorrect: _____

Task 10: Phonemic Awareness

Total Incorrect: _____

Task 11: Decoding Unfamiliar Words

Total Incorrect: _____

Results from Questionnaire Plus Screening Tasks

1. TOTAL (line 4) on Questionnaire _____

2. TOTAL incorrect answers on Screening Tasks _____

3. **GRAND TOTAL from lines 1 and 2** _____

Grade 3 Conclusions

If the GRAND TOTAL (line 3) **is 14 or greater**, then this student's performance is consistent with someone with dyslexia.

It can be assumed that the severity of dyslexia is in direct relation to **how much greater than 14** the GRAND TOTAL is (14 being mild and 204 being the most severe).

If the GRAND TOTAL **is less than 14**, then dyslexia is likely *not* the probable cause for the student's academic difficulties.

Grade 4 Screening Packet

This packet contains the following:

- Grade 4 Screening Questionnaire
- Grade 4 Questionnaire Answer Sheet
- Grade 4 Questionnaire Analysis
- Grade 4 Student Pages (for student's written answers)
- Grade 4 Instructions and Answer Sheets (for Tasks 1–11)
- Grade 4 Results
- Grade 4 Conclusions

Grade 4 Screening Questionnaire

(Mark answers on the answer sheet.)

Genetics

1. Does the student's mother have any trouble with reading or spelling?

2. Does the student's father have any trouble with reading or spelling?

3. Are there any other immediate family members who struggle with reading or spelling?

4. Are (or were) there any extended family members (parents, siblings, grandparents, cousins, aunts, uncles) who struggled in school?

Articulation/Speech

5. Did the student have a speech delay (were they a late talker)?

6. Does (did) the student have any articulation or speech issues?

7. Does (did) the student have problems forming certain words correctly?

8. Does (did) the student mispronounce words even after repeated correction?

9. Does (did) the student attend speech therapy?

10. Does (did) the student confuse *i/e*, *m/n*, or *f/th* when they speak?

11. Does (did) the person have difficulty saying words like *aluminum*, *cinnamon*, or *dyslexia*?

12. Does the student have difficulty expressing themself verbally?

13. Does the student have trouble retrieving words, use a lot of *um*s or *uh*s, or use grand gestures with their hands when speaking?

Directionality

14. Is (was) there any left/right confusion?

15. Are there any letter or number reversals continuing beyond the end of first grade, including *b/d* confusion?

16. Does (did) the student have difficulty learning to tie their shoes?

17. Does (did) the student have trouble telling time on an analog clock?

18. Does (did) the student have difficulty remembering the direction of mathematical operations, such as addition and subtraction moving right to left, or the directional movements in long division?

19. Does (did) the student transpose number sequences, such as writing *51* for *15*?

20. Does (did) the student reverse words when reading, such as reading *top* for *pot*?

Memory/Recall

21. Does (did) the student have trouble recalling the names of letters, numbers, or colors?

22. Does the student have difficulty remembering sequences (such as a list of directions, arithmetic steps, spelling sequences, days of the week, or months of the year in order)?

23. Does the student have difficulty on timed math tests?

24. Does the student have trouble with copying (copying slowly and inaccurately)?

25. Does the student have difficulty remembering names?

26. Does the student have trouble remembering important dates?

27. Does the student have difficulty remembering the order of the alphabet?

28. Does the student have trouble recalling the days of the week or months of the year in order?

29. Does the student have trouble recalling the names of familiar objects, instead replacing them with words like *stuff* or *things*?

30. Does the student have trouble remembering multiple-step directions?

31. Does the student have difficulty remembering an address or phone number?

32. Does the student have trouble with alphabetizing or with remembering the order of the alphabet?

33. Does the student have a hard time recalling math facts quickly?

Phonemic Awareness/Auditory Processing

34. Does (did) the student have difficulty learning nursery rhymes or playing rhyming games?

35. Does the student have problems repeating back sounds accurately and in order?

36. Does (did) the student have trouble breaking off the first or last sound of a word?

37. Does (did) the student have trouble identifying the vowel sound within a word?

38. Does (did) the student confuse the short *i* and the short *e* sound when saying or reading words?

39. Does (did) the student have trouble understanding the connection between letters and sounds?

40. Does (did) the student have trouble isolating and manipulating the sounds within a word?

Reading

41. Does (did) the student read below grade level?

42. Does the student have trouble decoding unfamiliar words?

43. Is the student's reading slow and labor intensive?

44. Does (did) the student have trouble reading sight words or high frequency words?

45. Does the student forget how to read a word from one moment to the next?

46. Does the student have trouble comprehending what they read?

47. Would the student prefer *not* to be called on to read aloud in class or in public? Would they prefer to avoid reading, especially aloud?

48. Does (did) the student guess at words based on the size, shape, context, or picture clues?

49. Does (did) the student skip or misread small, simple words when reading?

50. Is the student easily frustrated when reading?

51. Does the student spend an unusually long time completing tasks that involve reading?

52. Does the student omit the suffixes or endings of words?

53. Does the student have trouble recognizing their mistakes when reading?

54. Does the student rarely read for pleasure?

55. Does the student require multiple readings to comprehend the material?

56. Does the student omit, substitute, add, or transpose letters when reading?

Spelling/Writing

57. Does (did) the student have trouble with spelling?

58. Does (did) the student spend an unusually long time completing tasks that involve writing?

59. Does (did) the student have trouble spelling sight words or high frequency words?

60. Does (did) the student forget how to spell a word from one moment to the next?

61. Do others have trouble reading what the student wrote, due to spelling errors?

62. Is the student's intelligence not reflected in their writing?

63. When writing, will the student use words that they know how to spell, instead of those that they would prefer to use?

64. Does the student have trouble remembering and applying spelling rules?

65. Does (did) the student use unpredictable, illogical spelling?

66. Does (did) the student omit, substitute, add, or transpose letters when spelling?

67. Does the student have difficulty using spell check or a dictionary?

Additional Learning Experiences

68. Has the student attended special academic classes, reading groups, or had outside tutoring?

69. Does the student have trouble learning a foreign language in print (reading and writing in the foreign language)?

70. Does the student have difficulty reading printed music?

71. Does the student have trouble taking notes in class?

72. Does (has) the student pretended to be sick or otherwise unable to attend school/perform academically in a classroom?

73. Can the student answer questions orally, but be unable to adequately do so in print?

74. Does the student need more time than others to process verbal information?

75. Does (did) the student have poor self-esteem resulting from poor academic performance?

76. Does (did) the student experience anxiety or high levels of stress surrounding academics?

Strengths/Talents

77. Does the student have a high capacity for learning?

78. Is the student gifted athletically?

79. Is the student gifted musically?

80. Is the student gifted artistically?

81. Is the student extremely creative?

82. Is the student highly imaginative?

83. Does the student have surprising maturity?

84. Does the student enjoy, and is good at, puzzles (Excellent spatial reasoning)?

85. Is the student extremely curious?

86. Is the student able to easily comprehend stories that they HEAR or LISTEN TO?

87. Is the student able to easily remember song lyrics?

88. Is the student mechanically inclined (Good with their hands, such as working with Legos, building models, taking things apart and putting them back together again, etc.)?

89. Does the student have excellent creative writing skills?

90. Does the student have excellent thinking and reasoning skills?

91. Does the student have the ability to produce unique, out-of-the-box ideas?

92. Is the student gifted at seeing the big picture?

93. Is the student highly empathetic?

94. Is the student highly resilient?

95. Does the student have excellent interpersonal skills (maintains friendships easily)?

Grade 4 Questionnaire Answer Sheet

Genetics

1. Yes _____   Somewhat or Unsure _____   No _____
2. Yes _____   Somewhat or Unsure _____   No _____
3. Yes _____   Somewhat or Unsure _____   No _____
4. Yes _____   Somewhat or Unsure _____   No _____

Articulation/Speech

5. Yes _____   Somewhat or Unsure _____   No _____
6. Yes _____   Somewhat or Unsure _____   No _____
7. Yes _____   Somewhat or Unsure _____   No _____
8. Yes _____   Somewhat or Unsure _____   No _____
9. Yes _____   Somewhat or Unsure _____   No _____
10. Yes _____   Somewhat or Unsure _____   No _____
11. Yes _____   Somewhat or Unsure _____   No _____
12. Yes _____   Somewhat or Unsure _____   No _____
13. Yes _____   Somewhat or Unsure _____   No _____

Directionality

14. Yes _____   Somewhat or Unsure _____   No _____
15. Yes _____   Somewhat or Unsure _____   No _____
16. Yes _____   Somewhat or Unsure _____   No _____
17. Yes _____   Somewhat or Unsure _____   No _____
18. Yes _____   Somewhat or Unsure _____   No _____
19. Yes _____   Somewhat or Unsure _____   No _____
20. Yes _____   Somewhat or Unsure _____   No _____

Memory/Recall

21.	Yes _____	Somewhat or Unsure _____	No _____
22.	Yes _____	Somewhat or Unsure _____	No _____
23.	Yes _____	Somewhat or Unsure _____	No _____
24.	Yes _____	Somewhat or Unsure _____	No _____
25.	Yes _____	Somewhat or Unsure _____	No _____
26.	Yes _____	Somewhat or Unsure _____	No _____
27.	Yes _____	Somewhat or Unsure _____	No _____
28.	Yes _____	Somewhat or Unsure _____	No _____
29.	Yes _____	Somewhat or Unsure _____	No _____
30.	Yes _____	Somewhat or Unsure _____	No _____
31.	Yes _____	Somewhat or Unsure _____	No _____
32.	Yes _____	Somewhat or Unsure _____	No _____
33.	Yes _____	Somewhat or Unsure _____	No _____

Phonemic Awareness/Auditory Processing

34.	Yes _____	Somewhat or Unsure _____	No _____
35.	Yes _____	Somewhat or Unsure _____	No _____
36.	Yes _____	Somewhat or Unsure _____	No _____
37.	Yes _____	Somewhat or Unsure _____	No _____
38.	Yes _____	Somewhat or Unsure _____	No _____
39.	Yes _____	Somewhat or Unsure _____	No _____
40.	Yes _____	Somewhat or Unsure _____	No _____

Reading

41.	Yes _____	Somewhat or Unsure _____	No _____
42.	Yes _____	Somewhat or Unsure _____	No _____

43.	Yes _____	Somewhat or Unsure _____	No _____
44.	Yes _____	Somewhat or Unsure _____	No _____
45.	Yes _____	Somewhat or Unsure _____	No _____
46.	Yes _____	Somewhat or Unsure _____	No _____
47.	Yes _____	Somewhat or Unsure _____	No _____
48.	Yes _____	Somewhat or Unsure _____	No _____
49.	Yes _____	Somewhat or Unsure _____	No _____
50.	Yes _____	Somewhat or Unsure _____	No _____
51.	Yes _____	Somewhat or Unsure _____	No _____
52.	Yes _____	Somewhat or Unsure _____	No _____
53.	Yes _____	Somewhat or Unsure _____	No _____
54.	Yes _____	Somewhat or Unsure _____	No _____
55.	Yes _____	Somewhat or Unsure _____	No _____
56.	Yes _____	Somewhat or Unsure _____	No _____

Spelling/Writing

57.	Yes _____	Somewhat or Unsure _____	No _____
58.	Yes _____	Somewhat or Unsure _____	No _____
59.	Yes _____	Somewhat or Unsure _____	No _____
60.	Yes _____	Somewhat or Unsure _____	No _____
61.	Yes _____	Somewhat or Unsure _____	No _____
62.	Yes _____	Somewhat or Unsure _____	No _____
63.	Yes _____	Somewhat or Unsure _____	No _____
64.	Yes _____	Somewhat or Unsure _____	No _____
65.	Yes _____	Somewhat or Unsure _____	No _____
66.	Yes _____	Somewhat or Unsure _____	No _____
67.	Yes _____	Somewhat or Unsure _____	No _____

Additional Learning Experiences

68.   Yes _____   Somewhat or Unsure _____   No _____

69.   Yes _____   Somewhat or Unsure _____   No _____

70.   Yes _____   Somewhat or Unsure _____   No _____

71.   Yes _____   Somewhat or Unsure _____   No _____

72.   Yes _____   Somewhat or Unsure _____   No _____

73.   Yes _____   Somewhat or Unsure _____   No _____

74.   Yes _____   Somewhat or Unsure _____   No _____

75.   Yes _____   Somewhat or Unsure _____   No _____

76.   Yes _____   Somewhat or Unsure _____   No _____

Strengths/Talents

77.   Yes _____   Somewhat or Unsure _____   No _____

78.   Yes _____   Somewhat or Unsure _____   No _____

79.   Yes _____   Somewhat or Unsure _____   No _____

80.   Yes _____   Somewhat or Unsure _____   No _____

81.   Yes _____   Somewhat or Unsure _____   No _____

82.   Yes _____   Somewhat or Unsure _____   No _____

83.   Yes _____   Somewhat or Unsure _____   No _____

84.   Yes _____   Somewhat or Unsure _____   No _____

85.   Yes _____   Somewhat or Unsure _____   No _____

86.   Yes _____   Somewhat or Unsure _____   No _____

87.   Yes _____   Somewhat or Unsure _____   No _____

88.   Yes _____   Somewhat or Unsure _____   No _____

89.   Yes _____   Somewhat or Unsure _____   No _____

90.   Yes _____   Somewhat or Unsure _____   No _____

91.   Yes _____   Somewhat or Unsure _____   No _____

92.   Yes _____   Somewhat or Unsure _____   No _____

93.   Yes _____   Somewhat or Unsure _____   No _____

94.   Yes _____   Somewhat or Unsure _____   No _____

95.   Yes _____   Somewhat or Unsure _____   No _____

Grade 4 Questionnaire Analysis

All Areas Except Strengths/Talents

1.	Count the number of "yes" answers in all areas **except** Strengths/Talents.	_____
2.	Count the number of "somewhat" answers in these areas and divide by 2.	_____
3.	Add lines 1 and 2 for the **TOTAL** in these areas.	_____

If the **TOTAL** in these areas is **3 or more,** then the screener should proceed to the screening tasks.

Strengths/Talents

4.	Count the number of "yes" answers in Strengths/Talents.	_____
5.	Count the number of "somewhat" answers and divide by 2.	_____
6.	Add lines 4 and 5 for the **TOTAL** in these areas.	_____
7.	Add lines 3 and 6 for the **GRAND TOTAL.**	_____

Any number greater than 3 in line 7 (GRAND TOTAL) increases the likelihood that dyslexia is present.

Grade 4 Student Pages

(Copy these THREE pages for the student to write on during the screening.)

On these pages, the student will complete the work for tasks that involve writing: Tasks: 1, 2, 4, 5, 6, 9, and 11. (The remaining tasks require dictation only, which the screener will record on the Screener Answer Sheet.)

Task 1: Write the Alphabet

_____

_____

_____

Task 2: Spelling Sight Words

_____

1. _____

   _____

2. _____

   _____

3. _____

   _____

4. _____

   _____

5. _____

   _____

6. _____

   _____

7. _____

   _____

8. _____

   _____

9. _____

   _____

10. _____

   _____

Task 4: Reading Grade-Level Words

1.	*longitude*	6.	*synonym*
2.	*orphan*	7.	*numerical*
3.	*partial*	8.	*compatible*
4.	*organism*	9.	*architecture*
5.	*omnivore*	10.	*parentheses*

Task 5: Symbol to Sound Knowledge

1. d

2. u

3. q

4. y

5. a

6. w

7. i

8. x

9. e

10. o

Task 6: Write the Letter(s)

1.	_____	6.	_____
2.	_____	7.	_____
3.	_____	8.	_____
4.	_____	9.	_____
5.	_____	10.	_____

Task 9: Phonemic Awareness 2 (Isolation)

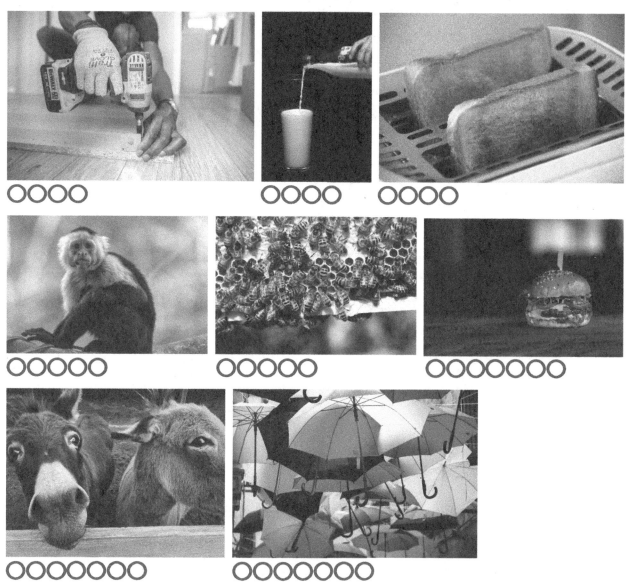

Source: https://docs.google.com/document/d/1v_W0fHCmiZ6Fm0VCZVPUsEWSAU8-YsknIDpwNJZroKY/edit

Task 11: Reading Unfamiliar Words

1.	*trats*	6.	*threlps*
2.	*flaspry*	7.	*drothplaits*
3.	*crilth*	8.	*thrimpstire*
4.	*chulps*	9.	*clampstandra*
5.	*sprisp*	10.	*shustrupa*

Grade 4 Instructions and Answer Sheets

Task 1 Screener Instructions

(This information for the screener is also offered in video format at https://courses.learnreading.com/courses/dyslexia-screening-videos.)

- Ask the student to write the alphabet in lowercase letters.
- There should be no help, no copying, and no erasing or crossing out.
- Watch for any hints of directionality confusion when they go to write a letter. Be aware of any pauses or hesitations, especially at *b/d/p/q*.
- Watch for confusion midway through, or if they need to start again at the beginning and use the alphabet song to help them determine the next letter.
- Watch for any reversals (writing a letter backward), inversions (writing a letter upside down), or errors (omitting a letter or writing it in the wrong sequence).
- After you have carefully watched the student complete the task, record their responses by answering "true" or "no" in the spaces provided.

Task 1 Student Instructions

(You may present this information to the student yourself, or show them the "Student Instructions" video at https://courses.learnreading.com/courses/dyslexia-screening-videos.)

"In this task, you're going to write the alphabet. You're going to use a pen (or a pencil without an eraser). This is because I want to see the way your brain works, and what you write down first. So, if you don't like what you wrote and are tempted to cross it out, don't worry! Just draw a box around the answer you didn't like, so I can still see what it was, and then put the answer you do want right next to or above it. And please use only lowercase letters in this screening. Okay! Let's get started!"

Task 1 Answer Sheet

Directions: Ask the student to write the alphabet in *lowercase letters* in the space provided on the Student Pages, with no help, no copying, and no erasing.

1.	The student made it to the end without any errors.	TRUE_____ NO_____
2.	The letters all faced the correct direction. (There were no reversals or inversions.)	TRUE_____ NO_____

3.	The student wrote the alphabet easily and quickly, with no hesitations, questions, or restarts.	TRUE_____ NO_____
4.	There was no hesitation at *b/d* or *p/q*. (The student did not wonder which way the letter faced.)	TRUE_____ NO_____

Task 2 Screener Instructions

(This information for the screener is also offered in video format at https://courses.learnreading.com/courses/dyslexia-screening-videos.)

- You will dictate sight words for the student to spell.
- You can repeat the word and/or use it in a sentence, but no hints as to the spelling.
- Mark "correct" or "incorrect" in the spaces provided.

Task 2 Student Instructions

(You may present this information to the student yourself, or show them the "Student Instructions" video at https://courses.learnreading.com/courses/dyslexia-screening-videos.)

"You might already know that sight words are words that don't follow typical spelling rules. They can sometimes be tricky to spell. I'm going to say a few of these sight words and I'd like for you to try to spell them the best that you can."

Task 2 Answer Sheet

Directions: Ask the student to spell the following words in the space provided on the Student Pages, with no erasing or changing. Mark "correct" or "incorrect." (If they spelled the word incorrectly at first, then changed their mind and went to fix it, mark it "incorrect" even if their second attempt was correct.)

1.	*gone*	CORRECT_____ INCORRECT_____
2.	*done*	CORRECT_____ INCORRECT_____
3.	*through* (as in "Put it through the hole.")	CORRECT_____ INCORRECT_____
4.	*right* (as in "Use your right hand.")	CORRECT_____ INCORRECT_____
5.	*again*	CORRECT_____ INCORRECT_____
6.	*any*	CORRECT_____ INCORRECT_____
7.	*find*	CORRECT_____ INCORRECT_____

8.	*move*		CORRECT_____ INCORRECT_____
9.	*wild*		CORRECT_____ INCORRECT_____
10.	*what*		CORRECT_____ INCORRECT_____

Task 3 Screener Instructions

(This information for the screener is also offered in video format at https://courses.learnreading.com/courses/dyslexia-screening-videos.)

- You will dictate words to the student and ask them to count how many sounds they hear in a word (not syllables or letters).
- Mark "correct" or "incorrect" in the spaces provided. (The answer is next to the word.)

Task 3 Student Instructions

(You may present this information to the student yourself, or show them the "Student Instructions" video at https://courses.learnreading.com/courses/dyslexia-screening-videos.)

"For this task, you are simply going to be counting sounds. I am going to say a word, and you will count how many sounds you hear in that word. If you know how to spell the word, try not to think about the letters because I don't want you to count the letters, just the sounds. Sometimes there are more letters in a word than there are sounds, so just focus on the sounds, and tell me how many you hear."

Task 3 Answer Sheet

Directions: Ask the student how many sounds are in each word. (Note: they are counting individual sounds, not syllables and not letters. For instance, *chicken* has 5 sounds.)

1.	*tan*	(answer: 3)	CORRECT_____ INCORRECT_____
2.	*blue*	(answer: 3)	CORRECT_____ INCORRECT_____
3.	*bench*	(answer: 4)	CORRECT_____ INCORRECT_____
4.	*truck*	(answer: 4)	CORRECT_____ INCORRECT_____
5.	*drill*	(answer: 4)	CORRECT_____ INCORRECT_____
6.	*straw*	(answer: 4)	CORRECT_____ INCORRECT_____
7.	*tractor*	(answer: 6)	CORRECT_____ INCORRECT_____
8.	*country*	(answer: 6)	CORRECT_____ INCORRECT_____

9.	*synonym*	(answer: 7)	CORRECT_____ INCORRECT_____
10.	*aluminum*	(answer: 8)	CORRECT_____ INCORRECT_____

Task 4 Screener Instructions

(This information for the screener is also offered in video format at https://courses.learnreading.com/courses/dyslexia-screening-videos.)

- Ask the student to read the words on their Student Pages.
- Mark "correct" or "incorrect" in the spaces provided.

If the student chose to skip a word, mark it incorrect.

Task 4 Student Instructions

(You may present this information to the student yourself, or show them the "Student Instructions" video at https://courses.learnreading.com/courses/dyslexia-screening-videos.)

"For this task, you are going to read a list of words as best as you can. It may be a little difficult, but just do your best. If you try and still feel like you can't read the word, it's okay to say, 'Skip it,' and move on to the next word."

Task 4 Answer Sheet

Directions: Ask the student to *read* each word as it is written for them on the Student Pages. If you are unsure of the pronunciation of any word, spell it into your cell phone and ask for the correct pronunciation. This is important because many words are easily missed, even by adults.

1.	*longitude*	CORRECT_____ INCORRECT_____
2.	*orphan*	CORRECT_____ INCORRECT_____
3.	*partial*	CORRECT_____ INCORRECT_____
4.	*organism*	CORRECT_____ INCORRECT_____
5.	*omnivore*	CORRECT_____ INCORRECT_____
6.	*synonym*	CORRECT_____ INCORRECT_____
7.	*numerical*	CORRECT_____ INCORRECT_____
8.	*compatible*	CORRECT_____ INCORRECT_____

9.	*architecture*	CORRECT_____ INCORRECT_____
10.	*parentheses*	CORRECT_____ INCORRECT_____

Task 5 Screener Instructions

(This information for the screener is also offered in video format at https://courses.learnreading.com/courses/dyslexia-screening-videos.)

- Ask the student to look at each letter on their Student Page, and tell you the sound that it makes.
- When they come to the vowels, ask the student to tell you the short, or most common, sound.
- If they hesitate for longer than three seconds on any letter, mark it "incorrect."
- Mark "correct" or "incorrect" in the spaces provided. (The correct answer is provided for you.)

Task 5 Student Instructions

(You may present this information to the student yourself, or show them the "Student Instructions" video at https://courses.learnreading.com/courses/dyslexia-screening-videos.)

"For this task, I'd like you to look at a letter and then tell me the sound that it makes. When you come to a vowel, tell me the short, or most common, sound."

Task 5 Answer Sheet

Directions: Ask the student to look at each letter and tell you the sound each one makes. If they hesitate for longer than three seconds, mark it "incorrect." For *a, e, i, o, u,* tell them you want the short, or most common, sound. If they have any questions, tell them to just do their best.

1.	*d*	(answer: /d/ as in *dog*)	CORRECT_____ INCORRECT_____
2.	*u*	(answer: /u/ as in *under*)	CORRECT_____ INCORRECT_____
3.	*q*	(answer: /kw/ as in *queen*)	CORRECT_____ INCORRECT_____
4.	*y*	(answer: /y/ as in *yellow*)	CORRECT_____ INCORRECT_____
5.	*a*	(answer: /ă/ as in *apple*)	CORRECT_____ INCORRECT_____
6.	*w*	(answer: /w/ as in *water*)	CORRECT_____ INCORRECT_____
7.	*i*	(answer: /ĭ/ as in *index*)	CORRECT_____ INCORRECT_____
8.	*x*	(answer: /ks/ as in *fox*)	CORRECT_____ INCORRECT_____

9.	*e*	(answer: /ĕ/ as in *exit*)	CORRECT_____ INCORRECT_____
10.	o	(answer: /ŏ/ as in *octopus*)	CORRECT_____ INCORRECT_____

Task 6 Screener Instructions

(This information for the screener is also offered in video format at https://courses.learnreading.com/courses/dyslexia-screening-videos.)

- You will dictate a sound to the student.
- Ask the student what letter, or set of letters, makes that sound.
- The "as in" hints are for the screener only and should *not* be given to the student.
- Ask the student to write their answers in lowercase letters.
- When the student writes their answer, the letters must be facing the correct way for the answer to be marked "correct." If any letters are reversed, mark it "incorrect."

Task 6 Student Instructions

(You may present this information to the student yourself, or show them the "Student Instructions" video at https://courses.learnreading.com/courses/dyslexia-screening-videos.)

"This time I'm going to give you the sound, and you're going to write down the letter or letters that makes that sound. For instance, if I said /m/ (the sound of *m*), you would write *m*. If I said /th/ (the sound of *th*), you would write *th*.

Task 6 Answer Sheet

Directions: For the following items, say to the student, "What letter, or letters, makes this sound?" then pronounce the sound for them. (Do *not* say "as in..." because that is only for you to read so you are sure which sound to make. The answer is the bold letter(s) in the example word. *Q* can be written as *Q* or *QU*. Both are correct.) Have them write down their answer in lowercase letters in the space provided on the Student Pages. The letters they write down must be facing the right direction to be marked "correct."

1.	/ch/	(as in **ch**air)	CORRECT_____ INCORRECT_____
2.	/ĕ/	(as in **e**xit)	CORRECT_____ INCORRECT_____
3.	/sh/	(as in **sh**ut)	CORRECT_____ INCORRECT_____

Is It Dyslexia?

4.	/ŏ/	(as in *octopus*)	CORRECT_____ INCORRECT_____
5.	/w/	(as in *wonder*)	CORRECT_____ INCORRECT_____
6.	/ĭ/	(as in *index*)	CORRECT_____ INCORRECT_____
7.	/y/	(as in *yellow*)	CORRECT_____ INCORRECT_____
8.	/ŭ/	(as in *under*)	CORRECT_____ INCORRECT_____
9.	/d/	(as in *door*)	CORRECT_____ INCORRECT_____
10.	/kw/	(as in *queen*)	CORRECT_____ INCORRECT_____

Task 7 Screener Instructions

(This information for the screener is also offered in video format at https://courses.learnreading.com/courses/dyslexia-screening-videos.)

- Dictate three distinct sounds to the student, with clean and clear *breaks* in between each sound.
- Ask the student to repeat the sounds back to you in order.
- The "as in" hints are for the screener only and should *not* be given to the student.
- The sounds must all be repeated back with exactness to be marked "correct." If the student mispronounced or omitted any sounds, or switched the order, mark the answer "incorrect."

Task 7 Student Instructions

(You may present this information to the student yourself, or show them the "Student Instructions" video at https://courses.learnreading.com/courses/dyslexia-screening-videos.)

"For this task, I am going to say three sounds and then you just repeat them exactly as I said them and in the same order. Listen very carefully because some of the sounds may sound similar. Repeat them back to me as best you can."

Task 7 Answer Sheet

Directions: Ask the student to repeat the following sound sequences after you. You will pronounce *all* three sounds, then they should repeat the three sounds back to you. If they ask you to repeat the sequence, you may repeat it one time. If they say all three sounds back to you *exactly* right, mark it "correct." If they mispronounced (or couldn't remember) even one of the three sounds, mark it "incorrect." (Do *not* say "as in..." because that is only for you so you are sure which sound to make.)

1.	/n/ /m/ /l/ (as in: *name, milk, leg*)	CORRECT_____	INCORRECT_____
2.	/ĭ/ /ŏ/ /ĕ/ (as in: *index, octopus, exit*)	CORRECT_____	INCORRECT_____
3.	/d/ /p/ /b/ (as in: *door, pie, box*)	CORRECT_____	INCORRECT_____
4.	/sh/ /s/ /z/ (as in: *ship, sun, zebra*)	CORRECT_____	INCORRECT_____
5.	/th/ /f/ /j/ (as in: *think, fish, jam*)	CORRECT_____	INCORRECT_____
6.	/ă/ /ĕ/ /ĭ/ (as in: *apple, exit, index*)	CORRECT_____	INCORRECT_____
7.	/ŭ/ /ŏ/ /ă/ (as in: *under, octopus, apple*)	CORRECT_____	INCORRECT_____
8.	/sh/ /ch/ /th/ (as in: *ship, chop, think*)	CORRECT_____	INCORRECT_____
9.	/r/ /l/ /n/ (as in: *run, leg, net*)	CORRECT_____	INCORRECT_____
10.	/w/ /y/ /p/ (as in: *water, yellow, pot*)	CORRECT_____	INCORRECT_____

Task 8 Screener Instructions

(This information for the screener is also offered in video format at https://courses.learnreading.com/courses/dyslexia-screening-videos.)

- Important note: when you see a letter in between two slanted lines, it means the sound that that letter makes. For instance, /f/ is the *sound* of *f*, not the letter itself.
- Read the questions to the student, making sure to only say the sound of the letter in between the slanted lines.
- Mark "correct" or "incorrect" in the spaces provided. (The correct answer is provided for you.)

Task 8 Student Instructions

(You may present this information to the student yourself, or show them the "Student Instructions" video at https://courses.learnreading.com/courses/dyslexia-screening-videos.)

"For this task, I am going to say a word. Then, I'm going to ask you to repeat the word but without one of the sounds. For example, I might say *camp*, and then ask you to say *camp* without the /m/. *Camp* without the /m/ is *Cap* (model how to do the task). So listen carefully, take your time, and try your best."

Task 8 Answer Sheet

Directions: Ask the student each question. When you do so, say the sound that they are to remove, not the letter. (FYI: a letter inside of slanted lines, like /f/, means the sound only, not the letter itself.) If

they ask you to repeat the question, you may do so one time. The student should tell you the answer, not write it down.

1.	"What would *cat* say without the /k/?" (answer: *at*)	CORRECT_____ INCORRECT_____
2.	"What would *bite* say without the /t/?" (answer: *by*)	CORRECT_____ INCORRECT_____
3.	"What would *flatten* say without the /l/?" (answer: *fatten*)	CORRECT_____ INCORRECT_____
4.	"What would *scram* say without the /r/?" (answer: *scam*)	CORRECT_____ INCORRECT_____
5.	"What would *feast* say without the /s/?" (answer: *feet*)	CORRECT_____ INCORRECT_____
6.	"What would *play* say without the /l/?" (answer: *pay*)	CORRECT_____ INCORRECT_____
7.	"What would *boost* say without the /s/?" (answer: *boot*)	CORRECT_____ INCORRECT_____
8.	"What would *trip* say without the /r/?" (answer: *tip*)	CORRECT_____ INCORRECT_____
9.	"What would *faxed* say without the /k/?" (answer: *fast*)	CORRECT_____ INCORRECT_____
10.	"What would *bottle* say without the /t/?" (answer: *ball*)	CORRECT_____ INCORRECT_____

Task 9 Screener Instructions

(This information for the screener is also offered in video format at https://courses.learnreading.com/courses/dyslexia-screening-videos.)

- Ask the student to look at a picture on their Student Page, say what it is a picture of and stretch out the sounds in that word (such as *milk* "mmmiiilllk").
- Ask the student to break apart each sound in that word and then mark the dot that represents the sound in the question that you will ask them.
- Mark "correct" or "incorrect" if they identified the correct dot that contained that sound.

Task 9 Student Instructions

(You may present this information to the student yourself, or show them the "Student Instructions" video at https://courses.learnreading.com/courses/dyslexia-screening-videos.)

"For this task, you're going to see some pictures. I want you to tell me what the picture is and then stretch out the sounds in that word. Then I want you to separate each sound in that word with nice, big breaks in between each sound. You will see dots under the picture. I'd like you to point to each dot when you say each sound in that word. Then I'm going to ask where a certain sound is, and you'll just point to, or color in, that dot."

Task 9 Answer Sheet

Directions: As you ask each question, ask the student to follow along with you on their Student Pages. Ask the student to look at each picture and 1) repeat what the picture is, 2) stretch out the sounds in the word, and then 3) separate the sounds within the word and mark the dot on their paper where they hear the sound in question.

1.	Where is the /r/ in *drill*?	(answer: 2nd dot	CORRECT_____ INCORRECT_____
2.	Where is the /l/ in *milk*?	(answer: 3rd dot)	CORRECT_____ INCORRECT_____
3.	Where is the /s/ in *toast*?	(answer: 3rd dot)	CORRECT_____ INCORRECT_____
4.	Where is the /k/ in *monkey*?	(answer: 4th dot)	CORRECT_____ INCORRECT_____
5.	Where is the /h/ in *beehive*?	(answer: 3rd dot)	CORRECT_____ INCORRECT_____
6.	Where is the /b/ in *hamburger*?	(answer: 4th dot)	CORRECT_____ INCORRECT_____
7.	Where is the /ŭ/ in *animals*?	(answer: 5th dot)	CORRECT_____ INCORRECT_____
8.	Where is the /r/ in *umbrella*?	(answer: 4th dot)	CORRECT_____ INCORRECT_____

- The student had difficulty **breaking off** one sound   CORRECT_____ INCORRECT_____
  from another in one or more of the words (if so, mark
  "incorrect" here).

- The student had difficulty **articulating** the correct sounds   CORRECT _____ INCORRECT _____
  within the word (if so, mark "incorrect" here).

Task 10 Screener Instructions

(This information for the screener is also offered in video format at https://courses.learnreading.com/courses/dyslexia-screening-videos.)

- Read the word to the student. Have them repeat the word and then try to say the word backward.
- Mark "correct" or "incorrect" in the spaces provided. (The correct answer is provided for you.)

Task 10 Student Instructions

(You may present this information to the student yourself, or show them the "Student Instructions" video at https://courses.learnreading.com/courses/dyslexia-screening-videos.)

"In this task, I'm going to say a word. You will repeat the word back to me, and then try to say the word backward. For example, if I said the word *cat*. You would repeat that word *cat* and then try to say it backward. That last letter in *cat* would be the first letter if it was said backward. So *cat*, backward, is *tac* (model how to do the task).

Task 10 Answer Sheet

Directions: 1) Read the word (or nonsense word) to the student. 2) Ask them to repeat the word back to you. Then 3) tell them to say the word BACKWARD. If they ask you to repeat the word, you may do so one time. They must say every sound in the reversed word *exactly* right to be marked "correct." (If you are unsure of the correct pronunciation of the word, a "rhymes with" word is provided for you. Please do *not* share this "rhymes with" word with the student. It is only to aid the administrator.)

1.	*tea* (rhymes with *see*) (answer: *eat*)	CORRECT_____ INCORRECT_____
2.	*air* (rhymes with *stare*) (answer: *ray*)	CORRECT_____ INCORRECT_____
3.	*ile* (rhymes with *mile*) (answer: *lie*)	CORRECT_____ INCORRECT_____
4.	*oot* (rhymes with *flute*) (answer: *to*)	CORRECT_____ INCORRECT_____
5.	*eem* (rhymes with *team*) (answer: *me*)	CORRECT_____ INCORRECT_____
6.	*cheap* (rhymes with *sheep*) (answer: *peach*)	CORRECT_____ INCORRECT_____
7.	*chum* (rhymes with *plum*) (answer: *much*)	CORRECT_____ INCORRECT_____
8.	*stop* (rhymes with *top*) (answer: *pots*)	CORRECT_____ INCORRECT_____
9.	*gums* (rhymes with *chums*) (answer: *smug*)	CORRECT_____ INCORRECT_____
10.	*klim* (rhymes with *slim*) (answer: *milk*)	CORRECT_____ INCORRECT_____

Task 11 Screener Instructions

(This information for the screener is also offered in video format at https://courses.learnreading.com/courses/dyslexia-screening-videos.)

- Ask the student to read aloud the nonsense words on their Student Pages.
- They must get each sound in the word *exactly* correct for it to be marked "correct."
- The "rhymes with" hints are for the screener only and should *not* be given to the student.

Task 11 Student Instructions

(You may present this information to the student yourself, or show them the "Student Instructions" video at https://courses.learnreading.com/courses/dyslexia-screening-videos.)

"On your Student Pages, you're going to see some nonsense words. These are crazy words that you've never seen before. To read them, just use your knowledge of what the letters say."

Task 11 Answer Sheet

Directions: Ask the student to READ each nonsense word on their Student Pages. The student must pronounce each sound in the word *exactly* right for the word to be marked "correct." (A "rhymes with" word is provided for the screener only. Do not give the "rhymes with" word to the student.)

1.	*trats* (rhymes with *rats*)	CORRECT_____ INCORRECT_____
2.	*flaspry* (rhymes with *clasp ree'*)	CORRECT_____ INCORRECT_____
3.	*crilth* (rhymes with *filth*)	CORRECT_____ INCORRECT____
4.	*chulps* (rhymes with *gulps*)	CORRECT_____ INCORRECT_____
5.	*sprisp* (rhymes with *crisp*)	CORRECT_____ INCORRECT_____
6.	*threlps* (rhymes with *helps*)	CORRECT_____ INCORRECT_____
7.	*drothplaits* (rhymes with *cloth plates*)	CORRECT_____ INCORRECT_____
8.	*thrimpstire* (rhymes with *shrimp fire*)	CORRECT_____ INCORRECT_____
9.	*clampstandra* (sounds like *clămp stănd ruh*)	CORRECT_____ INCORRECT_____
10.	*shustrupa* (sounds like *shŭs true puh*)	CORRECT_____ INCORRECT_____

Grade 4 Results

Task 1: Long-Term Memory

Total Incorrect (or "no" answers) _____

Task 2: Sight Words Knowledge

Total Incorrect: _____

Task 3: Phonemic Awareness

Total Incorrect: _____

Task 4: Reading Grade-Level Words

Total Incorrect: _____

Task 5: Symbol to Sound Knowledge

Total Incorrect: _____

Task 6: Sound to Symbol Knowledge

Total Incorrect: _____

Task 7: Auditory Discrimination/Memory

Total Incorrect: _____

Task 8: Phonemic Awareness

Total Incorrect: _____

Task 9: Phonemic Awareness

Total Incorrect: _____

Task 10: Phonemic Awareness

Total Incorrect: _____

Task 11: Decoding Unfamiliar Words

Total Incorrect: _____

Results from Questionnaire Plus Screening Tasks

1.	TOTAL (line 4) on Questionnaire	_____
2.	TOTAL incorrect answers on Screening Tasks	_____
3.	**GRAND TOTAL from lines 1 and 2**	_____

Is It Dyslexia?

Grade 4 Conclusions

If the GRAND TOTAL (line 3) **is 14 or greater**, then this student's performance is consistent with someone with dyslexia.

It can be assumed that the severity of dyslexia is in direct relation to **how much greater than 14** the GRAND TOTAL is (14 being mild and 205 being the most severe).

If the GRAND TOTAL **is less than 14**, then dyslexia is likely *not* the probable cause for the student's academic difficulties.

Grade 5 Screening Packet

This packet contains the following:

- Grade 5 Screening Questionnaire

- Grade 5 Questionnaire Answer Sheet

- Grade 5 Questionnaire Analysis

- Grade 5 Student Pages (for student's written answers)

- Grade 5 Instructions and Answer Sheets (for Tasks 1–11)

- Grade 5 Results

- Grade 5 Conclusions

Grade 5 Screening Questionnaire

(Mark answers on the answer sheet.)

Genetics

1. Does the student's mother have any trouble with reading or spelling?

2. Does the student's father have any trouble with reading or spelling?

3. Are there any other immediate family members who struggle with reading or spelling?

4. Are (or were) there any extended family members (parents, siblings, grandparents, cousins, aunts, uncles) who struggled in school?

Articulation/Speech

5. Did the student have a speech delay (were they a late talker)?

6. Does (did) the student have any articulation or speech issues?

7. Does (did) the student have problems forming certain words correctly?

8. Does (did) the student mispronounce words even after repeated correction?

9. Does (did) the student attend speech therapy?

10. Does (did) the student confuse *i/e*, *m/n*, or *f/th* when they speak?

11. Does (did) the person have difficulty saying words like *aluminum*, *cinnamon*, or *dyslexia*?

12. Does the student have difficulty expressing themself verbally?

13. Does the student have trouble retrieving words, use a lot of *um*s or *uh*s, or use grand gestures with their hands when speaking?

Directionality

14. Is (was) there any left/right confusion?

15. Are there any letter or number reversals continuing beyond the end of first grade, including *b/d* confusion?

16. Does (did) the student have difficulty learning to tie their shoes?

17. Does (did) the student have trouble telling time on an analog clock?

18. Does (did) the student have difficulty remembering the direction of mathematical operations, such as addition and subtraction moving right to left, or the directional movements in long division?

19. Does (did) the student transpose number sequences, such as writing *51* for *15*?

20. Does (did) the student reverse words when reading, such as reading *top* for *pot*?

Memory/Recall

21. Does (did) the student have trouble recalling the names of letters, numbers, or colors?

22. Does the student have difficulty remembering sequences (such as a list of directions, arithmetic steps, spelling sequences, days of the week, or months of the year in order)?

23. Does the student have difficulty on timed math tests?

24. Does the student have trouble with copying (copying slowly and inaccurately)?

25. Does the student have difficulty remembering names?

26. Does the student have trouble remembering important dates?

27. Does the student have difficulty remembering the order of the alphabet?

28. Does the student have trouble recalling the days of the week or months of the year in order?

29. Does the student have trouble recalling the names of familiar objects, instead replacing them with words like *stuff* or *things*?

30. Does the student have trouble remembering multiple-step directions?

31. Does the student have difficulty remembering an address or phone number?

32. Does the student have trouble with alphabetizing or with remembering the order of the alphabet?

33. Does the student have a hard time recalling math facts quickly?

Phonemic Awareness/Auditory Processing

34. Does the student have difficulty with rhyming?

35. Does the student have problems repeating back sounds accurately and in order?

36. Does (did) the student have trouble breaking off the first or last sound of a word?

37. Does (did) the student have trouble identifying the vowel sound within a word?

38. Does (did) the student confuse the short *i* and the short *e* sound when saying or reading words?

39. Does (did) the student have trouble understanding the connection between letters and sounds?

40. Does (did) the student have trouble isolating and manipulating the sounds within a word?

Reading

41. Does (did) the student read below grade level?

42. Does the student have trouble decoding unfamiliar words?

43. Is the student's reading slow and labor intensive?

44. Does (did) the student have trouble reading sight words or high frequency words?

45. Does the student forget how to read a word from one moment to the next?

46. Does the student have trouble comprehending what they read?

47. Would the student prefer *not* to be called on to read aloud in class or in public? Would they prefer to avoid reading, especially aloud?

48. Does (did) the student guess at words based on the size, shape, context, or picture clues?

49. Does (did) the student skip or misread small, simple words when reading?

50. Is the student easily frustrated when reading?

51. Does the student spend an unusually long time completing tasks that involve reading?

52. Does the student omit the suffixes or endings of words?

53. Does the student have trouble recognizing their mistakes when reading?

54. Does the student rarely read for pleasure?

55. Does the student require multiple readings to comprehend the material?

56. Does the student omit, substitute, add, or transpose letters when reading?

Spelling/Writing

57. Does (did) the student have trouble with spelling?

58. Does (did) the student spend an unusually long time completing tasks that involve writing?

59. Does (did) the student have trouble spelling sight words or high frequency words?

60. Does (did) the student forget how to spell a word from one moment to the next?

61. Do others have trouble reading what the student wrote, due to spelling errors?

62. Is the student's intelligence not reflected in their writing?

63. When writing, will the student use words that they know how to spell, instead of those that they would prefer to use?

64. Does the student have trouble remembering and applying spelling rules?

65. Does (did) the student use unpredictable, illogical spelling?

66. Does (did) the student omit, substitute, add, or transpose letters when spelling?

67. Does the student have difficulty using spell check or a dictionary?

Additional Learning Experiences

68. Has the student attended special academic classes, reading groups, or had outside tutoring?

69. Does the student have trouble learning a foreign language in print (reading and writing in the foreign language)?

70. Does the student have difficulty reading printed music?

71. Does the student have trouble taking notes in class?

72. Does (has) the student pretended to be sick or otherwise unable to attend school/perform academically in a classroom?

73. Can the student answer questions orally, but be unable to adequately do so in print?

74. Does the student need more time than others to process verbal information?

75. Does (did) the student have poor self-esteem resulting from poor academic performance?

76. Does (did) the student experience anxiety or high levels of stress surrounding academics?

Strengths/Talents

77. Does the student have a high capacity for learning?

78. Is the student gifted athletically?

79. Is the student gifted musically?

80. Is the student gifted artistically?

81. Is the student extremely creative?

82. Is the student highly imaginative?

83. Does the student have surprising maturity?

84. Does the student enjoy, and is good at, puzzles (excellent spatial reasoning)?

85. Is the student extremely curious?

86. Is the student able to easily comprehend stories that they *hear* or *listen to*?

87. Is the student able to easily remember song lyrics?

88. Is the student mechanically inclined (good with their hands, such as working with Legos, building models, taking things apart and putting them back together again, etc.)?

89. Does the student have excellent creative writing skills?

90. Does the student have excellent thinking and reasoning skills?

91. Does the student have the ability to produce unique, out-of-the-box ideas?

92. Is the student gifted at seeing the big picture?

93. Is the student highly empathetic?

94. Is the student highly resilient?

95. Does the student have excellent interpersonal skills (maintains friendships easily)?

Grade 5 Questionnaire Answer Sheet

Genetics

1.   Yes _____   Somewhat or Unsure _____   No _____
2.   Yes _____   Somewhat or Unsure _____   No _____
3.   Yes _____   Somewhat or Unsure _____   No _____
4.   Yes _____   Somewhat or Unsure _____   No _____

Articulation/Speech

5.   Yes _____   Somewhat or Unsure _____   No _____
6.   Yes _____   Somewhat or Unsure _____   No _____
7.   Yes _____   Somewhat or Unsure _____   No _____
8.   Yes _____   Somewhat or Unsure _____   No _____
9.   Yes _____   Somewhat or Unsure _____   No _____
10.   Yes _____   Somewhat or Unsure _____   No _____
11.   Yes _____   Somewhat or Unsure _____   No _____
12.   Yes _____   Somewhat or Unsure _____   No _____
13.   Yes _____   Somewhat or Unsure _____   No _____

Directionality

14.   Yes _____   Somewhat or Unsure _____   No _____
15.   Yes _____   Somewhat or Unsure _____   No _____
16.   Yes _____   Somewhat or Unsure _____   No _____
17.   Yes _____   Somewhat or Unsure _____   No _____
18.   Yes _____   Somewhat or Unsure _____   No _____
19.   Yes _____   Somewhat or Unsure _____   No _____
20.   Yes _____   Somewhat or Unsure _____   No _____

Is It Dyslexia?

Memory/Recall

21.	Yes _____	Somewhat or Unsure _____	No _____
22.	Yes _____	Somewhat or Unsure _____	No _____
23.	Yes _____	Somewhat or Unsure _____	No _____
24.	Yes _____	Somewhat or Unsure _____	No _____
25.	Yes _____	Somewhat or Unsure _____	No _____
26.	Yes _____	Somewhat or Unsure _____	No _____
27.	Yes _____	Somewhat or Unsure _____	No _____
28.	Yes _____	Somewhat or Unsure _____	No _____
29.	Yes _____	Somewhat or Unsure _____	No _____
30.	Yes _____	Somewhat or Unsure _____	No _____
31.	Yes _____	Somewhat or Unsure _____	No _____
32.	Yes _____	Somewhat or Unsure _____	No _____
33.	Yes _____	Somewhat or Unsure _____	No _____

Phonemic Awareness/Auditory Processing

34.	Yes _____	Somewhat or Unsure _____	No _____
35.	Yes _____	Somewhat or Unsure _____	No _____
36.	Yes _____	Somewhat or Unsure _____	No _____
37.	Yes _____	Somewhat or Unsure _____	No _____
38.	Yes _____	Somewhat or Unsure _____	No _____
39.	Yes _____	Somewhat or Unsure _____	No _____
40.	Yes _____	Somewhat or Unsure _____	No _____

Reading

41. Yes _____   Somewhat or Unsure _____   No _____

42. Yes _____   Somewhat or Unsure _____   No _____

43. Yes _____   Somewhat or Unsure _____   No _____

44. Yes _____   Somewhat or Unsure _____   No _____

45. Yes _____   Somewhat or Unsure _____   No _____

46. Yes _____   Somewhat or Unsure _____   No _____

47. Yes _____   Somewhat or Unsure _____   No _____

48. Yes _____   Somewhat or Unsure _____   No _____

49. Yes _____   Somewhat or Unsure _____   No _____

50. Yes _____   Somewhat or Unsure _____   No _____

51. Yes _____   Somewhat or Unsure _____   No _____

52. Yes _____   Somewhat or Unsure _____   No _____

53. Yes _____   Somewhat or Unsure _____   No _____

54. Yes _____   Somewhat or Unsure _____   No _____

55. Yes _____   Somewhat or Unsure _____   No _____

56. Yes _____   Somewhat or Unsure _____   No _____

Spelling/Writing

57. Yes _____   Somewhat or Unsure _____   No _____

58. Yes _____   Somewhat or Unsure _____   No _____

59. Yes _____   Somewhat or Unsure _____   No _____

60. Yes _____   Somewhat or Unsure _____   No _____

61. Yes _____   Somewhat or Unsure _____   No _____

62. Yes _____   Somewhat or Unsure _____   No _____

63. Yes _____   Somewhat or Unsure _____   No _____

64. Yes _____   Somewhat or Unsure _____   No _____

65. Yes _____   Somewhat or Unsure _____   No _____

66.   Yes _____   Somewhat or Unsure _____   No _____
67.   Yes _____   Somewhat or Unsure _____   No _____

Additional Learning Experiences

68.   Yes _____   Somewhat or Unsure _____   No _____
69.   Yes _____   Somewhat or Unsure _____   No _____
70.   Yes _____   Somewhat or Unsure _____   No _____
71.   Yes _____   Somewhat or Unsure _____   No _____
72.   Yes _____   Somewhat or Unsure _____   No _____
73.   Yes _____   Somewhat or Unsure _____   No _____
74.   Yes _____   Somewhat or Unsure _____   No _____
75.   Yes _____   Somewhat or Unsure _____   No _____
76.   Yes _____   Somewhat or Unsure _____   No _____

Strengths/Talents

77.   Yes _____   Somewhat or Unsure _____   No _____
78.   Yes _____   Somewhat or Unsure _____   No _____
79.   Yes _____   Somewhat or Unsure _____   No _____
80.   Yes _____   Somewhat or Unsure _____   No _____
81.   Yes _____   Somewhat or Unsure _____   No _____
82.   Yes _____   Somewhat or Unsure _____   No _____
83.   Yes _____   Somewhat or Unsure _____   No _____
84.   Yes _____   Somewhat or Unsure _____   No _____
85.   Yes _____   Somewhat or Unsure _____   No _____
86.   Yes _____   Somewhat or Unsure _____   No _____
87.   Yes _____   Somewhat or Unsure _____   No _____
88.   Yes _____   Somewhat or Unsure _____   No _____

89.	Yes _____	Somewhat or Unsure _____	No _____
90.	Yes _____	Somewhat or Unsure _____	No _____
91.	Yes _____	Somewhat or Unsure _____	No _____
92.	Yes _____	Somewhat or Unsure _____	No _____
93.	Yes _____	Somewhat or Unsure _____	No _____
94.	Yes _____	Somewhat or Unsure _____	No _____
95.	Yes _____	Somewhat or Unsure _____	No _____

Is It Dyslexia?

Grade 5 Questionnaire Analysis

All Areas except Strengths/Talents

1.	Count the number of "yes" answers in all areas **except** Strengths/Talents.	_____
2.	Count the number of "somewhat" answers in these areas and divide by 2.	_____
3.	Add lines 1 and 2 for the **TOTAL** in these areas.	_____

If the **TOTAL** in these areas is **3 or more,** then the screener should proceed to the screening tasks.

Strengths/Talents

4.	Count the number of "yes" answers in Strengths/Talents.	_____
5.	Count the number of "somewhat" answers and divide by 2.	_____
6.	Add lines 4 and 5 for the **TOTAL** in these areas.	_____
7.	Add lines 3 and 6 for the **GRAND TOTAL.**	_____

Any number greater than 3 in line 7 (GRAND TOTAL) increases the likelihood that dyslexia is present.

Grade 5 Student Pages

(Copy these three pages for the student to write on during the screening.)

On these pages, the student will complete the work for tasks that involve writing: Tasks 1, 2, 4, 5, 6, 9, and 11. (The remaining tasks require dictation only, which the screener will record on the Screener Answer Sheet.)

Task 1: Write the Alphabet

_____

_____

_____

Task 2: Spelling Sight Words

_____

1. _____

2. _____

3. _____

4. _____

5. _____

6. _____

7. _____

8. _____

9. _____

_____

10. _____

_____

Task 4: Reading Grade-Level Words

1.	*compliant*	6.	*awkward*
2.	*cathedral*	7.	*quadruple*
3.	*distinguishable*	8.	*authenticity*
4.	*hydrogen*	9.	*politician*
5.	*impatient*	10.	*circumstantial*

Task 5: Symbol to Sound Knowledge

1. d

2. u

3. q

4. y

5. a

6. w

7. i

8. x

9. e

10. o

Task 6: Write the Letter(s)

1.	_____	6.	_____
2.	_____	7.	_____
3.	_____	8.	_____
4.	_____	9.	_____
5.	_____	10.	_____

Task 9: Phonemic Awareness 2 (Isolation)

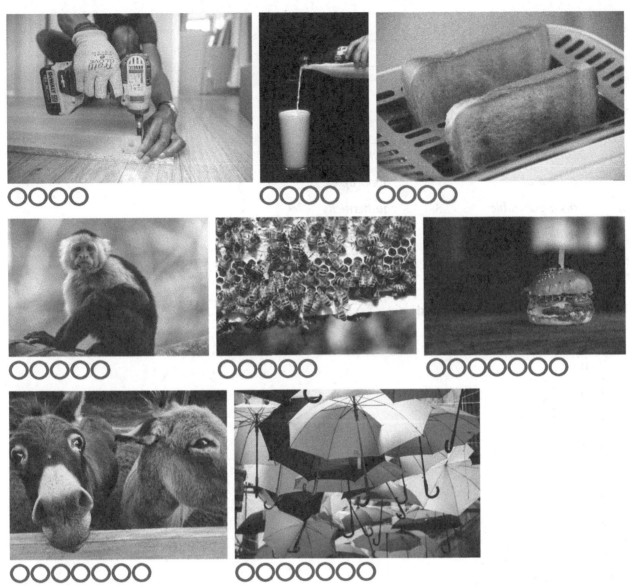

Source: https://docs.google.com/document/d/1v_W0fHCmiZ6Fm0VCZVPUsEWSAU8-YsknIDpwNJZroKY/edit

Task 11: Reading Unfamiliar Words

1.	*trats*	6.	*threlps*
2.	*flaspry*	7.	*drothplaits*
3.	*crilth*	8.	*thrimpstire*
4.	*chulps*	9.	*clampstandra*
5.	*sprisp*	10.	*shustrupa*

Grade 5 Instructions and Answer Sheets

Task 1 Screener Instructions

(This information for the screener is also offered in video format at https://courses.learnreading.com/courses/dyslexia-screening-videos.)

- Ask the student to write the alphabet in lowercase letters.
- There should be no help, no copying, and no erasing or crossing out.
- Watch for any hints of directionality confusion when they go to write a letter. Be aware of any pauses or hesitations, especially at *b/d/p/q*.
- Watch for confusion midway through, or if they need to start again at the beginning and use the alphabet song to help them determine the next letter.
- Watch for any reversals (writing a letter backward), inversions (writing a letter upside down), or errors (omitting a letter or writing it in the wrong sequence).
- After you have carefully watched the student complete the task, record their responses by answering "true" or "no" in the spaces provided.

Task 1 Student Instructions

(You may present this information to the student yourself, or show them the "Student Instructions" video at https://courses.learnreading.com/courses/dyslexia-screening-videos.)

"In this task, you're going to write the alphabet. You're going to use a pen (or a pencil without an eraser). This is because I want to see the way your brain works, and what you write down first. So, if you don't like what you wrote and are tempted to cross it out, don't worry! Just draw a box around the answer you didn't like, so I can still see what it was, and then put the answer you do want right next to or above it. And please use only lowercase letters in this screening. Okay! Let's get started!"

Task 1 Answer Sheet

Directions: Ask the student to write the alphabet in *lowercase letters* in the space provided on the Student Pages, with no help, no copying, and no erasing.

1.	The student made it to the end without any errors.	TRUE_____ NO_____
2.	The letters all faced the correct direction. (There were no reversals or inversions.)	TRUE_____ NO_____

3.	The student wrote the alphabet easily and quickly, with no hesitations, questions, or restarts.	TRUE_____ NO_____
4.	There was no hesitation at *b/d* or *p/q*. (The student did not wonder which way the letter faced.)	TRUE_____ NO_____

Task 2 Screenwwer Instructions

(This information for the screener is also offered in video format at https://courses.learnreading.com/courses/dyslexia-screening-videos.)

- You will dictate sight words for the student to spell.
- You can repeat the word and/or use it in a sentence, but no hints as to the spelling.
- Mark "correct" or "incorrect" in the spaces provided.

Task 2 Student Instructions

(You may present this information to the student yourself, or show them the "Student Instructions" video at https://courses.learnreading.com/courses/dyslexia-screening-videos.)

"You might already know that sight words are words that don't follow typical spelling rules. They can sometimes be tricky to spell. I'm going to say a few of these sight words and I'd like for you to try to spell them the best that you can."

Task 2 Answer Sheet

Directions: Ask the student to spell the following words in the space provided on the Student Pages, with no erasing or changing. Mark "correct" or "incorrect." (If they spelled the word incorrectly at first, then changed their mind and went to fix it, mark it "incorrect" even if their second attempt was correct.)

1.	*lose* (as in "I hope I don't lose the game.")	CORRECT_____ INCORRECT_____
2.	*change*	CORRECT_____ INCORRECT_____
3.	*answer*	CORRECT_____ INCORRECT_____
4.	*thought*	CORRECT_____ INCORRECT_____
5.	*world*	CORRECT_____ INCORRECT_____
6.	*high* (as in the opposite of *low*)	CORRECT_____ INCORRECT_____
7.	*country*	CORRECT_____ INCORRECT_____
8.	*earth*	CORRECT_____ INCORRECT_____

9.	*eyes* (as in used for seeing)	CORRECT_____ INCORRECT_____
10.	*light*	CORRECT_____ INCORRECT_____

Task 3 Screener Instructions

(This information for the screener is also offered in video format at https://courses.learnreading.com/courses/dyslexia-screening-videos.)

- You will dictate words to the student and ask them to count how many sounds they hear in a word (not syllables or letters).
- Mark "correct" or "incorrect" in the spaces provided. (The answer is next to the word.)

Task 3 Student Instructions

(You may present this information to the student yourself, or show them the "Student Instructions" video at https://courses.learnreading.com/courses/dyslexia-screening-videos.)

"For this task, you are simply going to be counting sounds. I am going to say a word, and you will count how many sounds you hear in that word. If you know how to spell the word, try not to think about the letters because I don't want you to count the letters, just the sounds. Sometimes there are more letters in a word than there are sounds, so just focus on the sounds, and tell me how many you hear."

Task 3 Answer Sheet

Directions: Ask the student how many SOUNDS are in each word. (Note: they are counting individual sounds, not syllables and not letters. For instance, chicken has 5 sounds.)

1.	*tan*	(answer: 3)	CORRECT_____ INCORRECT_____
2.	*blue*	(answer: 3)	CORRECT_____ INCORRECT_____
3.	*bench*	(answer: 4)	CORRECT_____ INCORRECT_____
4.	*truck*	(answer: 4)	CORRECT_____ INCORRECT_____
5.	*drill*	(answer: 4)	CORRECT_____ INCORRECT_____
6.	*straw*	(answer: 4)	CORRECT_____ INCORRECT_____
7.	*tractor*	(answer: 6)	CORRECT_____ INCORRECT_____
8.	*country*	(answer: 6)	CORRECT_____ INCORRECT_____

9.	*synonym*	(answer: 7)	CORRECT_____ INCORRECT_____
10.	*aluminum*	(answer: 8)	CORRECT_____ INCORRECT_____

Task 4 Screener Instructions

(This information for the screener is also offered in video format at https://courses.learnreading.com/courses/dyslexia-screening-videos.)

- Ask the student to read the words on their Student Pages.
- Mark "correct" or "incorrect" in the spaces provided.

If the student chose to skip a word, mark it incorrect.

Task 4 Student Instructions

(You may present this information to the student yourself, or show them the "Student Instructions" video at https://courses.learnreading.com/courses/dyslexia-screening-videos.)

"For this task, you are going to read a list of words as best as you can. It may be a little difficult, but just do your best. If you try and still feel like you can't read the word, it's okay to say, 'Skip it,' and move on to the next word."

Task 4 Answer Sheet

Directions: Ask the student to READ each word as it is written for them on the Student Pages. If you are unsure of the pronunciation of any word, spell it into your cell phone and ask for the correct pronunciation. This is important because many words are easily missed, even by adults.

1.	*compliant*	CORRECT_____ INCORRECT_____
2.	*cathedral*	CORRECT_____ INCORRECT_____
3.	*distinguishable*	CORRECT_____ INCORRECT_____
4.	*hydrogen*	CORRECT_____ INCORRECT_____
5.	*impatient*	CORRECT_____ INCORRECT_____
6.	*awkward*	CORRECT_____ INCORRECT_____
7.	*quadruple*	CORRECT_____ INCORRECT_____
8.	*authenticity*	CORRECT_____ INCORRECT_____

9.	*politician*	CORRECT_____ INCORRECT_____
10.	*circumstantial*	CORRECT_____ INCORRECT_____

Task 5 Screener Instructions

(This information for the screener is also offered in video format at https://courses.learnreading.com/courses/dyslexia-screening-videos.)

- Ask the student to look at each letter on their Student Page, and tell you the sound that it makes.
- When they come to the vowels, ask the student to tell you the short, or most common, sound.
- If they hesitate for longer than three seconds on any letter, mark it "incorrect."
- Mark "correct" or "incorrect" in the spaces provided. (The correct answer is provided for you.)

Task 5 Student Instructions

(You may present this information to the student yourself, or show them the "Student Instructions" video at https://courses.learnreading.com/courses/dyslexia-screening-videos.)

"For this task, I'd like you to look at a letter and then tell me the sound that it makes. When you come to a vowel, tell me the short, or most common, sound."

Task 5 Answer Sheet

Directions: Ask the student to look at each letter and tell you the sound each one makes. If they hesitate for longer than three seconds, mark it "incorrect." For *a, e, i, o, u*, tell them you want the short, or most common, sound. If they have any questions, tell them to just do their best.

1.	*d*	(answer: /d/ as in *dog*)	CORRECT_____ INCORRECT_____
2.	*u*	(answer: /u/ as in *under*)	CORRECT_____ INCORRECT_____
3.	*q*	(answer: /kw/ as in *queen*)	CORRECT_____ INCORRECT_____
4.	*y*	(answer: /y/ as in *yellow*)	CORRECT_____ INCORRECT_____
5.	*a*	(answer: /ă/ as in *apple*)	CORRECT_____ INCORRECT_____
6.	*w*	(answer: /w/ as in *water*)	CORRECT_____ INCORRECT_____
7.	*i*	(answer: /ĭ/ as in *index*)	CORRECT_____ INCORRECT_____
8.	*x*	(answer: /ks/ as in *fox*)	CORRECT_____ INCORRECT_____

| 9. | *e* | (answer: /ĕ/ as in *exit*) | CORRECT_____ INCORRECT_____ |
| 10. | *o* | (answer: /ŏ/ as in *octopus*) | CORRECT_____ INCORRECT_____ |

Task 6 Screener Instructions

(This information for the screener is also offered in video format at https://courses.learnreading.com/courses/dyslexia-screening-videos.)

- You will dictate a sound to the student.
- Ask the student what letter, or set of letters, makes that sound.
- The "as in" hints are for the screener only and should *not* be given to the student.
- Ask the student to write their answers in lowercase letters.
- When the student writes their answer, the letters must be facing the correct way for the answer to be marked "correct." If any letters are reversed, mark it "incorrect."

Task 6 Student Instructions

(You may present this information to the student yourself, or show them the "Student Instructions" video at https://courses.learnreading.com/courses/dyslexia-screening-videos.)

"This time I'm going to give you the sound, and you're going to write down the letter or letters that make that sound. For instance, if I said /m/ (the sound of *m*), you would write *m*. If I said /th/ (the sound of *th*), you would write *th*.

Task 6 Answer Sheet

Directions: For the following items, say to the student, "What letter, or letters, makes this sound?" then pronounce the sound for them. (Do *not* say "as in..." because that is only for you to read so you are sure which sound to make. The answer is the bold letter(s) in the example word. *Q* can be written as *Q* or *QU*. Both are correct.) Have them write down their answer in lowercase letters in the space provided on the Student Pages. The letters they write down must be facing the right direction to be marked "correct."

1.	/ch/	(as in **ch**air)	CORRECT_____ INCORRECT_____
2.	/ĕ/	(as in **e**xit)	CORRECT_____ INCORRECT_____
3.	/sh/	(as in **sh**ut)	CORRECT_____ INCORRECT_____

4.	/ŏ/	(as in **o**ctopus)	CORRECT_____ INCORRECT_____
5.	/w/	(as in **w**onder)	CORRECT_____ INCORRECT_____
6.	/ĭ/	(as in **i**ndex)	CORRECT_____ INCORRECT_____
7.	/y/	(as in **y**ellow)	CORRECT_____ INCORRECT_____
8.	/ŭ/	(as in **u**nder)	CORRECT_____ INCORRECT_____
9.	/d/	(as in **d**oor)	CORRECT_____ INCORRECT_____
10.	/kw/	(as in **qu**een)	CORRECT_____ INCORRECT_____

Task 7 Screener Instructions

(This information for the screener is also offered in video format at https://courses.learnreading.com/courses/dyslexia-screening-videos.)

- Dictate three distinct sounds to the student, with clean and clear breaks in between each sound.
- Ask the student to repeat the sounds back to you in order.
- The "as in" hints are for the screener only and should *not* be given to the student.
- The sounds must all be repeated back with exactness to be marked "correct." If the student mispronounced or omitted any sounds, or switched the order, mark the answer "incorrect."

Task 7 Student Instructions

(You may present this information to the student yourself, or show them the "Student Instructions" video at https://courses.learnreading.com/courses/dyslexia-screening-videos.)

"For this task, I am going to say three sounds and then you just repeat them exactly as I said them and in the same order. Listen very carefully, because some of the sounds may sound similar. Repeat them back to me as best you can."

Task 7 Answer Sheet

Directions: Ask the student to repeat the following sound sequences after you. You will pronounce all three sounds, then they should repeat the three sounds back to you. If they ask you to repeat the sequence, you may repeat it one time. If they say all three sounds back to you *exactly* right, mark it "correct." If they mispronounced (or couldn't remember) even one of the three sounds, mark it "incorrect." (Do *not* say "as in..." because that is only for you so you are sure which sound to make.)

Is It Dyslexia?

1.	/n/ /m/ /l/ (as in: *name, milk, leg*)	CORRECT_____ INCORRECT_____
2.	/ĭ/ /ŏ/ /ĕ/ (as in: *index, octopus, exit*)	CORRECT_____ INCORRECT_____
3.	/d/ /p/ /b/ (as in: *door, pie, box*)	CORRECT_____ INCORRECT_____
4.	/sh/ /s/ /z/ (as in: *ship, sun, zebra*)	CORRECT_____ INCORRECT_____
5.	/th/ /f/ /j/ (as in: *think, fish, jam*)	CORRECT_____ INCORRECT_____
6.	/ă/ /ĕ/ /ĭ / (as in: *apple, exit, index*)	CORRECT_____ INCORRECT_____
7.	/ŭ/ /ŏ/ /ă/ (as in: *under, octopus, apple*)	CORRECT_____ INCORRECT_____
8.	/sh/ /ch/ /th/ (as in: *ship, chop, think*)	CORRECT_____ INCORRECT___
9.	/r/ /l/ /n/ (as in: *run, leg, net*)	CORRECT_____ INCORRECT_____
10.	/w/ /y/ /p/ (as in: *water, yellow, pot*)	CORRECT_____ INCORRECT_____

Grade 5: Task 8
Phonemic Awareness/Deletion

Task 8 Screener Instructions

(This information for the screener is also offered in video format at https://courses.learnreading.com/courses/dyslexia-screening-videos.)

- Important note: when you see a letter in between two slanted lines, it means the sound that that letter makes. For instance, /f/ is the sound of *f*, not the letter itself.
- Read the questions to the student, making sure to only say the sound of the letter in between the slanted lines.
- Mark "correct" or "incorrect" in the spaces provided. (The correct answer is provided for you.)

Task 8 Student Instructions

(You may present this information to the student yourself, or show them the "Student Instructions" video at https://courses.learnreading.com/courses/dyslexia-screening-videos.)

"For this task, I am going to say a word. Then, I'm going to ask you to repeat the word but without one of the sounds. For example, I might say *camp*, and then ask you to say *camp* without the /m/. *Camp* without the /m/ is *Cap* (model how to do the task). So listen carefully, take your time, and try your best."

Task 8 Answer Sheet

Directions: Ask the student each question. When you do so, say the sound that they are to remove, not the letter. (FYI: a letter inside of slanted lines, like /f/, means the sound only, not the letter itself.) If they ask you to repeat the question, you may do so one time. The student should tell you the answer, not write it down.

1.	"What would *cat* say without the /k/?" (answer: *at*)	CORRECT_____ INCORRECT_____
2.	"What would *bite* say without the /t/?" (answer: *by*)	CORRECT_____ INCORRECT_____
3.	"What would *flatten* say without the /l/?" (answer: *fatten*)	CORRECT_____ INCORRECT_____
4.	"What would *scram* say without the /r/?" (answer: *scam*)	CORRECT_____ INCORRECT_____
5.	"What would *feast* say without the /s/?" (answer: *feet*)	CORRECT_____ INCORRECT_____
6.	"What would *play* say without the /l/?" (answer: *pay*)	CORRECT_____ INCORRECT_____
7.	"What would *boost* say without the /s/?" (answer: *boot*)	CORRECT_____ INCORRECT_____
8.	"What would *trip* say without the /r/?" (answer: *tip*)	CORRECT_____ INCORRECT_____
9.	"What would *faxed* say without the /k/?" (answer: *fast*)	CORRECT_____ INCORRECT_____
10.	"What would *bottle* say without the /t/?" (answer: *ball*)	CORRECT_____ INCORRECT_____

Task 9 Screener Instructions

(This information for the screener is also offered in video format at https://courses.learnreading.com/courses/dyslexia-screening-videos.)

- Ask the student to look at a picture on their Student Page, say what it is a picture of, and stretch out the sounds in that word (such as *milk* "mmmiiilllk").

- Ask the student to break apart each sound in that word and then mark the dot that represents the sound in the question that you will ask them.

- Mark "correct" or "incorrect" if they identified the correct dot that contained that sound.

Task 9 Student Instructions

(You may present this information to the student yourself, or show them the "Student Instructions" video at https://courses.learnreading.com/courses/dyslexia-screening-videos.)

"For this task, you're going to see some pictures. I want you to tell me what the picture is and then stretch out the sounds in that word. Then I want you to separate each sound in that word with nice, big breaks in between each sound. You will see dots under the picture. I'd like you to point to each

Is It Dyslexia?

dot when you say each sound in that word. Then I'm going to ask where a certain sound is, and you'll just point to, or color in, that dot."

Task 9 Answer Sheet

Directions: As you ask each question, ask the student to follow along with you on their Student Pages. Ask the student to look at each picture and 1) repeat what the picture is, 2) stretch out the sounds in the word, and then 3) separate the sounds within the word and mark the dot on their paper where they hear the sound in question.

1.	Where is the /r/ in *drill*?	(answer: 2nd dot)	CORRECT_____	INCORRECT_____
2.	Where is the /l/ in *milk*?	(answer: 3rd dot)	CORRECT_____	INCORRECT_____
3.	Where is the /s/ in *toast*?	(answer: 3rd dot)	CORRECT_____	INCORRECT_____
4.	Where is the /k/ in *monkey*?	(answer: 4th dot)	CORRECT_____	INCORRECT_____
5.	Where is the /h/ in *beehive*?	(answer: 3rd dot)	CORRECT_____	INCORRECT_____
6.	Where is the /b/ in *hamburger*?	(answer: 4th dot)	CORRECT_____	INCORRECT_____
7.	Where is the /ŭ/ in *animals*?	(answer: 5th dot)	CORRECT_____	INCORRECT_____
8.	Where is the /r/ in *umbrella*?	(answer: 4th dot)	CORRECT_____	INCORRECT_____

- If the student had difficulty **breaking off** one sound from another in one or more of the words or if the student chose to skip a word, mark it "incorrect" here.   CORRECT_____ INCORRECT_____

- If the student had difficulty **articulating** the correct sounds within the word or if the student chose to skip a word, mark it "incorrect" here.   CORRECT _____ INCORRECT _____

Task 10 Screener Instructions

(This information for the screener is also offered in video format at https://courses.learnreading.com/courses/dyslexia-screening-videos.)

- Read the word to the student. Have them repeat the word and then try to say the word backward.
- Mark "correct" or "incorrect" in the spaces provided. (The correct answer is provided for you.)

Task 10 Student Instructions

(You may present this information to the student yourself, or show them the "Student Instructions" video at https://courses.learnreading.com/courses/dyslexia-screening-videos.)

"In this task, I'm going to say a word. You will repeat the word back to me, and then try to say the word backward. For example, if I said the word *cat*. You would repeat that word *cat* and then try to say it backward. That last letter in *cat* would be the first letter if it was said backward. So *cat*, backward, is *tac* (model how to do the task).

Task 10 Answer Sheet

Directions: 1) Read the word (or nonsense word) to the student. 2) Ask them to repeat the word back to you. Then 3) tell them to say the word BACKWARD. If they ask you to repeat the word, you may do so one time. They must say every sound in the reversed word *exactly* right to be marked "correct." (If you are unsure of the correct pronunciation of the word, a "rhymes with" word is provided for you. Please do *not* share this "rhymes with" word with the student. It is only to aid the administrator.)

1.	*tea* (rhymes with *see*) (answer: *eat*)	CORRECT_____ INCORRECT_____
2.	*air* (rhymes with *stare*) (answer: *ray*)	CORRECT_____ INCORRECT_____
3.	*ile* (rhymes with *mile*) (answer: *lie*)	CORRECT_____ INCORRECT_____
4.	*oot* (rhymes with *flute*) (answer: *to*)	CORRECT_____ INCORRECT_____
5.	*eem* (rhymes with *team*) (answer: *me*)	CORRECT_____ INCORRECT_____
6.	*cheap* (rhymes with *sheep*) (answer: *peach*)	CORRECT_____ INCORRECT_____
7.	*chum* (rhymes with *plum*) (answer: *much*)	CORRECT_____ INCORRECT_____
8.	*stop* (rhymes with *top*) (answer: *pots*)	CORRECT_____ INCORRECT_____
9.	*gums* (rhymes with *chums*) (answer: *smug*)	CORRECT_____ INCORRECT_____
10.	*klim* (rhymes with *slim*) (answer: *milk*)	CORRECT_____ INCORRECT_____

Task 11 Screener Instructions

(This information for the screener is also offered in video format at https://courses.learnreading.com/courses/dyslexia-screening-videos.)

- Ask the student to read aloud the nonsense words on their Student Pages.
- They must get each sound in the word *exactly* correct for it to be marked "correct."
- The "rhymes with" hints are for the screener only and should *not* be given to the student.

Task 11 Student Instructions

(You may present this information to the student yourself, or show them the "Student Instructions" video at https://courses.learnreading.com/courses/dyslexia-screening-videos.)

"On your Student Pages, you're going to see some nonsense words. These are crazy words that you've never seen before. To read them, just use your knowledge of what the letters say."

Task 11 Answer Sheet

Directions: Ask the student to READ each nonsense word on their Student Pages. The student must pronounce each sound in the word *exactly* right for the word to be marked "correct." (A "rhymes with" word is provided for the screener only. Do *not* give the "rhymes with" word to the student.)

1.	*trats* (rhymes with *rats*)	CORRECT_____ INCORRECT_____
2.	*flaspry* (rhymes with *clasp ree'*)	CORRECT_____ INCORRECT_____
3.	*crilth* (rhymes with *filth*)	CORRECT_____ INCORRECT____
4.	*chulps* (rhymes with *gulps*)	CORRECT_____ INCORRECT_____
5.	*sprisp* (rhymes with *crisp*)	CORRECT_____ INCORRECT_____
6.	*threlps* (rhymes with *helps*)	CORRECT_____ INCORRECT_____
7.	*drothplaits* (rhymes with *cloth plates*)	CORRECT_____ INCORRECT_____
8.	*thrimpstire* (rhymes with *shrimp fire*)	CORRECT_____ INCORRECT_____
9.	*clampstandra* (sounds like *clămp stand ruh*)	CORRECT_____ INCORRECT_____
10.	*shustrupa* (sounds like *shŭs true puh*)	CORRECT_____ INCORRECT_____

Grade 5 Results

Task 1: Long-Term Memory

_____

Total Incorrect (or "no" answers) _____

Task 2: Sight Words Knowledge

_____

Total Incorrect: _____

Task 3: Phonemic Awareness

_____

Total Incorrect: _____

Task 4: Reading Grade-Level Words

_____

Total Incorrect: _____

Task 5: Symbol to Sound Knowledge

_____

Total Incorrect: _____

Task 6: Sound to Symbol Knowledge

_____

Total Incorrect: _____

Task 7: Auditory Discrimination/Memory

_____

Total Incorrect: _____

Task 8: Phonemic Awareness

_____

Total Incorrect: _____

Task 9: Phonemic Awareness

Total Incorrect: _____

Task 10: Phonemic Awareness

Total Incorrect: _____

Task 11: Decoding Unfamiliar Words

Total Incorrect: _____

Results from Questionnaire Plus Screening Tasks

1.   TOTAL (line 4) on Questionnaire   _____

2.   TOTAL incorrect answers on Screening Tasks   _____

3.   GRAND TOTAL from lines 1 and 2   _____

Grade 5 Conclusions

If the GRAND TOTAL (line 3) **is 14 or greater**, then this student's performance is consistent with someone with dyslexia.

It can be assumed that the severity of dyslexia is in direct relation to **how much greater than 14** the GRAND TOTAL is (14 being mild and 205 being the most severe).

If the GRAND TOTAL **is less than 14**, then dyslexia is likely *not* the probable cause for the student's academic difficulties.

Grade 6 Screening Packet

This packet contains the following:

- Grade 6 Screening Questionnaire
- Grade 6 Questionnaire Answer Sheet
- Grade 6 Questionnaire Analysis
- Grade 6 Student Pages (for student's written answers)
- Grade 6 Instructions and Answer Sheets (for Tasks 1–11)
- Grade 6 Results
- Grade 6 Conclusions

Grade 6 Screening Questionnaire

(Mark answers on the answer sheet.)

Genetics

1. Does the student's mother have any trouble with reading or spelling?

2. Does the student's father have any trouble with reading or spelling?

3. Are there any other immediate family members who struggle with reading or spelling?

4. Are (or were) there any extended family members (parents, siblings, grandparents, cousins, aunts, uncles) who struggled in school?

Articulation/Speech

5. Did the student have a speech delay (were they a late talker)?

6. Does (did) the student have any articulation or speech issues?

7. Does (did) the student have problems forming certain words correctly?

8. Does (did) the student mispronounce words even after repeated correction?

9. Does (did) the student attend speech therapy?

10. Does (did) the student confuse *i/e*, *m/n*, or *f/th* when they speak?

11. Does (did) the person have difficulty saying words like *aluminum*, *cinnamon*, or *dyslexia*?

12. Does the student have difficulty expressing themself verbally?

13. Does the student have trouble retrieving words, use a lot of *um*s or *uh*s, or use grand gestures with their hands when speaking?

Directionality

14. Is (was) there any left/right confusion?

15. Are there any letter or number reversals continuing beyond the end of first grade, including *b/d* confusion?

16. Does (did) the student have difficulty learning to tie their shoes?

17. Does (did) the student have trouble telling time on an analog clock?

18. Does (did) the student have difficulty remembering the direction of mathematical operations, such as addition and subtraction moving right to left, or the directional movements in long division?

19. Does (did) the student transpose number sequences, such as writing *51* for *15*?

20. Does (did) the student reverse words when reading, such as reading *top* for *pot*?

Memory/Recall

21. Does (did) the student have trouble recalling the names of letters, numbers, or colors?

22. Does the student have difficulty remembering sequences (such as a list of directions, arithmetic steps, spelling sequences, days of the week, or months of the year in order)?

23. Does the student have difficulty on timed math tests?

24. Does the student have trouble with copying (copying slowly and inaccurately)?

25. Does the student have difficulty remembering names?

26. Does the student have trouble remembering important dates?

27. Does the student have difficulty remembering the order of the alphabet?

28. Does the student have trouble recalling the days of the week or months of the year in order?

29. Does the student have trouble recalling the names of familiar objects, instead replacing them with words like *stuff* or *things*?

30. Does the student have trouble remembering multiple-step directions?

31. Does the student have difficulty remembering a pin number, address, or phone number?

32. Does the student have trouble with alphabetizing or with remembering the order of the alphabet?

33. Does the student have a hard time recalling math facts quickly?

Phonemic Awareness/Auditory Processing

34. Does (did) the student have difficulty with rhyming?

35. Does the student have problems repeating back sounds accurately and in order?

36. Does (did) the student have trouble breaking off the first or last sound of a word?

37. Does (did) the student have trouble identifying the vowel sound within a word?

38. Does (did) the student confuse the short *i* and the short *e* sound when saying or reading words?

39. Does (did) the student have trouble understanding the connection between letters and sounds?

40. Does (did) the student have trouble isolating and manipulating the sounds within a word?

Reading

41. Does (did) the student read below grade level?

42. Does the student have trouble decoding unfamiliar words?

43. Is the student's reading slow and labor intensive?

44. Does (did) the student have trouble reading sight words or high frequency words?

45. Does the student forget how to read a word from one moment to the next?

46. Does the student have trouble comprehending what they read?

47. Would the student prefer *not* to be called on to read aloud in class or in public? Would they prefer to avoid reading, especially aloud?

48. Does (did) the student guess at words based on the size, shape, context, or picture clues?

49. Does (did) the student skip or misread small, simple words when reading?

50. Is the student easily frustrated when reading?

51. Does the student spend an unusually long time completing tasks that involve reading?

52. Does the student omit the suffixes or endings of words?

53. Does the student have trouble recognizing their mistakes when reading?

54. Does the student rarely read for pleasure?

55. Does the student require multiple readings to comprehend the material?

56. Does the student omit, substitute, add, or transpose letters when reading?

Spelling/Writing

57. Does (did) the student have trouble with spelling?

58. Does (did) the student spend an unusually long time completing tasks that involve writing?

59. Does (did) the student have trouble spelling sight words or high frequency words?

60. Does (did) the student forget how to spell a word from one moment to the next?

61. Do others have trouble reading what the student wrote, due to spelling errors?

62. Is the student's intelligence not reflected in their writing?

63. When writing, will the student use words that they know how to spell, instead of those that they would prefer to use?

64. Does the student have trouble remembering and applying spelling rules?

65. Does (did) the student use unpredictable, illogical spelling?

66. Does (did) the student omit, substitute, add, or transpose letters when spelling?

67. Does the student have difficulty using spell check or a dictionary?

Additional Learning Experiences

68. Has the student attended special academic classes, reading groups, or had outside tutoring?

69. Does the student have trouble learning a foreign language in print (reading and writing in the foreign language)?

70. Does the student have difficulty reading printed music?

71. Does the student have trouble taking notes in class?

72. Does (has) the student pretended to be sick or otherwise unable to attend school/perform academically in a classroom?

73. Can the student answer questions orally, but be unable to adequately do so in print?

74. Does the student need more time than others to process verbal information?

75. Does (did) the student have poor self-esteem resulting from poor academic performance?

76. Does (did) the student experience anxiety or high levels of stress surrounding academics?

Strengths/Talents

77. Does the student have a high capacity for learning?

78. Is the student gifted athletically?

79. Is the student gifted musically?

80. Is the student gifted artistically?

81. Is the student extremely creative?

82. Is the student highly imaginative?

83. Does the student have surprising maturity?

84. Does the student enjoy, and are they good at, puzzles (excellent spatial reasoning)?

85. Is the student extremely curious?

86. Is the student able to easily comprehend stories that they *hear* or *listen* to?

87. Is the student able to easily remember song lyrics?

88. Is the student mechanically inclined (good with their hands, such as working with Legos, building models, taking things apart and putting them back together again, etc.)?

89. Does the student have excellent creative writing skills?

90. Does the student have excellent thinking and reasoning skills?

91. Does the student have the ability to produce unique, out-of-the-box ideas?

92. Is the student gifted at seeing the big picture?

93. Is the student highly empathetic?

94. Is the student highly resilient?

95. Does the student have excellent interpersonal skills (maintains friendships easily)?

Grade 6 Questionnaire Answer Sheet

Genetics

1.   Yes _____   Somewhat or Unsure _____   No _____

2.   Yes _____   Somewhat or Unsure _____   No _____

3.   Yes _____   Somewhat or Unsure _____   No _____

4.   Yes _____   Somewhat or Unsure _____   No _____

Articulation/Speech

5.   Yes _____   Somewhat or Unsure _____   No _____

6.   Yes _____   Somewhat or Unsure _____   No _____

7.   Yes _____   Somewhat or Unsure _____   No _____

8.   Yes _____   Somewhat or Unsure _____   No _____

9.   Yes _____   Somewhat or Unsure _____   No _____

10.   Yes _____   Somewhat or Unsure _____   No _____

11.   Yes _____   Somewhat or Unsure _____   No _____

12.   Yes _____   Somewhat or Unsure _____   No _____

13.   Yes _____   Somewhat or Unsure _____   No _____

Directionality

14.   Yes _____   Somewhat or Unsure _____   No _____

15.   Yes _____   Somewhat or Unsure _____   No _____

16.   Yes _____   Somewhat or Unsure _____   No _____

17.   Yes _____   Somewhat or Unsure _____   No _____

18.   Yes _____   Somewhat or Unsure _____   No _____

19.   Yes _____   Somewhat or Unsure _____   No _____

20.   Yes _____   Somewhat or Unsure _____   No _____

Memory/Recall

21.	Yes _____	Somewhat or Unsure _____	No _____
22.	Yes _____	Somewhat or Unsure _____	No _____
23.	Yes _____	Somewhat or Unsure _____	No _____
24.	Yes _____	Somewhat or Unsure _____	No _____
25.	Yes _____	Somewhat or Unsure _____	No _____
26.	Yes _____	Somewhat or Unsure _____	No _____
27.	Yes _____	Somewhat or Unsure _____	No _____
28.	Yes _____	Somewhat or Unsure _____	No _____
29.	Yes _____	Somewhat or Unsure _____	No _____
30.	Yes _____	Somewhat or Unsure _____	No _____
31.	Yes _____	Somewhat or Unsure _____	No _____
32.	Yes _____	Somewhat or Unsure _____	No _____
33.	Yes _____	Somewhat or Unsure _____	No _____

Phonemic Awareness/Auditory Processing

34.	Yes _____	Somewhat or Unsure _____	No _____
35.	Yes _____	Somewhat or Unsure _____	No _____
36.	Yes _____	Somewhat or Unsure _____	No _____
37.	Yes _____	Somewhat or Unsure _____	No _____
38.	Yes _____	Somewhat or Unsure _____	No _____
39.	Yes _____	Somewhat or Unsure _____	No _____
40.	Yes _____	Somewhat or Unsure _____	No _____

Reading

41.	Yes _____	Somewhat or Unsure _____	No _____
42.	Yes _____	Somewhat or Unsure _____	No _____
43.	Yes _____	Somewhat or Unsure _____	No _____
44.	Yes _____	Somewhat or Unsure _____	No _____
45.	Yes _____	Somewhat or Unsure _____	No _____
46.	Yes _____	Somewhat or Unsure _____	No _____
47.	Yes _____	Somewhat or Unsure _____	No _____
48.	Yes _____	Somewhat or Unsure _____	No _____
49.	Yes _____	Somewhat or Unsure _____	No _____
50.	Yes _____	Somewhat or Unsure _____	No _____
51.	Yes _____	Somewhat or Unsure _____	No _____
52.	Yes _____	Somewhat or Unsure _____	No _____
53.	Yes _____	Somewhat or Unsure _____	No _____
54.	Yes _____	Somewhat or Unsure _____	No _____
55.	Yes _____	Somewhat or Unsure _____	No _____
56.	Yes _____	Somewhat or Unsure _____	No _____

Spelling/Writing

57.	Yes _____	Somewhat or Unsure _____	No _____
58.	Yes _____	Somewhat or Unsure _____	No _____
59.	Yes _____	Somewhat or Unsure _____	No _____
60.	Yes _____	Somewhat or Unsure _____	No _____
61.	Yes _____	Somewhat or Unsure _____	No _____
62.	Yes _____	Somewhat or Unsure _____	No _____
63.	Yes _____	Somewhat or Unsure _____	No _____
64.	Yes _____	Somewhat or Unsure _____	No _____
65.	Yes _____	Somewhat or Unsure _____	No _____

| 66. | Yes _____ | Somewhat or Unsure _____ | No _____ |
| 67. | Yes _____ | Somewhat or Unsure _____ | No _____ |

Additional Learning Experiences

68.	Yes _____	Somewhat or Unsure _____	No _____
69.	Yes _____	Somewhat or Unsure _____	No _____
70.	Yes _____	Somewhat or Unsure _____	No _____
71.	Yes _____	Somewhat or Unsure _____	No _____
72.	Yes _____	Somewhat or Unsure _____	No _____
73.	Yes _____	Somewhat or Unsure _____	No _____
74.	Yes _____	Somewhat or Unsure _____	No _____
75.	Yes _____	Somewhat or Unsure _____	No _____
76.	Yes _____	Somewhat or Unsure _____	No _____

Strengths/Talents

77.	Yes _____	Somewhat or Unsure _____	No _____
78.	Yes _____	Somewhat or Unsure _____	No _____
79.	Yes _____	Somewhat or Unsure _____	No _____
80.	Yes _____	Somewhat or Unsure _____	No _____
81.	Yes _____	Somewhat or Unsure _____	No _____
82.	Yes _____	Somewhat or Unsure _____	No _____
83.	Yes _____	Somewhat or Unsure _____	No _____
84.	Yes _____	Somewhat or Unsure _____	No _____
85.	Yes _____	Somewhat or Unsure _____	No _____
86.	Yes _____	Somewhat or Unsure _____	No _____
87.	Yes _____	Somewhat or Unsure _____	No _____
88.	Yes _____	Somewhat or Unsure _____	No _____

89.	Yes _____	Somewhat or Unsure _____	No _____
90.	Yes _____	Somewhat or Unsure _____	No _____
91.	Yes _____	Somewhat or Unsure _____	No _____
92.	Yes _____	Somewhat or Unsure _____	No _____
93.	Yes _____	Somewhat or Unsure _____	No _____
94.	Yes _____	Somewhat or Unsure _____	No _____
95.	Yes _____	Somewhat or Unsure _____	No _____

Grade 6 Questionnaire Analysis

All Areas except Strengths/Talents

1. Count the number of "yes" answers in all areas **except** Strengths/Talents. _____

2. Count the number of "somewhat" answers in these areas and divide by 2. _____

3. Add lines 1 and 2 for the **TOTAL** in these areas. _____

If the **TOTAL** in these areas is **3 or more,** then the screener should proceed to the screening tasks.

Strengths/Talents

4. Count the number of "yes" answers in Strengths/Talents. _____

5. Count the number of "somewhat" answers and divide by 2. _____

6. Add lines 4 and 5 for the **TOTAL** in these areas. _____

7. Add lines 3 and 6 for the **GRAND TOTAL.** _____

Any number greater than 3 in line 7 (GRAND TOTAL) increases the likelihood that dyslexia is present.

Grade 6 Student Pages

(Copy these three pages for the student to write on during the screening.)

On these pages, the student will complete the work for tasks that involve writing: Tasks 1, 2, 4, 5, 6, 9, and 11. (The remaining tasks require dictation only, which the screener will record on the Screener Answer Sheet.)

Task 1: Write the Alphabet

_____

_____

_____

Task 2: Spelling Sight Words

_____

1. _____

2. _____

3. _____

4. _____

5. _____

6. _____

7. _____

8. _____

9. _____

    _____

10. _____

    _____

Task 4: Reading Grade-Level Words

1.	prejudice	6.	suspicion
2.	conscious	7.	choreography
3.	mischievous	8.	perennial
4.	pronunciation	9.	ambidextrous
5.	leisure	10.	compliant

Task 5: Symbol to Sound Knowledge

1. d		**6.** w	
2. u		**7.** i	
3. q		**8.** x	
4. y		**9.** e	
5. a		**10.** o	

Task 6: Write the Letter(s)

1.	_____	6.	_____
2.	_____	7.	_____
3.	_____	8.	_____
4.	_____	9.	_____
5.	_____	10.	_____

Task 9: Phonemic Awareness 2 (Isolation)

Source: https://docs.google.com/document/d/1v_W0fHCmiZ6Fm0VCZVPUsEWSAU8-YsknIDpwNJZroKY/edit

Task 11: Reading Unfamiliar Words

1.	trats	6.	threlps
2.	flaspry	7.	drothplaits
3.	crilth	8.	thrimpstire
4.	chulps	9.	clampstandra
5.	sprisp	10.	shustrupa

Grade 6 Instructions and Answer Sheets

Task 1 Screener Instructions

(This information for the screener is also offered in video format at https://courses.learnreading.com/courses/dyslexia-screening-videos.)

- Ask the student to write the alphabet in lowercase letters.

- There should be no help, no copying, and no erasing or crossing out.

- Watch for any hints of directionality confusion when they go to write a letter. Be aware of any pauses or hesitations, especially at *b/d/p/q*.

- Watch for confusion midway through, or if they need to start again at the beginning and use the alphabet song to help them determine the next letter.

- Watch for any reversals (writing a letter backward), inversions (writing a letter upside down), or errors (omitting a letter or writing it in the wrong sequence).

- After you have carefully watched the student complete the task, record their responses by answering "true" or "no" in the spaces provided.

Task 1 Student Instructions

(You may present this information to the student yourself, or show them the "Student Instructions" video at https://courses.learnreading.com/courses/dyslexia-screening-videos.)

"In this task, you're going to write the alphabet. You're going to use a pen (or a pencil without an eraser). This is because I want to see the way your brain works, and what you write down first. So, if you don't like what you wrote and are tempted to cross it out, don't worry! Just draw a box around the answer you didn't like, so I can still see what it was, and then put the answer you do want right next to or above it. And please use only lowercase letters in this screening. Okay! Let's get started!"

Task 1 Answer Sheet

Directions: Ask the student to write the alphabet in *lowercase letters* in the space provided on the Student Pages, with no help, no copying, and no erasing.

1.	The student made it to the end without any errors.	TRUE_____ NO_____
2.	The letters all faced the correct direction. (There were no reversals or inversions.)	TRUE_____ NO_____

3.	The student wrote the alphabet easily and quickly, with no hesitations, questions, or restarts.	TRUE_____ NO_____
4.	There was no hesitation at *b/d* or *p/q*. (The student did not wonder which way the letter faced.)	TRUE_____ NO_____

Task 2 Screener Instructions

(This information for the screener is also offered in video format at https://courses.learnreading.com/courses/dyslexia-screening-videos.)

- You will dictate sight words for the student to spell.
- You can repeat the word and/or use it in a sentence, but no hints as to the spelling.
- Mark "correct" or "incorrect" in the spaces provided.

Task 2 Student Instructions

(You may present this information to the student yourself, or show them the "Student Instructions" video at https://courses.learnreading.com/courses/dyslexia-screening-videos.)

"You might already know that sight words are words that don't follow typical spelling rules. They can sometimes be tricky to spell. I'm going to say a few of these sight words and I'd like for you to try to spell them the best that you can."

Task 2 Answer Sheet

Directions: Ask the student to spell the following words in the space provided on the Student Pages, with no erasing or changing. Mark "correct" or "incorrect." (If they spelled the word incorrectly at first, then changed their mind and went to fix it, mark it "incorrect" even if their second attempt was correct.)

1.	*together*	CORRECT_____ INCORRECT_____
2.	*daughter*	CORRECT_____ INCORRECT_____
3.	*walk*	CORRECT_____ INCORRECT_____
4.	*enough*	CORRECT_____ INCORRECT_____
5.	*Tuesday*	CORRECT_____ INCORRECT_____
6.	*know* (as in "I know that")	CORRECT_____ INCORRECT_____
7.	*enough*	CORRECT_____ INCORRECT_____
8.	*listen*	CORRECT_____ INCORRECT_____

9.	*though* (as in "even though")	CORRECT_____ INCORRECT_____
10.	*hour* (as in relating to time)	CORRECT_____ INCORRECT_____

Task 3 Screener Instructions

(This information for the screener is also offered in video format at https://courses.learnreading.com/courses/dyslexia-screening-videos.)

- You will dictate words to the student and ask them to count how many sounds they hear in a word (not syllables or letters).
- Mark "correct" or "incorrect" in the spaces provided. (The answer is next to the word.)

Task 3 Student Instructions

(You may present this information to the student yourself, or show them the "Student Instructions" video at https://courses.learnreading.com/courses/dyslexia-screening-videos.)

"For this task, you are simply going to be counting sounds. I am going to say a word, and you will count how many sounds you hear in that word. If you know how to spell the word, try not to think about the letters because I don't want you to count the letters, just the sounds. Sometimes there are more letters in a word then there are sounds, so just focus on the sounds, and tell me how many you hear."

Task 3 Answer Sheet

Directions: Ask the student how many SOUNDS are in each word. (Note: they are counting individual sounds, not syllables and not letters. For instance, *chicken* has 5 sounds.)

1.	*tan*	(answer: 3)	CORRECT_____ INCORRECT_____
2.	*blue*	(answer: 3)	CORRECT_____ INCORRECT_____
3.	bench	(answer: 4)	CORRECT_____ INCORRECT_____
4.	*truck*	(answer: 4)	CORRECT_____ INCORRECT_____
5.	*drill*	(answer: 4)	CORRECT_____ INCORRECT_____
6.	*straw*	(answer: 4)	CORRECT_____ INCORRECT_____
7.	tractor	(answer: 6)	CORRECT_____ INCORRECT_____
8.	*country*	(answer: 6)	CORRECT_____ INCORRECT_____
9.	*synonym*	(answer: 7)	CORRECT_____ INCORRECT_____
10.	*aluminum*	(answer: 8)	CORRECT_____ INCORRECT_____

Task 4 Screener Instructions

(This information for the screener is also offered in video format at https://courses.learnreading.com/courses/dyslexia-screening-videos.)

- Ask the student to read the words on their Student Pages.
- Mark "correct" or "incorrect" in the spaces provided.
- If the student chose to skip a word, mark it incorrect.

Task 4 Student Instructions

(You may present this information to the student yourself, or show them the "Student Instructions" video at https://courses.learnreading.com/courses/dyslexia-screening-videos.)

"For this task, you are going to read a list of words as best as you can. It may be a little difficult, but just do your best. If you try and still feel like you can't read the word, it's okay to say, 'Skip it,' and move on to the next word."

Task 4 Answer Sheet

Directions: Ask the student to READ each word as it is written for them on the Student Pages. If you are unsure of the pronunciation of any word, spell it into your cell phone and ask for the correct pronunciation. This is important because many words are easily missed, even by adults.

1.	*prejudice*	CORRECT_____	INCORRECT_____
2.	*conscious*	CORRECT_____	INCORRECT_____
3.	*mischievous*	CORRECT_____	INCORRECT_____
4.	*pronunciation*	CORRECT_____	INCORRECT_____
5.	*leisure*	CORRECT_____	INCORRECT_____
6.	*suspicion*	CORRECT_____	INCORRECT_____
7.	*choreography*	CORRECT_____	INCORRECT_____
8.	*perennial*	CORRECT_____	INCORRECT_____
9.	*ambidextrous*	CORRECT_____	INCORRECT_____
10.	*compliant*	CORRECT_____	INCORRECT_____

Task 5 Screener Instructions

(This information for the screener is also offered in video format at https://courses.learnreading.com/courses/dyslexia-screening-videos.)

- Ask the student to look at each letter on their Student Page, and tell you the sound that it makes.
- When they come to the vowels, ask the student to tell you the short, or most common, sound.
- If they hesitate for longer than three seconds on any letter, mark it "incorrect."
- Mark "correct" or "incorrect" in the spaces provided. (The correct answer is provided for you.)

Task 5 Student Instructions

(You may present this information to the student yourself, or show them the "Student Instructions" video at https://courses.learnreading.com/courses/dyslexia-screening-videos.)

"For this task, I'd like you to look at a letter and then tell me the sound that it makes. When you come to a vowel, tell me the short, or most common, sound."

Task 5 Answer Sheet

Directions: Ask the student to look at each letter and tell you the sound each one makes. If they hesitate for longer than three seconds, mark it "incorrect." For *a, e, i, o, u*, tell them you want the short, or most common, sound. If they have any questions, tell them to just do their best.

1.	*d*	(answer: /d/ as in *dog*)	CORRECT_____ INCORRECT_____
2.	*u*	(answer: /u/ as in *under*)	CORRECT_____ INCORRECT_____
3.	*q*	(answer: /kw/ as in *queen*)	CORRECT_____ INCORRECT_____
4.	*y*	(answer: /y/ as in *yellow*)	CORRECT_____ INCORRECT_____
5.	*a*	(answer: /ă/ as in *apple*)	CORRECT_____ INCORRECT_____
6.	*w*	(answer: /w/ as in *water*)	CORRECT_____ INCORRECT_____
7.	*i*	(answer: /ĭ/ as in *index*)	CORRECT_____ INCORRECT_____
8.	*x*	(answer: /ks/ as in *fox*)	CORRECT_____ INCORRECT_____
9.	*e*	(answer: /ĕ/ as in *exit*)	CORRECT_____ INCORRECT_____
10.	*o*	(answer: /ŏ/ as in *octopus*)	CORRECT_____ INCORRECT_____

Task 6 Screener Instructions

(This information for the screener is also offered in video format at https://courses.learnreading.com/courses/dyslexia-screening-videos.)

- You will dictate a sound to the student.

- Ask the student what letter, or set of letters, makes that sound.

- The "as in" hints are for the screener only and should *not* be given to the student.

- Ask the student to write their answers in lowercase letters.

- When the student writes their answer, the letters must be facing the correct way for the answer to be marked "correct." If any letters are reversed, mark it "incorrect."

Task 6 Student Instructions

(You may present this information to the student yourself, or show them the "Student Instructions" video at https://courses.learnreading.com/courses/dyslexia-screening-videos.)

"This time I'm going to give you the sound, and you're going to write down the letter or letters that make that sound. For instance, if I said /m/ (the sound of *m*), you would write *m*. If I said /th/ (the sound of *th*), you would write *th*.

Task 6 Answer Sheet

Directions: For the following items, say to the student, "What letter, or letters, makes this sound?" then pronounce the sound for them. (Do *not* say "as in..." because that is only for you to read so you are sure which sound to make. The answer is the bold letter(s) in the example word. *Q* can be written as *Q* or *QU*. Both are correct.) Have them write down their answer in lowercase letters in the space provided on the Student Pages. The letters they write down must be facing the right direction to be marked "correct."

1.	/ch/	(as in **ch**air)	CORRECT_____	INCORRECT_____
2.	/ĕ/	(as in **e**xit)	CORRECT_____	INCORRECT_____
3.	/sh/	(as in **sh**ut)	CORRECT_____	INCORRECT_____
4.	/ŏ/	(as in **o**ctopus)	CORRECT_____	INCORRECT_____
5.	/w/	(as in **w**onder)	CORRECT_____	INCORRECT_____
6.	/ĭ/	(as in **i**ndex)	CORRECT_____	INCORRECT_____
7.	/y/	(as in **y**ellow)	CORRECT_____	INCORRECT_____

8.	/ŭ/	(as in **u**nder)	CORRECT_____ INCORRECT_____
9.	/d/	(as in **d**oor)	CORRECT_____ INCORRECT_____
10.	/kw/	(as in **qu**een)	CORRECT_____ INCORRECT_____

Task 7 Screener Instructions

(This information for the screener is also offered in video format at https://courses.learnreading.com/courses/dyslexia-screening-videos.)

- Dictate three distinct sounds to the student, with clean and clear *breaks* in between each sound.
- Ask the student to repeat the sounds back to you in order.
- The "as in" hints are for the screener only and should *not* be given to the student.
- The sounds must all be repeated back with exactness to be marked "correct." If the student mispronounced or omitted any sounds, or switched the order, mark the answer "incorrect."

Task 7 Student Instructions

(You may present this information to the student yourself, or show them the "Student Instructions" video at https://courses.learnreading.com/courses/dyslexia-screening-videos.)

"For this task, I am going to say three sounds and then you just repeat them exactly as I said them and in the same order. Listen very carefully because some of the sounds may sound similar. Repeat them back to me as best you can."

Task 7 Answer Sheet

Directions: Ask the student to repeat the following sound sequences after you. You will pronounce all three sounds, then they should repeat the three sounds back to you. If they ask you to repeat the sequence, you may repeat it one time. If they say all three sounds back to you *exactly* right, mark it "correct." If they mispronounced (or couldn't remember) even one of the three sounds, mark it "incorrect." (Do *not* say "as in..." because that is only for you so you are sure which sound to make.)

1.	/n/ /m/ /l/ (as in: *name, milk, leg*)	CORRECT_____ INCORRECT_____
2.	/ĭ/ /ŏ/ /ĕ/ (as in: *index, octopus, exit*)	CORRECT_____ INCORRECT_____
3.	/d/ /p/ /b/ (as in: *door, pie, box*)	CORRECT_____ INCORRECT_____
4.	/sh/ /s/ /z/ (as in: *ship, sun, zebra*)	CORRECT_____ INCORRECT_____
5.	/th/ /f/ /j/ (as in: *think, fish, jam*)	CORRECT_____ INCORRECT_____

6.	/ă/ /ĕ/ /ĭ/ (as in: *apple, exit, index*)	CORRECT_____ INCORRECT_____
7.	/ŭ/ /ŏ/ /ă/ (as in: *under, octopus, apple*)	CORRECT_____ INCORRECT_____
8.	/sh/ /ch/ /th/ (as in: *ship, chop, think*)	CORRECT_____ INCORRECT____
9.	/r/ /l/ /n/ (as in: *run, leg, net*)	CORRECT_____ INCORRECT_____
10.	/w/ /y/ /p/ (as in: *water, yellow, pot*)	CORRECT_____ INCORRECT_____

Task 8 Screener Instructions

(This information for the screener is also offered in video format at https://courses.learnreading.com/courses/dyslexia-screening-videos.)

- Important note: when you see a letter in between two slanted lines, it means the sound that that letter makes. For instance, /f/ is the *sound* of *f*, not the letter itself.
- Read the questions to the student, making sure to only say the sound of the letter in between the slanted lines.
- Mark "correct" or "incorrect" in the spaces provided. (The correct answer is provided for you.)

Task 8 Student Instructions

(You may present this information to the student yourself, or show them the "Student Instructions" video at https://courses.learnreading.com/courses/dyslexia-screening-videos.)

"For this task, I am going to say a word. Then, I'm going to ask you to repeat the word but without one of the sounds. For example, I might say *camp*, and then ask you to say *camp* without the /m/. *Camp* without the /m/ is *Cap* (model how to do the task). So listen carefully, take your time, and try your best."

Task 8 Answer Sheet

Directions: Ask the student each question. When you do so, say the sound that they are to remove, not the letter. (FYI: a letter inside of slanted lines, like /f/, means the sound only, not the letter itself.) If they ask you to repeat the question, you may do so one time. The student should tell you the answer, not write it down.

1.	"What would *cat* say without the /k/?" (answer: *at*)	CORRECT_____ INCORRECT_____
2.	"What would *bite* say without the /t/?" (answer: *by*)	CORRECT_____ INCORRECT_____
3.	"What would *flatten* say without the /l/?" (answer: *fatten*)	CORRECT_____ INCORRECT_____

4.	"What would *scram* say without the /r/?" (answer: *scam*)	CORRECT_____	INCORRECT_____
5.	"What would *feast* say without the /s/?" (answer: *feet*)	CORRECT_____	INCORRECT_____
6.	"What would *play* say without the /l/?" (answer: *pay*)	CORRECT_____	INCORRECT_____
7.	"What would *boost* say without the /s/?" (answer: *boot*)	CORRECT_____	INCORRECT_____
8.	"What would *trip* say without the /r/?" (answer: *tip*)	CORRECT_____	INCORRECT_____
9.	"What would *faxed* say without the /k/?" (answer: *fast*)	CORRECT_____	INCORRECT_____
10.	"What would *bottle* say without the /t/?" (answer: *ball*)	CORRECT_____	INCORRECT_____

Task 9 Screener Instructions

(This information for the screener is also offered in video format at https://courses.learnreading.com/courses/dyslexia-screening-videos.)

- Ask the student to look at a picture on their Student Page, say what it is a picture of, and stretch out the sounds in that word (such as *milk* "mmmiiilllk").

- Ask the student to break apart each sound in that word and then mark the dot that represents the sound in the question that you will ask them.

- Mark "correct" or "incorrect" if they identified the correct dot that contained that sound.

Task 9 Student Instructions

(You may present this information to the student yourself, or show them the "Student Instructions" video at https://courses.learnreading.com/courses/dyslexia-screening-videos.)

"For this task, you're going to see some pictures. I want you to tell me what the picture is and then stretch out the sounds in that word. Then I want you to separate each sound in that word with nice, big breaks in between each sound. You will see dots under the picture. I'd like you to point to each dot when you say each sound in that word. Then I'm going to ask where a certain sound is, and you'll just point to, or color in, that dot."

Task 9 Answer Sheet

Directions: As you ask each question, ask the student to follow along with you on their Student Pages. Ask the student to look at each picture and 1) repeat what the picture is, 2) stretch out the sounds in the word, and then 3) separate the sounds within the word and mark the dot on their paper where they hear the sound in question.

1.	Where is the /r/ in *drill*?	(answer: 2nd dot	CORRECT_____ INCORRECT_____
2.	Where is the /l/ in *milk*?	(answer: 3rd dot)	CORRECT_____ INCORRECT_____
3.	Where is the /s/ in *toast*?	(answer: 3rd dot)	CORRECT_____ INCORRECT_____
4.	Where is the /k/ in *monkey*?	(answer: 4th dot)	CORRECT_____ INCORRECT_____
5.	Where is the /h/ in *beehive*?	(answer: 3rd dot)	CORRECT_____ INCORRECT_____
6.	Where is the /b/ in *hamburger*?	(answer: 4th dot)	CORRECT_____ INCORRECT_____
7.	Where is the /ŭ/ in *animals*?	(answer: 5th dot)	CORRECT_____ INCORRECT_____
8.	Where is the /r/ in *umbrella*?	(answer: 4th dot)	CORRECT_____ INCORRECT_____

- The student had difficulty **breaking off** one sound from another in one or more of the words (if so, mark "incorrect" here).   CORRECT_____ INCORRECT_____

- The student had difficulty **articulating** the correct sounds within the word (if so, mark "incorrect" here).   CORRECT _____ INCORRECT _____

Task 10 Screener Instructions

(This information for the screener is also offered in video format at https://courses.learnreading.com/courses/dyslexia-screening-videos.)

- Read the word to the student. Have them repeat the word and then try to say the word backward.
- Mark "correct" or "incorrect" in the spaces provided. (The correct answer is provided for you.)

Task 10 Student Instructions

(You may present this information to the student yourself, or show them the "Student Instructions" video at https://courses.learnreading.com/courses/dyslexia-screening-videos.)

"In this task, I'm going to say a word. You will repeat the word back to me, and then try to say the word backward. For example, if I said the word *cat*. You would repeat that word *cat* and then try to say it backward. That last letter in *cat* would be the first letter if it was said backward. So *cat*, backward, is *tac* (model how to do the task).

Task 10 Answer Sheet

Directions: 1) Read the word (or nonsense word) to the student. 2) Ask them to repeat the word back to you. Then 3) tell them to say the word backward. If they ask you to repeat the word, you may do so one time. They must say every sound in the reversed word *exactly* right to be marked "correct."

(If you are unsure of the correct pronunciation of the word, a "rhymes with" word is provided for you. Please do *not* share this "rhymes with" word with the student. It is only to aid the administrator.)

1.	*tea* (rhymes with *see*) (answer: *eat*)	CORRECT_____ INCORRECT_____
2.	*air* (rhymes with *stare*) (answer: *ray*)	CORRECT_____ INCORRECT_____
3.	*ile* (rhymes with *mile*) (answer: *lie*)	CORRECT_____ INCORRECT_____
4.	*oot* (rhymes with *flute*) (answer: *to*)	CORRECT_____ INCORRECT_____
5.	*eem* (rhymes with *team*) (answer: *me*)	CORRECT_____ INCORRECT_____
6.	*cheap* (rhymes with *sheep*) (answer: *peach*)	CORRECT_____ INCORRECT_____
7.	chum (rhymes with *plum*) (answer: *much*)	CORRECT_____ INCORRECT_____
8.	*stop* (rhymes with *top*) (answer: *pots*)	CORRECT_____ INCORRECT_____
9.	*gums* (rhymes with *chums*) (answer: *smug*)	CORRECT_____ INCORRECT_____
10.	*klim* (rhymes with *slim*) (answer: *milk*)	CORRECT_____ INCORRECT_____

Task 11 Screener Instructions

(This information for the screener is also offered in video format at https://courses.learnreading.com/courses/dyslexia-screening-videos.)

- Ask the student to read aloud the nonsense words on their Student Pages.
- They must get each sound in the word *exactly* correct for it to be marked "correct."
- The "rhymes with" hints are for the screener only and should *not* be given to the student.

Task 11 Student Instructions

(You may present this information to the student yourself, or show them the "Student Instructions" video at https://courses.learnreading.com/courses/dyslexia-screening-videos.)

"On your Student Pages, you're going to see some nonsense words. These are crazy words that you've never seen before. To read them, just use your knowledge of what the letters say."

Task 11 Answer Sheet

Directions: Ask the student to READ each nonsense word on their Student Pages. The student must pronounce each sound in the word *exactly* right for the word to be marked "correct." (A "rhymes with" word is provided for the screener only. Do *not* give the "rhymes with" word to the student.)

1.	*trats* (rhymes with *rats*)	CORRECT_____ INCORRECT_____
2.	*flaspry* (rhymes with *clasp ree'*)	CORRECT_____ INCORRECT_____
3.	*crilth* (rhymes with *filth*)	CORRECT_____ INCORRECT_____
4.	*chulps* (rhymes with *gulps*)	CORRECT_____ INCORRECT_____
5.	*sprisp* (rhymes with *crisp*)	CORRECT_____ INCORRECT_____
6.	*threlps* (rhymes with *helps*)	CORRECT_____ INCORRECT_____
7.	*drothplaits* (rhymes with *cloth plates*)	CORRECT_____ INCORRECT_____
8.	*thrimpstire* (rhymes with *shrimp fire*)	CORRECT_____ INCORRECT_____
9.	*clampstandra* (sounds like *clămp stand rŭh*)	CORRECT_____ INCORRECT_____
10.	*shustrupa* (sounds like *shŭs true pŭh*)	CORRECT_____ INCORRECT_____

Is It Dyslexia?

Grade 6 Results

Task 1: Long-Term Memory

Total Incorrect (or "no" answers): _____

Task 2: Sight Words Knowledge

Total Incorrect: _____

Task 3: Phonemic Awareness

Total Incorrect: _____

Task 4: Reading Grade-Level Words

Total Incorrect: _____

Task 5: Symbol to Sound Knowledge

Total Incorrect: _____

Task 6: Sound to Symbol Knowledge

Total Incorrect: _____

Task 7: Auditory Discrimination/Memory

Total Incorrect: _____

Task 8: Phonemic Awareness

Total Incorrect: _____

Task 9: Phonemic Awareness

Total Incorrect: _____

Task 10: Phonemic Awareness

Total Incorrect: _____

Task 11: Decoding Unfamiliar Words

Total Incorrect: _____

Results from Questionnaire Plus Screening Tasks

1. TOTAL (line 4) on Questionnaire _____
2. TOTAL incorrect answers on Screening Tasks _____
3. **GRAND TOTAL from lines 1 and 2** _____

Grade 6 Conclusions

If the GRAND TOTAL (line 3) **is 14 or greater**, then this student's performance is consistent with someone with dyslexia.

It can be assumed that the severity of dyslexia is in direct relation to **how much greater than 14** the GRAND TOTAL is (14 being mild and 205 being the most severe).

If the GRAND TOTAL **is less than 14**, then dyslexia is likely *not* the probable cause for the student's academic difficulties.

Grade 7 to Adult Screening Packet

This packet contains the following:

- Grade 7 to Adult Screening Questionnaire
- Grade 7 to Adult Screening Questionnaire Answer Sheet
- Grade 7 to Adult Questionnaire Analysis
- Grade 7 to Adult Student Pages (for student's written answers)
- Grade 7 to Adult Tasks Instructions and Answer Sheets (for Tasks 1–11)
- Grade 7 to Adult Results
- Grade 7 to Adult Conclusions

Grade 7 to Adult Screening Questionnaire

(Mark answers on the answer sheet.)

Genetics

1. Does the person's mother have any trouble with reading or spelling?

2. Does the person's father have any trouble with reading or spelling?

3. Are there any other immediate family members who struggle with reading or spelling?

4. Are (or were) there any extended family members (parents, siblings, grandparents, cousins, aunts, uncles) who struggled in school?

Articulation/Speech

5. Did the person have a speech delay (were they a late talker)?

6. Does (did) the person have any articulation or speech issues?

7. Does (did) the person have problems forming certain words correctly?

8. Does (did) the person mispronounce words even after repeated correction?

9. Does (did) the person attend speech therapy?

10. Does (did) the person confuse *i/e*, *m/n*, or *f/th* when they speak?

11. Does (did) the person have difficulty saying words like *aluminum*, *cinnamon*, or *dyslexia*?

12. Does the person have difficulty expressing themself verbally?

13. Does the person have trouble retrieving words, use a lot of *um*s or *uh*s, or use grand gestures with their hands when speaking?

Directionality

14. Is (was) there any left/right confusion?

15. Are there any letter or number reversals continuing beyond the end of first grade, including *b/d* confusion?

16. Does (did) the person have difficulty learning to tie their shoes?

17. Does (did) the person have trouble telling time on an analog clock?

18. Does (did) the person have difficulty remembering the direction of mathematical operations, such as addition and subtraction moving right to left, or the directional movements in long division?

19. Does (did) the person transpose number sequences, such as writing *51* for *15*?

20. Does (did) the person reverse words when reading, such as reading *top* for *pot*?

Memory/Recall

21. Does (did) the person have trouble recalling the names of letters, numbers, or colors?

22. Does the student have difficulty remembering sequences (such as a list of directions, arithmetic steps, spelling sequences, days of the week, or months of the year in order)?

23. Does the student have difficulty on timed math tests?

24. Does the student have trouble with copying (copying slowly and inaccurately)?

25. Does the student have difficulty remembering names?

26. Does the person have trouble remembering important dates?

27. Does the student have difficulty remembering the order of the alphabet?

28. Does the student have trouble recalling the days of the week or months of the year in order?

29. Does the student have trouble recalling the names of familiar objects, instead replacing them with words like *stuff* or *things*?

30. Does the student have trouble remembering multiple-step directions?

31. Does the person have difficulty remembering a pin number, address, or phone number?

32. Does the person have trouble with alphabetizing or with remembering the order of the alphabet?

33. Does the person have a hard time recalling math facts quickly?

Phonemic Awareness/Auditory Processing

34. Does (did) the person have difficulty with rhyming?

35. Does the person have problems repeating back sounds accurately and in order?

36. Does (did) the person have trouble breaking off the first or last sound of a word?

37. Does (did) the person have trouble identifying the vowel sound within a word?

38. Does (did) the person confuse the short *i* and the short *e* sound when saying or reading words?

39. Does (did) the person have trouble understanding the connection between letters and sounds?

40. Does (did) the person have trouble isolating and manipulating the sounds within a word?

Reading

41. Does (did) the person read below grade level?

42. Does the person have trouble decoding unfamiliar words?

43. Is the person's reading slow and labor intensive?

44. Does (did) the person have trouble reading sight words or high frequency words?

45. Does the person forget how to read a word from one moment to the next?

46. Does the person have trouble comprehending what they read?

47. Would the person prefer *not* to be called on to read aloud in class or in public? Would they prefer to avoid reading, especially aloud?

48. Does (did) the person guess at words based on the size, shape, context, or picture clues?

49. Does (did) the person skip or misread small, simple words when reading?

50. Is the student easily frustrated when reading?

51. Does the person spend an unusually long time completing tasks that involve reading?

52. Does (did) the person omit the suffixes or endings of words?

53. Does (did) the person have trouble recognizing their mistakes when reading?

54. Does the person rarely read for pleasure?

55. Does the person require multiple readings to comprehend the material?

56. Does (did) the person omit, substitute, add, or transpose letters when reading?

Spelling/Writing

57. Does (did) the person have trouble with spelling?

58. Does (did) the person spend an unusually long time completing tasks that involve writing?

59. Does (did) the person have trouble spelling sight words or high frequency words?

60. Does (did) the person forget how to spell a word from one moment to the next?

61. Do (did) others have trouble reading what the student wrote, due to spelling errors?

62. Is the person's intelligence not reflected in their writing?

63. When writing, will the person use words that they know how to spell, instead of those that they would prefer to use?

64. Does the person have trouble remembering and applying spelling rules?

65. Does (did) the person use unpredictable, illogical spelling?

66. Does (did) the person omit, substitute, add, or transpose letters when spelling?

67. Does the person have difficulty using spell check or a dictionary?

Additional Learning Experiences

68. Has the person attended special academic classes, reading groups, or had outside tutoring?

69. Does (did) the person have trouble learning a foreign language in print (reading and writing in the foreign language)?

70. Does (did) the person have difficulty reading printed music?

71. Does (did) the person have trouble taking notes in class?

72. Has the person pretended to be sick or otherwise unable to attend school or perform academically?

73. Can the person answer questions orally better than in print?

74. Does the person need more time than others to process verbal information?

75. Does (did) the person have poor self-esteem resulting from poor academic performance?

76. Does (did) the person experience anxiety or high levels of stress surrounding academics?

Strengths/Talents

77. Does the person have a high capacity for learning?

78. Is the person gifted athletically?

79. Is the person gifted musically?

80. Is the person gifted artistically?

81. Is the person extremely creative?

82. Is the person highly imaginative?

83. Does (did) the person have surprising maturity?

84. Does the person enjoy, and are they good at, puzzles (excellent spatial reasoning)?

85. Is the person extremely curious?

86. Is the person able to easily comprehend stories that they *hear* or *listen to*?

87. Is the person able to easily remember song lyrics?

88. Is the person mechanically inclined (good with their hands, such as working with Legos, building models, taking things apart and putting them back together again, etc.)?

89. Does the person have excellent creative writing skills?

90. Does the person have excellent thinking and reasoning skills?

91. Does the person have the ability to produce unique, out-of-the-box ideas?

92. Is the person gifted at seeing the big picture?

93. Is the person highly empathetic?

94. Is the person highly resilient?

95. Does the person have excellent interpersonal skills (maintains friendships easily)?

Grade 7 to Adult Questionnaire Answer Sheet

Genetics

1.	Yes _____	Somewhat or Unsure _____	No _____
2.	Yes _____	Somewhat or Unsure _____	No _____
3.	Yes _____	Somewhat or Unsure _____	No _____
4.	Yes _____	Somewhat or Unsure _____	No _____

Articulation/Speech

5.	Yes _____	Somewhat or Unsure _____	No _____
6.	Yes _____	Somewhat or Unsure _____	No _____
7.	Yes _____	Somewhat or Unsure _____	No _____
8.	Yes _____	Somewhat or Unsure _____	No _____
9.	Yes _____	Somewhat or Unsure _____	No _____
10.	Yes _____	Somewhat or Unsure _____	No _____
11.	Yes _____	Somewhat or Unsure _____	No _____
12.	Yes _____	Somewhat or Unsure _____	No _____
13.	Yes _____	Somewhat or Unsure _____	No _____

Directionality

14.	Yes _____	Somewhat or Unsure _____	No _____
15.	Yes _____	Somewhat or Unsure _____	No _____
16.	Yes _____	Somewhat or Unsure _____	No _____
17.	Yes _____	Somewhat or Unsure _____	No _____
18.	Yes _____	Somewhat or Unsure _____	No _____
19.	Yes _____	Somewhat or Unsure _____	No _____
20.	Yes _____	Somewhat or Unsure _____	No _____

Memory/Recall

21. Yes _____   Somewhat or Unsure _____   No _____
22. Yes _____   Somewhat or Unsure _____   No _____
23. Yes _____   Somewhat or Unsure _____   No _____
24. Yes _____   Somewhat or Unsure _____   No _____
25. Yes _____   Somewhat or Unsure _____   No _____
26. Yes _____   Somewhat or Unsure _____   No _____
27. Yes _____   Somewhat or Unsure _____   No _____
28. Yes _____   Somewhat or Unsure _____   No _____
29. Yes _____   Somewhat or Unsure _____   No _____
30. Yes _____   Somewhat or Unsure _____   No _____
31. Yes _____   Somewhat or Unsure _____   No _____
32. Yes _____   Somewhat or Unsure _____   No _____
33. Yes _____   Somewhat or Unsure _____   No _____

Phonemic Awareness/Auditory Processing

34. Yes _____   Somewhat or Unsure _____   No _____
35. Yes _____   Somewhat or Unsure _____   No _____
36. Yes _____   Somewhat or Unsure _____   No _____
37. Yes _____   Somewhat or Unsure _____   No _____
38. Yes _____   Somewhat or Unsure _____   No _____
39. Yes _____   Somewhat or Unsure _____   No _____
40. Yes _____   Somewhat or Unsure _____   No _____

Reading

41. Yes _____   Somewhat or Unsure _____   No _____
42. Yes _____   Somewhat or Unsure _____   No _____
43. Yes _____   Somewhat or Unsure _____   No _____

44.	Yes _____	Somewhat or Unsure _____	No _____
45.	Yes _____	Somewhat or Unsure _____	No _____
46.	Yes _____	Somewhat or Unsure _____	No _____
47.	Yes _____	Somewhat or Unsure _____	No _____
48.	Yes _____	Somewhat or Unsure _____	No _____
49.	Yes _____	Somewhat or Unsure _____	No _____
50.	Yes _____	Somewhat or Unsure _____	No _____
51.	Yes _____	Somewhat or Unsure _____	No _____
52.	Yes _____	Somewhat or Unsure _____	No _____
53.	Yes _____	Somewhat or Unsure _____	No _____
54.	Yes _____	Somewhat or Unsure _____	No _____
55.	Yes _____	Somewhat or Unsure _____	No _____
56.	Yes _____	Somewhat or Unsure _____	No _____

Spelling/Writing

57.	Yes _____	Somewhat or Unsure _____	No _____
58.	Yes _____	Somewhat or Unsure _____	No _____
59.	Yes _____	Somewhat or Unsure _____	No _____
60.	Yes _____	Somewhat or Unsure _____	No _____
61.	Yes _____	Somewhat or Unsure _____	No _____
62.	Yes _____	Somewhat or Unsure _____	No _____
63.	Yes _____	Somewhat or Unsure _____	No _____
64.	Yes _____	Somewhat or Unsure _____	No _____
65.	Yes _____	Somewhat or Unsure _____	No _____
66.	Yes _____	Somewhat or Unsure _____	No _____
67.	Yes _____	Somewhat or Unsure _____	No _____

Is It Dyslexia?

Additional Learning Experiences

68. Yes _____   Somewhat or Unsure _____   No _____
69. Yes _____   Somewhat or Unsure _____   No _____
70. Yes _____   Somewhat or Unsure _____   No _____
71. Yes _____   Somewhat or Unsure _____   No _____
72. Yes _____   Somewhat or Unsure _____   No _____
73. Yes _____   Somewhat or Unsure _____   No _____
74. Yes _____   Somewhat or Unsure _____   No _____
75. Yes _____   Somewhat or Unsure _____   No _____
76. Yes _____   Somewhat or Unsure _____   No _____

Strengths/Talents

77. Yes _____   Somewhat or Unsure _____   No _____
78. Yes _____   Somewhat or Unsure _____   No _____
79. Yes _____   Somewhat or Unsure _____   No _____
80. Yes _____   Somewhat or Unsure _____   No _____
81. Yes _____   Somewhat or Unsure _____   No _____
82. Yes _____   Somewhat or Unsure _____   No _____
83. Yes _____   Somewhat or Unsure _____   No _____
84. Yes _____   Somewhat or Unsure _____   No _____
85. Yes _____   Somewhat or Unsure _____   No _____
86. Yes _____   Somewhat or Unsure _____   No _____
87. Yes _____   Somewhat or Unsure _____   No _____
88. Yes _____   Somewhat or Unsure _____   No _____
89. Yes _____   Somewhat or Unsure _____   No _____
90. Yes _____   Somewhat or Unsure _____   No _____
91. Yes _____   Somewhat or Unsure _____   No _____
92. Yes _____   Somewhat or Unsure _____   No _____

93.   Yes _____   Somewhat or Unsure _____   No _____

94.   Yes _____   Somewhat or Unsure _____   No _____

95.   Yes _____   Somewhat or Unsure _____   No _____

Grade 7 to Adult Questionnaire Analysis

All Areas except Strengths/Talents

1.	Count the number of "yes" answers in all areas **except** Strengths/Talents.	_____
2.	Count the number of "somewhat" answers in these areas and divide by 2.	_____
3.	Add lines 1 and 2 for the **TOTAL** in these areas.	_____

If the **TOTAL** in these areas is **3 or more,** then the screener should proceed to the screening tasks.

Strengths/Talents

4.	Count the number of "yes" answers in Strengths/Talents.	_____
5.	Count the number of "somewhat" answers and divide by 2.	_____
6.	Add lines 4 and 5 for the **TOTAL** in these areas.	_____
7.	Add lines 3 and 6 for the **GRAND TOTAL.**	_____

Any number greater than 3 in line 7 (GRAND TOTAL) increases the likelihood that dyslexia is present.

Grade 7 to Adult Student Pages

(Copy these three pages for the student to write on during the screening.)

On these pages, the student will complete the work for tasks that involve writing: Tasks 1, 2, 4, 5, 6, 9, and 11. (The remaining tasks require dictation only, which the screener will record on the Screener Answer Sheet.)

Task 1: Write the Alphabet

_____

_____

_____

Task 2: Spelling Sight Words

_____

1. _____

   _____

2. _____

   _____

3. _____

   _____

4. _____

   _____

5. _____

   _____

6. _____

   _____

7. _____

   _____

8. _____

   _____

9. _____

    _____

10. _____

    _____

Task 4: Reading Grade-Level Words

1.	*ambivalent*	6.	*heterogenous*
2.	*calumny*	7.	*surreptitious*
3.	*constituent*	8.	*ubiquitous*
4.	*eclectic*	9.	*virtuoso*
5.	*egregious*	10.	*zephyr*

Task 5: Symbol to Sound Knowledge

1. d

2. u

3. q

4. y

5. a

6. w

7. i

8. x

9. e

10. o

Task 6: Write the Letter(s)

1.	_____	6.	_____
2.	_____	7.	_____
3.	_____	8.	_____
4.	_____	9.	_____
5.	_____	10.	_____

Task 9: Phonemic Awareness 2 (Isolation)

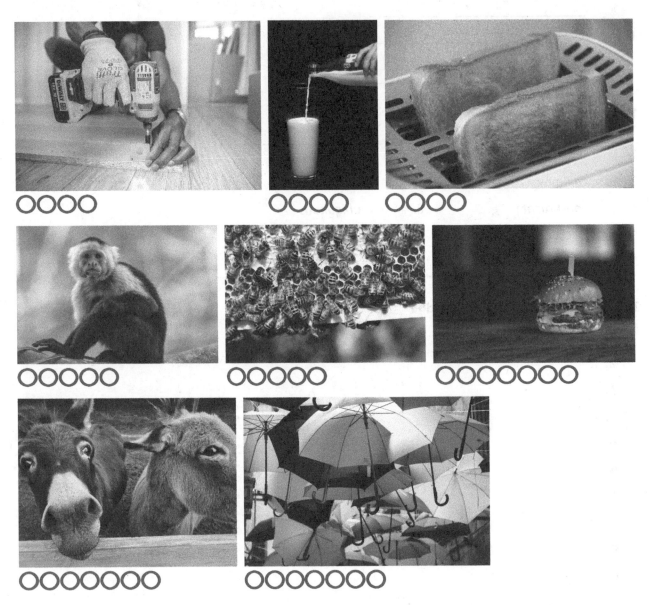

Source: https://docs.google.com/document/d/1v_W0fHCmiZ6Fm0VCZVPUsEWSAU8-YsknIDpwNJZroKY/edit

Is It Dyslexia?

Task 11: Reading Unfamiliar Words

1.	*phlendriplond*	6.	*fancitrinder*
2.	*cemaplidroid*	7.	*phlumpy*
3.	*blyndroama*	8.	*chastidoolander*
4.	*cystaclandrophy*	9.	*thrompolistry*
5.	*drompilpha*	10.	*flestoppler*

Grade 7 to Adult Instructions and Answer Sheets

Task 1 Screener Instructions

(This information for the screener is also offered in video format at https://courses.learnreading.com/courses/dyslexia-screening-videos.)

- Ask the student to write the alphabet in lowercase letters.
- There should be no help, no copying, and no erasing or crossing out.
- Watch for any hints of directionality confusion when they go to write a letter. Be aware of any pauses or hesitations, especially at *b/d/p/q*.
- Watch for confusion midway through, or if they need to start again at the beginning and use the alphabet song to help them determine the next letter.
- Watch for any reversals (writing a letter backward), inversions (writing a letter upside down), or errors (omitting a letter or writing it in the wrong sequence).
- After you have carefully watched the student complete the task, record their responses by answering "true" or "no" in the spaces provided.

Task 1 Student Instructions

(You may present this information to the student yourself, or show them the "Student Instructions" video at https://courses.learnreading.com/courses/dyslexia-screening-videos.)

"In this task, you're going to write the alphabet. You're going to use a pen (or a pencil without an eraser). This is because I want to see the way your brain works, and what you write down first. So, if you don't like what you wrote and are tempted to cross it out, don't worry! Just draw a box around the answer you didn't like, so I can still see what it was, and then put the answer you do want right next to or above it. And please use only lowercase letters in this screening. Okay! Let's get started!"

Task 1 Answer Sheet

Directions: Ask the student to write the alphabet in *lowercase letters* in the space provided on the Student Pages, with no help, no copying, and no erasing.

1.	The student made it to the end without any errors.	TRUE_____ NO_____
2.	The letters all faced the correct direction. (There were no reversals or inversions.)	TRUE_____ NO_____

3.	The student wrote the alphabet easily and quickly, with no hesitations, questions, or restarts.	TRUE_____ NO_____
4.	There was no hesitation at *b/d* or *p/q*. (The student did not wonder which way the letter faced.)	TRUE_____ NO____

Task 2 Screener Instructions

(This information for the screener is also offered in video format at https://courses.learnreading.com/courses/dyslexia-screening-videos.)

- You will dictate sight words for the student to spell.
- You can repeat the word and/or use it in a sentence, but no hints as to the spelling.
- Mark "correct" or "incorrect" in the spaces provided.

Task 2 Student Instructions

(You may present this information to the student yourself, or show them the "Student Instructions" video at https://courses.learnreading.com/courses/dyslexia-screening-videos.)

"You might already know that sight words are words that don't follow typical spelling rules. They can sometimes be tricky to spell. I'm going to say a few of these sight words and I'd like for you to try to spell them the best that you can."

Task 2 Answer Sheet

Directions: Ask the student to spell the following words in the space provided on the Student Pages, with no erasing or changing. Mark "correct" or "incorrect." (If they spelled the word incorrectly at first, then changed their mind and went to fix it, mark it "incorrect" even if their second attempt was correct.)

1.	*thorough* (as in complete)	CORRECT_____ INCORRECT_____
2.	*Wednesday*	CORRECT_____ INCORRECT_____
3.	*ocean*	CORRECT_____ INCORRECT_____
4.	*people*	CORRECT_____ INCORRECT_____
5.	*honest*	CORRECT_____ INCORRECT_____
6.	*ocean*	CORRECT_____ INCORRECT_____
7.	*half*	CORRECT_____ INCORRECT_____

8.	*laugh*	CORRECT_____ INCORRECT_____
9.	*machine*	CORRECT_____ INCORRECT_____
10.	*language*	CORRECT_____ INCORRECT_____

Task 3 Screener Instructions

(This information for the screener is also offered in video format at https://courses.learnreading.com/courses/dyslexia-screening-videos).

- You will dictate words to the student and ask them to count how many sounds they hear in a word (not syllables or letters).
- Mark "correct" or "incorrect" in the spaces provided. (The answer is next to the word.)

Task 3 Student Instructions

(You may present this information to the student yourself, or show them the "Student Instructions" video at https://courses.learnreading.com/courses/dyslexia-screening-videos.)

"For this task, you are simply going to be counting sounds. I am going to say a word, and you will count how many sounds you hear in that word. If you know how to spell the word, try not to think about the letters because I don't want you to count the letters, just the sounds. Sometimes there are more letters in a word than there are sounds, so just focus on the sounds, and tell me how many you hear."

Task 3 Answer Sheet

Directions: Ask the student how many SOUNDS are in each word. (Note: they are counting individual sounds, not syllables and not letters. For instance, *chicken* has 5 sounds.)

1.	*tan*	(answer: 3)	CORRECT_____ INCORRECT_____
2.	*blue*	(answer: 3)	CORRECT_____ INCORRECT_____
3.	*bench*	(answer: 4)	CORRECT_____ INCORRECT_____
4.	*truck*	(answer: 4)	CORRECT_____ INCORRECT_____
5.	*drill*	(answer: 4)	CORRECT_____ INCORRECT_____
6.	*straw*	(answer: 4)	CORRECT_____ INCORRECT_____
7.	*tractor*	(answer: 6)	CORRECT_____ INCORRECT_____

8.	*country*	(answer: 6)	CORRECT_____ INCORRECT_____
9.	*synonym*	(answer: 7)	CORRECT_____ INCORRECT_____
10.	*aluminum*	(answer: 8)	CORRECT_____ INCORRECT_____

Task 4 Screener Instructions

(This information for the screener is also offered in video format at https://courses.learnreading.com/courses/dyslexia-screening-videos.)

- Ask the student to read the words on their Student Pages.
- Mark "correct" or "incorrect" in the spaces provided.

If the student chose to skip a word, mark it incorrect.

Task 4 Student Instructions

(You may present this information to the student yourself, or show them the "Student Instructions" video at https://courses.learnreading.com/courses/dyslexia-screening-videos.)

"For this task, you are going to read a list of words as best as you can. It may be a little difficult, but just do your best. If you try and still feel like you can't read the word, it's okay to say, 'Skip it,' and move on to the next word."

Task 4 Answer Sheet

Directions: Ask the student to READ each word as it is written for them on the Student Pages. If you are unsure of the pronunciation of any word, spell it into your cell phone and ask for the correct pronunciation. This is important because some words are easily missed, even by adults.

1.	*ambivalent*	CORRECT_____ INCORRECT_____
2.	*calumny*	CORRECT_____ INCORRECT_____
3.	*constituent*	CORRECT_____ INCORRECT_____
4.	*eclectic*	CORRECT_____ INCORRECT_____
5.	*egregious*	CORRECT_____ INCORRECT_____
6.	*heterogenous*	CORRECT_____ INCORRECT_____
7.	*surreptitious*	CORRECT_____ INCORRECT_____

8.	_ubiquitous_	CORRECT_____ INCORRECT_____
9.	_virtuoso_	CORRECT_____ INCORRECT_____
10.	_zephyr_	CORRECT_____ INCORRECT_____

Task 5 Screener Instructions

(This information for the screener is also offered in video format at https://courses.learnreading.com/courses/dyslexia-screening-videos.)

- Ask the student to look at each letter on their Student Page and tell you the sound that it makes.
- When they come to the vowels, ask the student to tell you the short, or most common, sound.
- If they hesitate for longer than three seconds on any letter, mark it "incorrect."
- Mark "correct" or "incorrect" in the spaces provided. (The correct answer is provided for you.)

Task 5 Student Instructions

(You may present this information to the student yourself, or show them the "Student Instructions" video at https://courses.learnreading.com/courses/dyslexia-screening-videos.)

"For this task, I'd like you to look at a letter and then tell me the sound that it makes. When you come to a vowel, tell me the short, or most common, sound."

Task 5 Answer Sheet

Directions: Ask the student to look at each letter and tell you the sound each one makes. If they hesitate for longer than three seconds, mark it "incorrect." For _a, e, i, o, u_, tell them you want the short, or most common, sound. If they have any questions, tell them to just do their best.

1.	_d_	(answer: /d/ as in _dog_)	CORRECT_____ INCORRECT_____
2.	_u_	(answer: /u/ as in _under_)	CORRECT_____ INCORRECT_____
3.	_q_	(answer: /kw/ as in _queen_)	CORRECT_____ INCORRECT_____
4.	_y_	(answer: /y/ as in _yellow_)	CORRECT_____ INCORRECT_____
5.	_a_	(answer: /ă/ as in _apple_)	CORRECT_____ INCORRECT_____
6.	_w_	(answer: /w/ as in _water_)	CORRECT_____ INCORRECT_____
7.	_i_	(answer: /ĭ/ as in _index_)	CORRECT_____ INCORRECT_____
8.	_x_	(answer: /ks/ as in _fox_)	CORRECT_____ INCORRECT_____

9.	e	(answer: /ĕ/ as in *exit*)	CORRECT_____ INCORRECT_____
10.	o	(answer: /ŏ/ as in *octopu*s)	CORRECT_____ INCORRECT_____

Task 6 Screener Instructions

(This information for the screener is also offered in video format at https://courses.learnreading.com/courses/dyslexia-screening-videos.)

- You will dictate a sound to the student.
- Ask the student what letter, or set of letters, makes that sound.
- The "as in" hints are for the screener only and should *not* be given to the student.
- Ask the student to write their answers in lowercase letters.
- When the student writes their answer, the letters must be facing the correct way for the answer to be marked "correct." If any letters are reversed, mark it "incorrect."

Task 6 Student Instructions

(You may present this information to the student yourself, or show them the "Student Instructions" video at https://courses.learnreading.com/courses/dyslexia-screening-videos.)

"This time I'm going to give you the sound, and you're going to write down the letter or letters that make that sound. For instance, if I said /m/ (the sound of *m*), you would write *m*. If I said /th/ (the sound of *th*), you would write *th*.

Task 6 Answer Sheet

Directions: For the following items, say to the student, "What letter, or letters, makes this sound?" then pronounce the sound for them. (Do *not* say "as in..." because that is only for you to read so you are sure which sound to make. The answer is the bold letter(s) in the example word. *Q* can be written as *Q* or *QU*. Both are correct.) Have them write down their answer in lowercase letters in the space provided on the Student Pages. The letters they write down must be facing the right direction to be marked "correct."

1.	/ch/	(as in **ch**air)	CORRECT_____ INCORRECT_____
2.	/ĕ/	(as in **e**xit)	CORRECT_____ INCORRECT_____
3.	/sh/	(as in **sh**ut)	CORRECT_____ INCORRECT_____

4.	/ŏ/	(as in *octopus*)	CORRECT_____ INCORRECT_____
5.	/w/	(as in *wonder*)	CORRECT_____ INCORRECT_____
6.	/ĭ/	(as in *index*)	CORRECT_____ INCORRECT_____
7.	/y/	(as in *yellow*)	CORRECT_____ INCORRECT_____
8.	/ŭ/	(as in *under*)	CORRECT_____ INCORRECT_____
9.	/d/	(as in *door*)	CORRECT_____ INCORRECT_____
10.	/kw/	(as in *queen*)	CORRECT_____ INCORRECT_____

Task 7 Screener Instructions

(This information for the screener is also offered in video format at https://courses.learnreading.com/courses/dyslexia-screening-videos.)

- Dictate three distinct sounds to the student, with clean and clear *break*s in between each sound.
- Ask the student to repeat the sounds back to you in order.
- The "as in" hints are for the screener only and should *not* be given to the student.
- The sounds must all be repeated back with exactness to be marked "correct." If the student mispronounced or omitted any sounds, or switched the order, mark the answer "incorrect."

Task 7 Student Instructions

(You may present this information to the student yourself, or show them the "Student Instructions" video at https://courses.learnreading.com/courses/dyslexia-screening-videos.)

"For this task, I am going to say three sounds and then you just repeat them exactly as I said them and in the same order. Listen very carefully because some of the sounds may sound similar. Repeat them back to me as best you can."

Task 7 Answer Sheet

Directions: Ask the student to repeat the following sound sequences after you. You will pronounce all three sounds, then they should repeat the three sounds back to you. If they ask you to repeat the sequence, you may repeat it one time. If they say all three sounds back to you *exactly* right, mark it "correct." If they mispronounced (or couldn't remember) even one of the three sounds, mark it "incorrect." (Do *not* say "as in..." because that is only for you so you are sure which sound to make.)

Is It Dyslexia?

1.	/n/ /m/ /l/ (as in: *name, milk, leg*)	CORRECT_____ INCORRECT_____
2.	/ĭ/ /ŏ/ /ĕ/ (as in: *index, octopus, exit*)	CORRECT_____ INCORRECT_____
3.	/d/ /p/ /b/ (as in: *door, pie, box*)	CORRECT_____ INCORRECT_____
4.	/sh/ /s/ /z/ (as in: *ship, sun, zebra*)	CORRECT_____ INCORRECT_____
5.	/th/ /f/ /j/ (as in: *think, fish, jam*)	CORRECT_____ INCORRECT_____
6.	/ă/ /ĕ/ /ĭ/ (as in: *apple, exit, index*)	CORRECT_____ INCORRECT_____
7.	/ŭ/ /ŏ/ /ă/ (as in: *under, octopus, apple*)	CORRECT_____ INCORRECT_____
8.	/sh/ /ch/ /th/ (as in: *ship, chop, think*)	CORRECT_____ INCORRECT_____
9.	/r/ /l/ /n/ (as in: *run, leg, net*)	CORRECT_____ INCORRECT_____
10.	/w/ /y/ /p/ (as in: *water, yellow, pot*)	CORRECT_____ INCORRECT_____

Task 8 Screener Instructions

(This information for the screener is also offered in video format at https://courses.learnreading.com/ courses/dyslexia-screening-videos.)

- Important note: when you see a letter in between two slanted lines, it means the sound that that letter makes. For instance, /f/ is the *sound* of *f*, not the letter itself.
- Read the questions to the student, making sure to only say the sound of the letter in between the slanted lines.
- Mark "correct" or "incorrect" in the spaces provided. (The correct answer is provided for you.)

Task 8 Student Instructions

(You may present this information to the student yourself, or show them the "Student Instructions" video at https://courses.learnreading.com/courses/dyslexia-screening-videos.)

"For this task, I am going to say a word. Then, I'm going to ask you to repeat the word but without one of the sounds. For example, I might say *camp*, and then ask you to say *camp* without the /m/. *Camp* without the /m/ is *Cap* (model how to do the task). So listen carefully, take your time, and try your best."

Task 8 Answer Sheet

Directions: Ask the student each question. When you do so, say the sound that they are to remove, not the letter. (FYI: a letter inside of slanted lines, like /f/, means the sound only, not the letter itself.) If

they ask you to repeat the question, you may do so one time. The student should tell you the answer, not write it down.

1.	"What would *cat* say without the /k/?" (answer: *at*)	CORRECT_____	INCORRECT_____
2.	"What would *bite* say without the /t/?" (answer: *by*)	CORRECT_____	INCORRECT_____
3.	"What would *flatten* say without the /l/?" (answer: *fatten*)	CORRECT_____	INCORRECT_____
4.	"What would *scram* say without the /r/?" (answer: *scam*)	CORRECT_____	INCORRECT_____
5.	"What would *feast* say without the /s/?" (answer: *feet*)	CORRECT_____	INCORRECT_____
6.	"What would *play* say without the /l/?" (answer: *pay*)	CORRECT_____	INCORRECT_____
7.	"What would *boost* say without the /s/?" (answer: *boot*)	CORRECT_____	INCORRECT_____
8.	"What would *trip* say without the /r/?" (answer: *tip*)	CORRECT_____	INCORRECT_____
9.	"What would *faxed* say without the /k/?" (answer: *fast*)	CORRECT_____	INCORRECT_____
11.	"What would *bottle* say without the /t/?" (answer: *ball*)	CORRECT_____	INCORRECT_____

Task 9 Screener Instructions

(This information for the screener is also offered in video format at https://courses.learnreading.com/courses/dyslexia-screening-videos.)

- Ask the student to look at a picture on their Student Page, say what it is a picture of, and stretch out the sounds in that word (such as *milk* "mmmiiillllk").
- Ask the student to break apart each sound in that word and then mark the dot that represents the sound in the question that you will ask them.
- Mark "correct" or "incorrect" if they identified the correct dot that contained that sound.

Task 9 Student Instructions

(You may present this information to the student yourself, or show them the "Student Instructions" video at https://courses.learnreading.com/courses/dyslexia-screening-videos.)

"For this task, you're going to see some pictures. I want you to tell me what the picture is and then stretch out the sounds in that word. Then I want you to separate each sound in that word with nice, big breaks in between each sound. You will see dots under the picture. I'd like you to point to each dot when you say each sound in that word. Then I'm going to ask where a certain sound is, and you'll just point to, or color in, that dot."

Task 9 Answer Sheet

Directions: As you ask each question, ask the student to follow along with you on their Student Pages. Ask the student to look at each picture and 1) repeat what the picture is, 2) stretch out the sounds in the word, and then 3) separate the sounds within the word and mark the dot on their paper where they hear the sound in question.

1.	Where is the /r/ in *drill*?	(answer: 2nd dot)	CORRECT_____	INCORRECT_____
2.	Where is the /l/ in *milk*?	(answer: 3rd dot)	CORRECT_____	INCORRECT_____
3.	Where is the /s/ in *toast*?	(answer: 3rd dot)	CORRECT_____	INCORRECT_____
4.	Where is the /k/ in *monkey*?	(answer: 4th dot)	CORRECT_____	INCORRECT_____
5.	Where is the /h/ in *beehive*?	(answer: 3rd dot)	CORRECT_____	INCORRECT_____
6.	Where is the /b/ in *hamburger*?	(answer: 4th dot)	CORRECT_____	INCORRECT_____
7.	Where is the /ŭ/ in *animals*?	(answer: 5th dot)	CORRECT_____	INCORRECT_____
8.	Where is the /r/ in *umbrella*?	(answer: 4th dot)	CORRECT_____	INCORRECT_____

- The student had difficulty **breaking off** one sound from another   CORRECT_____ INCORRECT_____
  in one or more of the words (if so, mark "incorrect" here).

- The student had difficulty **articulating** the correct sounds   CORRECT _____ INCORRECT _____
  within the word (if so, mark "incorrect" here).

Task 10 Screener Instructions

(This information for the screener is also offered in video format at https://courses.learnreading.com/courses/dyslexia-screening-videos.)

- Read the word to the student. Have them repeat the word and then try to say the word backward.

- Mark "correct" or "incorrect" in the spaces provided. (The correct answer is provided for you.)

Task 10 Student Instructions

(You may present this information to the student yourself, or show them the "Student Instructions" video at https://courses.learnreading.com/courses/dyslexia-screening-videos.)

"In this task, I'm going to say a word. You will repeat the word back to me, and then try to say the word backward. For example, if I said the word *cat*. You would repeat that word *cat* and then try to say it backward. That last letter in *cat* would be the first letter if it was said backward. So *cat*, backward, is *tac* (model how to do the task).

Task 10 Answer Sheet

Directions: 1) Read the word (or nonsense word) to the student. 2) Ask them to repeat the word back to you. Then 3) tell them to say the word backward. If they ask you to repeat the word, you may do so one time. They must say every sound in the reversed word *exactly* right to be marked "correct." (If you are unsure of the correct pronunciation of the word, a "rhymes with" word is provided for you. Please do *not* share this "rhymes with" word with the student. It is only to aid the administrator.)

1.	*tea* (rhymes with *see*)	(answer: *eat*)	CORRECT_____	INCORRECT_____
2.	*air* (rhymes with *stare*)	(answer: *ray*)	CORRECT_____	INCORRECT_____
3.	*ile* (rhymes with *mile*)	(answer: *lie*)	CORRECT_____	INCORRECT_____
4.	*oot* (rhymes with *flute*)	(answer: *to*)	CORRECT_____	INCORRECT_____
5.	*eem* (rhymes with *team*)	(answer: *me*)	CORRECT_____	INCORRECT_____
6.	*cheap* (rhymes with *sheep*)	(answer: *peach*)	CORRECT_____	INCORRECT_____
7.	*chum* (rhymes with *plum*)	(answer: *much*)	CORRECT_____	INCORRECT_____
8.	*stop* (rhymes with *top*)	(answer: *pots*)	CORRECT_____	INCORRECT_____
9.	*gums* (rhymes with *chums*)	(answer: *smug*)	CORRECT_____	INCORRECT_____
10.	*klim* (rhymes with *slim*)	(answer: *milk*)	CORRECT_____	INCORRECT___

Task 11 Screener Instructions

(This information for the screener is also offered in video format at https://courses.learnreading.com/courses/dyslexia-screening-videos.)

- Ask the student to read aloud the nonsense words on their Student Pages.
- They must get each sound in the word *exactly* correct for it to be marked "correct."
- The "rhymes with" hints are for the screener only and should *not* be given to the student.

Task 11 Student Instructions

(You may present this information to the student yourself, or show them the "Student Instructions" video at https://courses.learnreading.com/courses/dyslexia-screening-videos.)

"On your Student Pages, you're going to see some nonsense words. These are crazy words that you've never seen before. To read them, just use your knowledge of what the letters say."

Task 11 Answer Sheet

Directions: Ask the student to READ each nonsense word on their Student Pages. The student must pronounce each sound in the word *exactly* right for the word to be marked "correct." (A "rhymes with" word is provided for the screener only. Do *not* give the "rhymes with" word to the student.)

1.   *phlendriplond* (sounds like: *flĕn drĭp lŏnd*)   CORRECT_____ INCORRECT_____

2.   *cemaplidroid* (sounds like: *sĕm ăp lĭh droid*)   CORRECT_____ INCORRECT_____

3.   *blyndroama* (sounds like: *blĭn drō mā*)   CORRECT_____ INCORRECT____

4.   *cystaclandrophy* (sounds like: *sĭs tŭh clăn drō fee*) CORRECT_____ INCORRECT_____

5.   *drompilpha* (sounds like: *drŏm pĭll fŭh*)   CORRECT_____ INCORRECT_____

6.   *fancitrinder* (sounds like: *făn sĭh trĭn der*)   CORRECT_____ INCORRECT_____

7.   *phlumpy* (sounds like: *flŭm pee*)   CORRECT_____ INCORRECT_____

8.   *chastidoolander* (sounds like: *chăs tĭh doo lănd er*) CORRECT_____ INCORRECT_____

9.   *thrompolistry* (sounds like: *thrŏm pō lĭst ree*)   CORRECT_____ INCORRECT_____

10.   *flestoppler* (sounds like: *flĕs tŏp ler*)   CORRECT_____ INCORRECT_____

Grade 7 to Adult Results

Task 1: Long-Term Memory

Total Incorrect (or "no" answers):   _____

Task 2: Sight Words Knowledge

Total Incorrect: _____

Task 3: Phonemic Awareness

Total Incorrect: _____

Task 4: Reading Grade-Level Words

Total Incorrect: _____

Task 5: Symbol to Sound Knowledge

Total Incorrect: _____

Task 6: Sound to Symbol Knowledge

Total Incorrect: _____

Task 7: Auditory Discrimination/Memory

Total Incorrect: _____

Task 8: Phonemic Awareness

Total Incorrect: _____

Is It Dyslexia?

Task 9: Phonemic Awareness

Total Incorrect: _____

Task 10: Phonemic Awareness

Total Incorrect: _____

Task 11: Decoding Unfamiliar Words

Total Incorrect: _____

Results from Questionnaire Plus Screening Tasks

1. TOTAL (line 4) on Questionnaire _____
2. TOTAL incorrect answers on Screening Tasks _____
3. **GRAND TOTAL from lines 1 and 2** _____

Grade 7 to Adult Conclusions

If the GRAND TOTAL (line 3) **is 14 or greater**, then this student's performance is consistent with someone with dyslexia.

It can be assumed that the severity of dyslexia is in direct relation to **how much greater than 14** the GRAND TOTAL is (14 being mild and 205 being the most severe).

If the GRAND TOTAL **is less than 14**, then dyslexia is likely *not* the probable cause for the student's academic difficulties.

Moving Forward with Dyslexia

Chapter 8

Taking 7 Steps after Screening

You've now learned about dyslexia and administered the screening, so in this chapter, we'll talk about next steps. If the screening results indicate that the student is likely dyslexic, then the following steps are recommended.

Step 1: Talk to Your Student

Play the "Congratulations!" video for the student at https://courses.learnreading.com/courses/dyslexia-screening-videos.

This video discusses the talents and strengths that are typical in a person with dyslexia, as well as what they might find challenging. This video, and thoughtful conversations with you, will help them better understand themselves, their strengths and their weaknesses, and will give them hope for a bright future!

If you do not have access to the video, here is a transcript that you can use for a reference when you talk to your student.

You may say something like:

According to your screening results, it looks like you may have dyslexia, congratulations! Here's why that's a good thing. It's a good thing because if you have dyslexia that means you likely have many talents and strengths that center in the right hemisphere of the brain.

You might be very gifted in athletics. Maybe you are super-fast or super good at sports. Or, maybe you are gifted in art. Maybe you know how to draw or paint or create things really well. And speaking of creating, maybe you're really good with your hands. Kids and adults with dyslexia are really good at working with their hands and creating things. Maybe you know how to create wonderful things with Legos or painting or working with wood. Maybe you're good at taking things apart and putting them back together or putting puzzles together. Anything that has to do with your hands, you might be really good at. As you get older, you might notice some talents or areas of strength. Pay attention to the things you are good at and that you enjoy doing.

You might also be gifted in music. Maybe you can hear a song and easily remember the lyrics. Maybe you're really good at singing. Or maybe you're really good at playing the piano by ear. Sometimes reading printed music can be difficult for a dyslexic student but often you can just pick up how to play music a little easier than others.

Now, you're probably not gifted in all of those areas, but there might be one that you have special talents in.

Another area that dyslexics are often gifted in is they are really good with people. They know how to really show empathy and they're good at making friends. They're also really good leaders. They know how to think outside of the box and think of plans in a way that kind of sets you apart from others.

So, there's probably something that you are really good at. And that is because dyslexics are really good at those things.

You also might have trouble with some things, like telling time on a clock with hands or memorizing math facts. Maybe the times tables don't come as easy to you as they do to others. Or maybe you have difficulty on timed math tests. Maybe left versus right might be kind of difficult for you.

There are some things that might be a little more difficult for someone with dyslexia, but it is dyslexia that is making those things difficult. It is not because you are any less intelligent than anybody else. It is just because your brain works a little differently. You are gifted in some areas and some things are challenging for you, which is the same for anybody. None of us are good at everything. Some of us have trouble with some things and some people have trouble with other things.

But the good news is that there is a plan! If you have dyslexia, you just need to learn to read and spell in a way that is specific for your brain. Your parents will be learning how to provide you with that kind of instruction so that you can learn to read and spell in a way that makes sense.

All you need to know is the "why," or the reason why words are spelled the way they are and why they sound the way they do when you read. When you know the why of words, you'll be able to apply that knowledge to figure out what the words say without memorization or guessing.

So you will be able to read and spell just as well as your peers. Plus, you'll also have all of those other talents and strengths that dyslexics have. And that is why I said, "Congratulations! You are amazing!"

Step 2: Celebrate!

Some parents choose to celebrate this new knowledge because there is much to celebrate! Not only is there an answer to why your student struggles, but there is a plan to conquer their challenges moving forward. There is hope and help just around the corner! You may also choose to celebrate the gifts that your student has been given—because they have dyslexia!

Step 3: Evaluate Your Current Reading Program

If you educate your student at home, please assess your reading instruction program to ensure it is a structured literacy program appropriate for dyslexic learners. This information should be on the reading curriculum website.

- Learn Reading is one example of a comprehensive reading program designed specifically for the dyslexic learner. However, there are several structured literacy programs that may work for a dyslexic student.

- If your child is educated at a public or private school and is not receiving direct, explicit, structured, and code-based literacy instruction, then a specialized tutor who uses a reading program as previously described is recommended. You may provide this additional instruction yourself or hire a tutor who uses a dyslexia-appropriate reading program.

- A possible resource for online and in-person tutors can be found at LearnReading.com.

Step 4: Study the Effective Literacy Instruction and Recommendations in the Following Pages

Choose which accommodations you feel would best help your learner at this time. Note, not all recommendations or accommodations need to be implemented at once. Instead, choose those that you feel would make the biggest and quickest impact on your child's learning experience, and start with those.

Step 5: Talk to Your Child's Teacher

If your child attends public or private school, their teacher may benefit from knowing that your student is most likely dyslexic and what works best for dyslexic learners. Though conversations regarding this screening and any resulting accommodations should be informal, the result of these discussions may facilitate a significant improvement for your learner in the classroom.

- You may refer to the recommendations in the following pages to determine which may be appropriate for your child's teacher to easily and informally include as part of your child's instruction.

- Please remember, the results of this screening are not to be used to demand formal accommodations on an Individualized Education Program (IEP) or 504 plan. The report is for personal and informational purposes only. However, the results may be discussed with your child's teacher informally to determine what simple, free, and easy ways there are to help your child succeed at school.

Step 6: Read at Home

If your child enjoys reading, yet struggles:

- The student should be provided with stories with controlled text (decodable readers) to eliminate their dependence on guessing, until the student can apply the reading rules that they will encounter in most books. Please read to your child or allow them to listen to stories often. This is essential for vocabulary development and comprehension, and will aid in developing a love for reading and literature. There are several audio book apps available as well as free videos of volunteers reading books to children on YouTube or other online media sources.

If your child does NOT enjoy reading:

- As they progress through a dyslexia-designed reading program and experience continued success, they will begin to lose the fear that accompanies reading.

- It is imperative that they are not required to read text that they have not learned how to read, or "uncontrolled text." Present them with appropriate decodable readers or passages that only contain words that they have learned the reading rules for.

- Please read to your child, or allow them to listen to stories, often. This will help to strengthen vocabulary development and comprehension, and will aid in developing a love for reading and literature.

Step 7: Educate Yourself Further on the Topic of Dyslexia

A reliable online resource is the International Dyslexia Association. You can learn more at dyslexiaida.org.

An easy-to-read yet extremely comprehensive book on the topic of dyslexia is *Overcoming Dyslexia* by Sally Shaywitz, M.D.

Summary

You have learned seven steps that will help a dyslexic reader after a screening has been completed. Now that you are on the path to success, you will next learn what effective literacy instruction looks like for children with dyslexia.

Chapter 9

Effective Literacy Instruction for Students with Dyslexia

In this chapter, we'll cover what effective literacy instruction looks like for children with dyslexia. Parents can use the information to find or confirm a reading program meets their needs.

A student who fits the dyslexia profile should receive structured, direct, explicit, code-based literacy instruction. An effective and comprehensive reading program for dyslexic students will include each of the following elements:

- Phonemic awareness.

- Phonics.

- Fluency.

- Vocabulary.

- Comprehension.

There are several effective reading programs that are appropriate for students with dyslexia. My company, Learn Reading, fulfills all of these requirements and can be found at LearnReading.com. This program was designed to build all of the essential reading skills. In addition to Learn Reading, there are several programs that include the specific type of reading instruction designed for the dyslexic learner. If used as designed, each one should help a dyslexic student understand how to unlock the reading code.

It is recommended that an appropriate literacy instruction program be implemented immediately, often (at least twice weekly), and consistently. Several reading programs are designed to be used at home with parental guidance and supervision. Or, a tutor can be hired to provide this important instruction.

A complete and effective reading program will include each of the preceding components, which can be expanded even further into the following:

- Phonological awareness.
- Phonemic awareness.
- Knowledge of the correct sounds of each grapheme, especially vowels.
- Proper teaching of phonetically irregular words.

- Phonics instruction (systematic, direct, synthetic, explicit, code-based phonics instruction).
- The importance of connected and controlled text.
- Fluency development.
- Vocabulary development.
- Comprehension development.

Phonological Awareness

A solid foundation in reading, whether a child is dyslexic or not, begins with phonological awareness. This is an awareness that spoken language can be broken into smaller parts. For instance, a child would come to learn that sentences are broken into words, words are broken into syllables, and syllables contain even smaller units of sounds, called phonemes.

Phonological awareness includes the ability to recognize and produce words that rhyme. A child developing phonological awareness will begin to grasp the similarities and differences between and within words. For instance, a child will begin to recognize that *cat*, *mat*, and *sat* all have similar word parts. Soon, these word parts will be able to be broken into the smallest units of sound (phonemes). Students will then be able to recognize even the smallest similarities and differences within words, such as recognizing the initial sound similarities in *slide* and *sand*, and the vowel sound differences in *pet* and *pit*.

Phonological awareness is an essential part of reading readiness. Understanding that the spoken word can be broken into sounds will prepare them to understand the alphabetic principle. The alphabetic principle is an understanding that the words we speak have sounds that are represented by written letters—which, when combined, create that same spoken word.

There are several ways to develop and strengthen a young child's phonological awareness. Reading nursery rhymes is an excellent way to help them hear similar endings within words and experience the predictability of rhyme. Singing simple songs to and with them will also help them hear those similar word sounds.

You can also play games that draw attention to the different parts within sentences, phrases, words, and syllables. Children can count words within a spoken sentence, repeat similar phrases within sentences, and clap or jump to experience the cadence of syllables. Then they will be ready to strengthen their phonemic awareness by breaking apart, isolating, and manipulating the smallest units of spoken sound: phonemes.

Phonemic Awareness

The skill that will yield the most significant improvement in reading is phonemic awareness. *Phonemic awareness* is the ability to hear, isolate, discriminate, and manipulate the smallest units of sound (phonemes) within a word. Almost all struggling readers have weak phonemic awareness to some degree.

A little-known but all-important fact about reading is that there is an auditory component as well as a visual component, and it's the auditory processing component (phonemic awareness) that is actually the most important skill needed to read accurately, fluently, and with confidence. Without solid phonemic awareness, readers will likely experience confusion when faced with an unknown word and will struggle to decode the word accurately.

One way to develop and strengthen phonemic awareness (once phonological awareness has been established) is to begin pulling words apart into their individual phonemes, and then pushing (or blending) those phonemes back into words. Activities for segmenting words into their separate phonemes can include counting the number of phonemes within a word, separating and locating a specific sound, or isolating and then changing a specific sound to create a new word. There are also activities that can strengthen a student's blending skills, such as the "pencil reading" technique as taught in the Learn Reading program and discussed in the "Phonics Instruction" section that follows.

Knowledge of the Correct Sounds of Each Grapheme, Especially Vowels

In order for a student to use their phonemic awareness skills to apply phonics accurately, they will need a solid knowledge of the correct sound that each grapheme will make, including (and especially) vowels. The student will need to know exactly what each letter, or grapheme, will say in order to accurately read the word. The challenge for many students lies in the fact that several letters make several sounds. Too often, students are left to wonder, guess, or simply try all the sounds a letter can make in order to figure out which sound fits best in that word. This guess-and-try method is dangerous. It teaches students to guess, rather than teaches them to read. The "Vowel Placement Strategy" as taught in the Learn Reading program (described in more detail later) eliminates this reliance on guessing and puts the student in control of each word.

Students need to be taught the pure sounds of all the consonants and vowel sounds. A good way to teach these sounds is to allow the students to see and feel the shape of their mouth and tongue when they create the intended sound. Knowledge of the pure sounds of the letters involves articulating the sounds tightly, cleanly, and clipping any potentially lingering schwa sound off the end of it. Students need to be taught the difference between sustained or continuous sounds, and quick or stop sounds. They must also learn the difference between voiced and voiceless sounds. Being aware of how the sound feels and looks, based on what their mouth and tongue are doing, is an excellent way to teach the pure sounds of the graphemes.

The sounds that vowels will make requires intensive instruction because the sound will change based on where the vowel sits within a word and the letters that surround it. Learn Reading's "Vowel Placement Strategy" teaches the student exactly *what* each vowel will say and *when* the vowel will say each of its sounds. This understanding of what each grapheme will say, and when, is an important step to enable a student to approach an unknown word with confidence.

Proper Teaching of Phonetically Irregular Words

True sight words are words that break typical phonetic patterns at the time an emerging reader would encounter them. True sight words are different from high frequency words. High frequency words (often lumped into the "sight words" category) can often be decoded and should, in that case, be taught with typical phonetic reading rules. True sight words, or words with phonetically irregular spellings, should be taught as rule-breakers.

There are several ways to teach phonetically irregular words. One way is to memorize the word as a whole unit. Memorizing the word as a whole (with clues) can be advantageous for dyslexic learners because there can be several meaningful attachments associated with the word. First, it is difficult (if not impossible after ample experience) to "turn off" the automatic response of the brain to make connections between the first letter or two of a word and its initial pronunciation. Even if the student was instructed to look at the word as a unit and not decode it, they will most likely be unable to avoid making the phoneme-grapheme connection in the onset of the word, which would give them a clue as to what the word is. Usually the onset of a sight word makes the sound that you would expect, and is therefore a phonetic clue to the first part of the word. There is also the context of the text itself that would give a clue to the word that would make sense in that spot. A student can also create their own meaningful attachment to the sight word by writing the word in isolation and then drawing or sketching the meaning, using the word itself *in* the drawing. This kind of logical attachment can give the student yet another layer of meaningful links to decipher what the word is. The pro for this method is the availability of meaningful attachments to serve as memory triggers, whether in the context of the sentence or within the word itself. One con is that it is difficult for dyslexic students to remember which words are true sight words and which are not. They would have to rely on memory to associate that word as a rule-breaker and approach it with a different reading strategy. This would take ample training and practice, but it is possible.

A second way to teach true sight words is to teach the student that the word should be decoded just like any other word, except one or two graphemes ("tricky parts") that break the rules of reading. The student is taught to sound out all the decodable parts of the word and then to memorize the rule-breaking sound(s) only. There are pros and cons to teaching dyslexics true sight words this way. The pro is that students are learning to apply the alphabetic principle. They are learning that each part of a word has a job and a sound, even if the sound is an unusual or seemingly random one. The difficulty with this method, especially for dyslexics, is that a student would have to rely on memory, with no meaningful attachment triggers for three separate things.

- Is this a true sight word?
- What was the undecodable grapheme(s) within it?
- What was the *sound* that that rule-breaking grapheme(s) was supposed to make?

The student cannot rely on the letter itself as a clue to which sound it should make. It would also be very difficult to draw a linking attachment from the letter to a random sound that is not typically associated with that letter. So, although this method of teaching sight words has merit in the fact that the student is learning that each grapheme has an associated phoneme, it also leaves the memorization of an unknown, random sound to memory without any meaningful attachments or memory triggers to help the student recall the sound and then ultimately the word. This requirement to recall a random sound from 44 phoneme choices, without any links or meaningful triggers, can be especially difficult for dyslexic students.

The first method requires the memorization of a word. The second method requires the memorization of a sound. Both require memorization.

A good way to teach true sight words to dyslexic students is to teach them that the word is a "sight word" because there is at least one grapheme that breaks the rules of reading. Therefore, the word should not be "sounded out" in its entirety, but should be looked at instead as a "unit with clues." Students should be taught that there are several meaningful attachments that can be made to figure out the word. Typically, the word will follow the rules of reading for the initial consonant(s) up to the vowel sound (the onset) and they can typically depend on that initial clue to know the beginning sound of the word. It is often the vowel sound that will be the rule-breaker, so the student can typically rely on the sound of the first letter, consonant digraph, or consonant blend to give them a clue as to how the word starts. Second, they can then use the context of the passage or other creative memory triggers, such as a related picture, to decipher the word with confidence.

Dyslexic students often struggle with memorizing rote, random facts. Creating meaningful attachments to anything requiring memorization is the best way for a dyslexic student to learn.

Phonics Instruction

Students with dyslexia (and it could be argued all students) will benefit the greatest from direct, explicit, systematic, synthetic, code-based phonics instruction. The term *phonics* generally refers to linking written letters to spoken sounds, and then using that knowledge to decode and encode words from speech to print and vice versa.

- *Direct instruction* occurs when a teacher directly teaches the student(s). The teacher teaches exactly what they want their students to know. Direct instruction can include lectures, modeling, and feedback.

- *Explicit instruction* means that the teacher explicitly states exactly what they want the student to know, leaving nothing to chance or to subliminal acquisition. Specific knowledge is explicitly taught and not left to happenstance, hopeful absorption, or as a result of experimentation.

- *Systematic phonics* means lessons are taught using a formal outline with specific and sequential goals. This type of teaching progressively introduces grapheme-phoneme relationships beginning with the simplest and building to the more complex pairings. Systematic phonics is taught in an organized, planned sequence that provides a solid framework for future knowledge.

Students are taught that individual sounds, represented by letters, can be blended together to create spoken words. Students learn to identify the individual sounds within spoken and written words, together with their associated graphemes, and then how to blend, or synthesize, those sounds together to create words.

One way students can learn phonics directly, explicitly, systematically, and synthetically is to teach them the "pencil reading" method as taught in the Learn Reading program. "Pencil reading" requires a student to look at an unknown word carefully, placing a dot with a pencil underneath each grapheme while saying its corresponding phoneme, and then slowly pushing those sounds together as they connect the dots. The "pencil reading" strategy allows the student to use three different senses while they read. They are listening to themselves pronounce each phoneme as they say the sound. They are seeing each separate grapheme as they articulate it and placing it in the right order. And they are using their sense of touch as they physically segment and then blend the graphemes back together to read the word.

In order for a student to be successful and confident while using the "pencil reading" technique, they will require a firm knowledge of the correct sounds of each grapheme, including the sounds that each vowel will make in the word. The "Vowel Placement Strategy," another technique in the Learn Reading program, teaches the student exactly what each vowel will say based on where it sits in a word and the letters that surround it.

If a student is going to be successful at applying phonics knowledge, they must know when the vowels will say each of their respective sounds. Students should not be asked to try all of the sounds to figure out which sound makes a real word, or to ultimately guess. For a student to read accurately and with confidence, they must be taught not only what the different sounds are that each vowel makes, but when they will make each sound.

For instance, in the Learn Reading program, one of the most useful elements in the "Vowel Placement Strategy" is called the "Tap 2" rule. This rule teaches students when a vowel will make its long sound versus its short sound. The "Tap 2" rule states: "When you come to a vowel, tap (touch) the next two letters. If either one of them is another vowel, then the vowel that you are on will probably say its name, or its long sound. If not, it will probably say its short sound." That "Tap 2" rule alone changes the reading game for many struggling readers who feel they have no option but to guess at what a vowel will say. The word *probably* is intentionally placed in that rule, twice. But, the student is not left to wonder about the exceptions. There are actually very few exceptions to phonics rules. The remainder of rules found in the "Vowel Placement Strategy" also teach students when the vowels will say their other sounds, besides their long and short sounds. It teaches them when the vowel will change to the schwa sound, what happens if there is an *R* or a *W* after it, and so on.

Dyslexic students must know the "why" of letters. Only then can they use their intellect to apply that phonics knowledge to read unknown words with confidence. The students are not left to memorize or guess. Instead, they are given the tools to read with success.

The Importance of Connected and Controlled Text

Words are not meant to be read in isolation only. While we teach emerging readers to read words one grapheme at a time, it is important to put those words into connected text and have them read phrases, sentences, and stories as soon as possible.

Words are intended to convey meaning, not just to be read as standalone objects to be conquered. Therefore, reading words in context is the essential and obvious pathway to reading for meaning. The sooner a child can begin reading words in meaningful passages, the sooner their fluency, vocabulary, and comprehension will strengthen.

It is important that this connected text also be carefully controlled. Controlled text means that the passages they are asked to read should *only* contain words that they have learned the reading rules for and sight words that they have already learned. When a student is presented with reading material that they know contains only words that they are capable of reading, then the student will begin to relinquish their dependence on guessing.

If a student is presented with a book or passage with just any text, or if they are simply asked to read any book off the shelf, then we are setting them up for confusion and guessing, not confidence and success. We must teach students how to read, not how to guess. To ensure a student is set up for success, we must ask them to read only very carefully controlled text. These passages are often found in decodable readers. These readers are particularly helpful if they correspond directly to the reading curriculum used and on a scaffolded, lesson-by-lesson basis.

Fluency Development

An often overlooked but important skill for readers to develop is fluency. Fluency is the degree of skill in which a reader can scan and read words, ultimately in context or connected text. Fluency includes reading words accurately and quickly, and comprehending what they read. Fluent readers also are able to read with expression and proper phrasing. Because there is not a great deal of energy required for decoding, fluent readers are free to relax and read for pleasure.

Fluency is a skill that should be incorporated in any reading program because it is the all-important bridge from accuracy to comprehension. The more fluently a student reads, the quicker and easier they will be able to attach meaning to what they are reading. For instance, a child might read a sentence accurately, but this was only accomplished after several minutes of significant effort decoding each word. Once the last word in the sentence has been read, the student has by that time spent so much energy figuring out what each word is, that they have no idea what the sentence is about, nor can they remember what the previous words were in the sentence. This is why fluency can be the bridge to comprehension. If a student does not have to spend all of their energy decoding each individual word, that energy is then freed up to ponder on the meaning of the passage. Fluency allows the student to read for meaning, which is the ultimate purpose of words.

There are several activities that can be used to promote fluency. Consistent, repetitive, positive exposure is the key. Repetitive, positive exposure means that the student experiences reading the word accurately, over and over, so the correct pronunciation is more easily and quickly established in their brain. Reading the word inaccurately will set their fluency goals back several steps. Flashcards and paired word cards can be used in a multitude of games and activities to incorporate this repetitive, positive exposure.

Oral reading helps develop fluency in significant ways. When a student reads orally, they are forced to articulate each sound within the word and in the correct sequence. The students will hear themselves blending each sound to form the correct word, using another sense (in addition to sight) that the brain can draw on to establish a solid knowledge of the word.

An example of this intense oral reading instruction is incorporated in the "Give a Goal" strategy in the Learn Reading program. If a student makes an error when reading, the "Give a Goal" strategy encourages parents and teachers to not tell the child the word, but rather, tell them the error that was made, and then let the student correct the word on their own. If a student is told exactly what letter was missing, inserted, or transposed when reading, and exactly where the error occurred, then when the student tries again, they will focus on that specific part of the word and apply the counsel they were given. In most cases, this is all it takes for the student to read the word correctly, thus allowing the student to take charge of their own reading progress. This "Give a Goal" strategy to strengthen reading skills results in significant gains in phonemic awareness, and ultimately, fluency. When fluency is strengthened, comprehension and an enjoyment of reading will follow.

Another effective way to strengthen fluency is to develop their expression and phrasing skills. When a student learns to read with expression and proper phrasing, then words no longer remain as though they were in isolation, but instead become a small part of a great, meaningful whole.

One way to develop expression is to have the student scan the text and look for a word or phrase that they feel should be emphasized. Then, when they read the passage orally, they will add emphasis to important details. This scanning, considering the text, and determining which parts should be read with emphasis will also considerably strengthen their comprehension.

To develop good phrasing skills, readers may be asked to scan the text beforehand, marking or highlighting all the punctuation marks. The teacher would directly teach students how to read with phrasing, pausing at commas and controlling voice inflections at the different end marks. Then, the student would read orally, paying special attention to the punctuation marks that are intended to help a student read fluently.

Reading with expression and phrasing strengthens fluency—and fluency is the bridge from accuracy to comprehension.

Vocabulary Development

Vocabulary and comprehension are two parts of a continuous cycle in reading. A reader will come to a text with some foundational knowledge of the vocabulary they will encounter. However, there will likely also be many words that a reader will meet that they will learn the meaning of *as* they read and comprehend the passage. Therefore, previous knowledge of vocabulary improves comprehension, and comprehension in turn improves vocabulary. This important cycle is essential for all emerging and advancing readers. One cannot entirely comprehend what they are reading without a solid understanding of the vocabulary involved, and vocabulary grows as one encounters and comprehends new words in context. The link between the two is inseparable.

There are many ways to increase a student's vocabulary. For instance, in the Learn Reading lessons, students are given a page of new vocabulary words and are asked to pronounce each word correctly into a smart device to request the definition. Using technology this way forces the student to articulate each grapheme correctly and in the right order, otherwise the AI will not know what word the student needs the definition of. This dual purpose of using technology, which relies on the correct pronunciation of the word, and in turn, provides the needed definition, is an excellent way to build a student's knowledge bank.

In the Learn Reading lessons, once the student has discovered the meaning of each word, they then are invited to draw a picture of the meaning of it right next to the word. This helps the student to spend time pondering the meaning of the word, which will help to solidify its definition in the brain. Their illustration also serves as a reminder of what that word meant when they encounter it in the upcoming sentences and stories.

After the student has discovered the meaning of each new vocabulary word and has sketched the meaning of it, they then search for that word on the "Sentences" page and place a box around it in the sentence. Then, when the student comes to the "Sentences" page in the lesson, they will notice that they have already circled the new sight word in every sentence, they've underlined all the new words (from the "pencil reading" page), and have boxed each new vocabulary word. So by the time they get to the "Sentences" page, they are not faced with an assortment of seemingly random, daunting words on a page. Instead, they are faced with a visual reminder that they have already successfully read almost every word in every sentence. This realization alleviates fear and provides comfort knowing that they do have the necessary skills to read the sentences with confidence. This head start into reading the sentences successfully leads to a smoother and more assured path to comprehension.

Comprehension Development

An excellent way to develop and strengthen comprehension, especially for students with dyslexia, is to use their talents and strengths to build on prior knowledge. As an example, in the Learn Reading lessons, after a student has read a sentence or a story, they are asked to pick one of three ways to more completely understand what they just read. They are asked to either draw a picture of what is happening, retell what they just read in their own words, or physically act out what the passage was about. There are also other ways to elaborate on the meaning of a passage, but these three ways appeal to those who enjoy art, verbal expression, or drama and theater. Students with dyslexia often fall into one of those categories. Being invited to pursue comprehension activities that draw on a student's strengths is one way to create meaningful connections to the text. This technique of utilizing strengths to strengthen comprehension also helps students who struggle with reading to be allowed to perform in ways in which they feel strong, comfortable, and confident.

Phonemic awareness, phonics, fluency, vocabulary, and comprehension are all interconnected parts of the reading process. One does not typically read words solely for the sake of reading words. One reads to understand. Comprehension, and ultimately, an enjoyment of the process, which is why we teach reading in the first place.

Summary

Now that you have learned what type of literacy instruction works for people with dyslexia, you are now equipped to find a reading program that will best help your child. It typically does not take long for a dyslexic student, once they begin this type of specialized instruction, to make quick and remarkable strides in reading.

Chapter 10

Recommendations for School and Home

In this chapter, you will learn what can help a dyslexic learner at home and at school. You will discover simple, free, and informal accommodations that can make a big impact on how a dyslexic student learns. You will also learn what you can do, personally, to help your child thrive academically.

Recommendations for School

The following are academic recommendations that a school may offer for students with dyslexia.

Please note that the results of this screening should not be used to demand formal accommodations in a public school. However, the results of this screening and the following possible accommodations may be discussed informally with the student's teacher so the student may experience more success in the classroom.

Accommodations allow all students to access information and prove their knowledge without altering the academic standard. Academic adjustments do not decrease expectations, but change the way a student's knowledge and ability are demonstrated. They do not give a dyslexic student an unfair advantage, but rather they level the playing field and give all students an opportunity to prove their knowledge of a subject. Academic adjustments should be made to ensure a dyslexic student can access information as easily as their peers as well as prove their knowledge of it. These adjustments do not alter the validity of assessments. In fact, without appropriate accommodations, assessments may be less valid in measuring the extent of a dyslexic student's knowledge.

This list of possible accommodations is not exhaustive. There are many ways a student with dyslexia may receive fair access to instruction and assessments. The following are just a few examples.

Academic accommodations may only be needed until the student has received enough specialized instruction to bridge the gap between their ability and their achievement. With the right instruction, accommodations may only be needed temporarily.

As a reminder, the screenings in this book are not intended to be used to demand or request formal accommodations in a public school. However, if you are in a homeschool or private school situation, the following accommodations may be used to improve your child's academic experience. If your child attends a public school, these accommodations may be informally discussed with the teacher, but should not be expected without a formal, comprehensive dyslexia assessment administered by a professional.

Possible academic accommodations may include:

- Auditory access to instructional materials.
- Additional time on tests.
- Allow technology to assist with reading and spelling.
- The use of a calculator on math assignments and tests where quick memorization of facts is not the main objective.
- Oral testing.
- Reduced homework load when the objective is quality and not quantity.
- No copying required, but a peer note-taker or copies of the material may be provided instead.
- Instructions presented verbally in addition to in print.

For additional accommodations and recommendations, parents may visit the International Dyslexia Association website at dyslexiaida.org.

Recommendations for Home

The following are recommendations for parents.

Accentuate Their Strengths

Trouble processing language is not the only effect of dyslexia. Dyslexia also often accompanies several talents and strengths that can unfortunately be overlooked.

One of the best things you can do for a dyslexic student is to point out these strengths to the student and encourage their development.

Dyslexics often spend all day at school in a state of stress, anxiety, and sometimes depression. Being able to come home from school with a reasonable amount of homework and ample time to enjoy the things they are good at will help to balance that stress load, provide much needed relief, and restore their self-confidence.

Tutor Them

To improve a dyslexic student's reading skills, it is recommended that tutoring be done as soon and as frequently as is reasonably possible, without encroaching on the student's free and much needed leisure and play time.

However, it is imperative that it not be just any tutor, not just any tutoring program, and not just any tutoring clinic.

A student who is presumed to be dyslexic must receive highly specialized instruction designed especially for a dyslexic learner. This type of literacy instruction must be systematic, explicit, and phonics-based. It should also include all of the elements as described in the previous "Literacy Instruction" section.

There are many tutors, schools, and tutoring clinics that specialize in the dyslexic learner. Or, parents may decide to teach their own child using an appropriate tutoring program designed for home use. One such possible resource is www.LearnReading.com. It provides lessons that parents can use at home with their child as well as a database of tutors who are licensed and certified to tutor using the Learn Reading lessons with students online.

Practice Patience

Dyslexics travel a difficult road. It is hard for people without dyslexia to understand just how difficult their life path is. If you don't have dyslexia, it is almost impossible to see the world through their perspective. A student with dyslexia wakes up knowing that they will have to go to school and struggle in front of their peers and teacher. They are under a constant state of stress and fear and confusion as they wonder why they can't do the things that their peers can. Then, they come home to what they hope will be a sanctuary of peace and relaxation. But oftentimes that sanctuary can turn into school part two, with more of the same stress, fear, and disappointment. However, this time they are, in their eyes, failing in front of the people they care about the most—their parents.

The best thing you can do for your dyslexic child at home is to remember Learn Reading's "Rule No. 1" when teaching. Rule No. 1 is: "You are teaching the child, not the lesson." The child comes first. The child is the highest priority. The lesson, as important as it may be, cannot be as important as the child for whom the lesson is taught.

Please be patient, kind, and understanding as you work with your dyslexic child. They have a stress load and fear that is difficult to understand if you do not struggle with dyslexia yourself. Their parents and teachers must be safe places.

If there comes a time when the parent or the student is frustrated, take a break. Remember, the child is more important than the lesson. An important teaching technique to remember is to end each lesson on a positive note, prior to any potential frustration happening. If you even sense that the child is beginning to become frustrated (or yourself), talk about something positive for a few minutes. Talk about their strengths, what they are good at. Tell them how proud of them you are! Tell them all the things that you have noticed that they are doing remarkably well! Remind them how far they have come. Point out how hard they are working, and that they should be very proud of their efforts. Tell them that you might not understand what it's like to have dyslexia, but you are there to help and support them. Be their safe place.

Educate, Advocate, and Spread the Word

Now that you know the signs and symptoms of dyslexia and understand the condition with more clarity, it is time to help others and spread the word.

There are countless parents out there who are worried about their underachieving readers and are desperate for help, like you probably were when you began this book.

They need what you now have.

Please educate the public about the good news of dyslexia! Dyslexia is not an obstacle as much as it is an answer! Understanding what dyslexia is and how the dyslexic brain operates is hopeful! If a person knows they are dyslexic, then they can begin to conquer the obstacles that are causing their confusion—and conquer them! Discovering dyslexia can be an incredibly liberating experience.

Please tell the world about dyslexia and the hope and help that accompany it! If your child has dyslexia (or if you do yourself), then it is highly likely that other family members also struggle with the condition. Whether they be old or young, it is never too late to discover the answer to their challenges and begin anew.

Dyslexia is nothing to be ashamed about. It is an extremely common condition that occurs in people of all levels of intelligence, including the extremely bright and gifted. There should be no shame associated with this common brain difference.

If you share with the world that dyslexics *can* learn to read and write well, that they *can* perform just as well as their peers, that they *are* just as intelligent as their friends and acquaintances, then you *will* change the world for the better.

Your knowledge and influence will impact not only your own family, but it can change the lives of other students and their families—for generations.

Summary

You have been on a learning journey and have discovered what the world looks like from a dyslexic perspective. You have watched Michael, John, Emma, and their families as they have navigated knowing, and not knowing, the answer to the question: "is it dyslexia?" You have been provided with screening tools, instructional frameworks, and accommodations to help a dyslexic learner thrive. You, your child, and future generations can now be joyfully set on the path to reading success.